Dennis Bergkamp was born in Amsterdam in 1969, and played for Ajax and Inter Milan before joining Arsenal in 1995 for a fee of £7.5 million. Over the next 11 years, he made more than 400 appearances for the club and won three league titles with the Gunners, including two Doubles in 1998 and 2002, and was part of the 'Invincibles' side of 2004. He won 79 caps for the Netherlands. He retired in 2006, and now works as the assistant manager at Ajax.

David Winner, who worked with Dennis Bergkamp on the writing of the book, is the author of *Brilliant Orange: The Neurotic Genius of Dutch Football*, which was shortlisted for the William Hill Sports Book of the Year prize, as well as many other books on the sport.

Jaap Visser also worked on the writing of the book, and is one of the leading sports writers in the Netherlands.

STILLNESS
AND SPEED

MY STORY

DENNIS BERGKAMP
WITH DAVID WINNER

**SIMON &
SCHUSTER**

London · New York · Sydney · Toronto · New Delhi

A CBS COMPANY

First published in Great Britain by Simon & Schuster UK Ltd, 2013
This paperback edition published by Simon & Schuster UK Ltd, 2014
A CBS COMPANY

1 3 5 7 9 10 8 6 4 2

Simon & Schuster UK Ltd
1st Floor
222 Gray's Inn Road
London WC1X 8HB

www.simonandschuster.co.uk

Simon & Schuster Australia, Sydney
Simon & Schuster India, New Delhi

A CIP catalogue record for this book
is available from the British Library

ISBN: 978-1-47112-953-7
Ebook ISBN: 978-1-47112-954-4

Typeset in UK by M Rules
Printed and bound by CPI Group (UK) Ltd, Croydon, CR0 4YY

CONTENTS

A NOTE ON THE
ENGLISH EDITION

I NEVER SAW THE 1980s comedy *Twins* but the poster was fantastic. It showed tiny, squidgy-looking Danny DeVito leaning into muscle-bound giant Arnold Schwarzenegger under the tagline 'Only Their Mother Can Tell Them Apart'.

The object you hold in your hands is basically Danny DeVito. Its giant twin – remarkably similar yet entirely different – is the Dutch edition of this book, written by my esteemed colleague Jaap Visser. He has created a coffee-table colossus covering every aspect of Dennis Bergkamp's life and career chronologically. That version is illustrated with many hundreds of colour pictures and will surely one day govern California.

Dennis, naturally, is the biological parent of both editions.

The form, we feel, fits the man. A footballer like no other ought to have a book (or books) no less distinctive. In the film, the brothers share genetic material. We did something similar. Broadly speaking, Jaap's research and interviews with Dennis covered his Dutch years while I dealt with his time in Italy and England. Then we pooled everything.

The Dutch edition is in the classic tradition of football biography.

The English one is more experimental, its structure influenced, among other things, by *Puskas on Puskas*, Rogan Taylor and Klara Jamrich's wonderful book of interviews with and about Ferenc Puskas, and by Francois Truffaut's book of interviews with Alfred Hitchcock. I am not remotely comparable to Truffaut and Dennis is certainly much nicer than the Master of Suspense. But, like him, he is a unique and influential genius in his chosen art form. Much of the book concerns Dennis's technique and creative process.

On the field, Dennis usually played as a deft and original 'shadow striker', operating between the lines, using his skills and understanding of space to help colleagues and create moments of beauty that won football matches. In print, he now does much the same, playing off interviews with colleagues, coaches and fellow footballing greats like Johan Cruyff, Arsene Wenger, Thierry Henry and Tony Adams. The result, we hope, is both unique and revealing.

When he retired from Arsenal in 2006, Dennis had no plans to write a book. But the more he moved into coaching with his boyhood club Ajax, the more he realised he had something of value to say. That turned out to be an understatement ...

David Winner
London, 2013

THE WALL

'**Y**OU GET USED TO the noise,' says Dennis, smiling. 'You hardly notice it'.

We are standing a few yards from Dennis's childhood home beside the A10 motorway that circles Amsterdam. Up until the 1950s the road was a muddy field where cows grazed on the extreme western edge of the city. By the time the Bergkamp family moved here in 1970 construction had begun. As a toddler, Dennis, watching from his high chair by the window, was enchanted by the sand trucks, bulldozers and cranes at work. These days, mature trees and glass barriers reduce the sound of traffic but in the seventies nothing stood between the flat and the roaring torrent of cars and lorries. Yet the recollection delights him. Dennis even remembers how the road ended up being useful. 'When it was finished it ran all the way around the city, so it took me six minutes to get to training. Through town it would have taken me forty-five minutes.' As we stroll through his old neighbourhood his memories are all happy ones.

Dennis was the youngest of four sons in a hard-working and devoutly Catholic family. Wim, his dad, was a modest, twinkly-eyed craftsman and perfectionist. He worked as an electrician, played football with the Wilskracht club (the name means 'Willpower') and loved making and repairing things: furniture, toys, puzzles, anything. Dennis's mum, Tonny, an accomplished amateur gymnast in her youth, ran the family home here on James Rosskade (the 'Kade'), adored all her boys and was renowned for her warmth, strength and neighbourliness.

Dennis crosses the wide pavement towards the entrance to number 22. 'Look up there on the first floor: that was my bedroom. And this is where we played football, here on the pavement.' His old building appears rundown but Dennis doesn't mind. He gazes contentedly up at the wall of brick and messy balconies. He is beaming. 'It's fair to say I had a perfect childhood here.'

Football was a huge part of it. The Bergkamp boys – Wim Jr, Ronald, Marcel and Dennis – played not only here in the street, but in the corridor of the flat and on local patches of grass. When the security guy with the large dog guarding it were away, they even used the real grass pitch on the far side of the motorway, reached through a tunnel and over a wooden plank across a ditch. Televised football was rare by today's standards. On Saturday evenings the family would hurry to Mass at nearby St Joseph's Church – but only after watching German football on television. The FA Cup final, one of the few English games shown live, was a special treat. Legend has it that Dennis was named after his father's favourite player, Denis Law. The legend is true. For the different spelling, though, we have to thank Wim Jr, ten years old at the time, and Ronald, aged seven, who thought 'Dennis' sounded 'less girly' than 'Denis'. Their little brother grew up to like Glenn Hoddle better. 'I'm not sure why, but the thing that always interested me most was *controlling* the ball, especially when it was in the air. I wasn't interested in dribbling or doing tricks or scoring goals. Control. That was my thing. We saw some English football on TV and the player who really stood out for me was Glenn Hoddle, because he was always in balance. I loved the way he plucked the ball out of the air and controlled it. Instant control. His touch was perfect.'

At school Dennis's teacher, Mr De Boer, let the kids play five-a-side in the gym. 'We finished school at twelve, ran home as fast as we could for a quick sandwich and then went straight back to school. At half-past twelve we'd be back in the gym playing *paalt-jesvoetbal* (literally, 'little-stick football'). Everyone had their own stick and you had to defend that against the ball. My stick was Maradona. I made him in my arts and crafts class. I filed the wood away so he had a neck, a head and a torso and I painted him in blue and white stripes with a number 10 on the back.

'We played football all the time, especially here. The Kade was wider in those days, and there weren't so many cars. It was real street football: four against five or five against five or four against four. You had to have a certain level of skill and balance because the concrete was hard and if you fell, you'd hurt yourself. One goal was that tree over there. It was a brilliant feeling to score there. The tree was a small target so you had to be so precise. And this door would be the other goal. You had to be clever and use what was around. You could play a one-two off the wall, or a car, but you weren't allowed to hit the door of the car so you aimed for the wheel. Be precise, invent ... that was the idea. You were always looking for solutions.'

Not that there was anything wrong with just sticking down jumpers for goalposts and spending most of your time running to collect the ball after a goal. 'We did that too! And in the evenings we'd have games on the grass behind the flats. With all the Dutch kids and Turkish and Moroccan kids living here, then it would be Holland v Morocco, or Holland v Turkey or whatever. It was really interesting. With the apartments all around and people watching from their balconies after dinner, it was like a stadium.'

Later, as his brothers had done, he joined Wilskracht. His all-round athletic talent had been obvious from an early age. 'I enjoyed cross-country runs in the park during PE lessons. In fact I loved all PE, except gymnastics which just wasn't my thing and Mum was disappointed about that. But rope-climbing, baseball, basketball ... I was good at everything.' At the age of nine, he joined the nearby AAC athletics club and proceeded to win medals for sprinting, the 1500 metres, the long jump, everything. One of his favourite events was the shot putt. 'We used to take the shot and measuring tape with us on holidays. When we had to do the washing-up after dinner, I'd say to my brothers, "Sorry guys, but I have to go outside with Dad and practise my shot putting." Mum would stand and watch, and after every throw she would call out, "Nice throw, Den."'

It has been said that Johan Cruyff, Louis Van Gaal or one of the youth trainers at Ajax must have taught or developed Dennis's unique touch with a football. But it turns out Dennis taught himself. 'I'm not the "product" of any manager. My best trainers were the ones who let me do my own thing: Cruyff, Wenger and Guus Hiddink in the national team. They understood me.' He gives greater credit to his brothers. 'They acted as a sounding board, and I needed that more than I needed a manager. I never had many friends as a kid. I didn't need any because I had my best three at home.'

The brothers themselves – Wim, now an accountant, molecular biologist Ronald and Marcel, an IT expert – seem stunned into silence when they hear Dennis regards them as more significant to his development than the likes of Cruyff and Van Gaal. Eventually Ronald reacts: 'Dennis does us a great honour. We were never trainers. We were always there for him and that made him feel comfortable, that's all,' Wim adds: 'Dennis is always there for us too, you know', and Marcel completes the thought: 'We're always there for each other.' The brothers insist that Dennis was an auto-didact. For Marcel, the key was his powers of observation. 'When he came to see me playing he saw everything down to the smallest detail. Afterwards he could always tell you exactly how situations had unfolded and who was standing where. Dennis was always an excellent observer. He plays golf, but he's never had lessons. He learned by watching. It was the same with tennis and snooker, too.' Wim confirms: 'Dennis would watch and watch and watch, then he'd do it himself. Dennis wanted to achieve perfection. He got that from Dad, who was never content with the work he'd done or the things he'd made. Dad's motto was: *you can always do better*. And that became Dennis's motto, too.'

No one in the history of football has had a touch quite as soft, precise, masterful and elegant as Dennis. When he retired in 2006, the *Financial Times* writer Simon Kuper recalled a dinner he had attended in Amsterdam the previous year with 'some legends of Dutch football'. Around midnight the conversation turned to an old question: who was the best Dutch footballer ever? According to Kuper: 'Dutchmen have been voted European Footballer of the Year seven times, more than any other nationality except Germans. Yet Jan Mulder, a great centre-forward turned writer, chose a player who had never even threatened to win the award nor, at the time, a Champions' League. "Bergkamp. He had the finest technique." Guus Hiddink, the great Dutch manager, nodded, and so the matter was settled.'

A few years later, in a Dutch TV interview, Robin van Persie explained what Bergkamp's example meant to him. Speaking with the writer Henk Spaan, he recalled an afternoon at the Arsenal training ground when he was a youngster and Dennis was a veteran. Van Persie had finished earlier and was sitting in a Jacuzzi which happened to be by a window. Out on the field he noticed Dennis doing a complicated exercise involving shooting, and receiving and giving passes at speed. Robin decided to get out of the bath as soon as Dennis made a mistake.

'That man, he's just bizarre!' says Van Persie. 'He'd been injured and he was on his way back, and he was training with one boy of about fifteen and with another boy of sixteen or seventeen and with the fitness coach. They were doing some passing and kicking with those mannequins. It was a forty-five-minute session and there wasn't one pass Dennis gave that wasn't perfect. He just didn't make a single mistake! And he did everything one hundred per cent, to the max, shooting as hard as possible, controlling, playing, direct passing ... That was so beautiful! To me it was plainly art. My hands got all wrinkled in the bath but I just stayed there. I sat and watched and I waited, looking for one single mistake. But the mistake never came. And that was the answer for me.

'Watching that training session answered so many questions I had. I can pass the ball well, too. I'm a good football player as well. But this man did it so well and with such drive. He had such total focus. I found myself thinking: "OK, wait a minute, I can play football well enough, but I've still got an enormous step to take to get to that level." And that's when I realised, if I want to become really good, then I have to be able to do that, too. From that moment on I started doing every exercise with total commitment. With every simple passing or kicking practice, I did everything at one hundred per cent, just so I wouldn't make mistakes. And when I did make a mistake I was angry. Because I wanted to be like Bergkamp.'

So Dennis's search for perfection began below his bedroom window on the James Rosskade, where he would kick a ball against a wall. Hour after hour. Day after day. Year after year.

* * *

I'M TRYING TO picture you aged about eight, kicking a ball against this wall. What would you be thinking?

Dennis: 'It's not thinking. It's *doing*. And in doing, I find my way. I used the brickwork around the entrance to the building. You see that line of vertical bricks, like a crossbar? Most of the time I was by myself, just kicking the ball against the wall, seeing how it bounces, how it comes back, just controlling it. I found that so interesting! Trying it different ways: first one foot, then the other foot, looking for new things: inside of the foot, outside of the foot, laces ... getting a sort of rhythm going, speeding it up, slowing it down. Sometimes I'd aim at a certain brick, or at the crossbar. Left foot, right foot, making the ball spin. Again and again. It was just fun. I was enjoying it. It interested me. Maybe other people wouldn't bother. Maybe they wouldn't find it interesting. But I was fascinated. Much later, you could give a pass in a game and you could maybe look back and see: "Oh, wait a minute, I know where that touch comes from." But as a kid you're just kicking a ball against the wall. You're not thinking of a pass. You're just enjoying the mechanics of it, the pleasure of doing it.

'Later, I'd say: "With every pass, there needs to be a message or a thought behind it." But that was there from very early, in my body and in my mind. When I was kicking the ball against the wall I'd be trying to hit a certain brick or trying to control the ball in a certain way. You play around with the possibilities, with bounces, for example. You hit the wall and the ball comes back with one bounce. Then you say, "Let's try to do it with two bounces," so you hit it against the wall a little bit softer, a little bit higher. With two bounces, it means probably that both bounces are a little bit higher, so you have to control it again, in a different way. You're always playing around. I wasn't obsessed. I was just very intrigued by how the ball moves, how the spin worked, what you could do with spin.

'In every sport with a ball, it's the same thing. If you watch Roger Federer play tennis against a big serve-and-volley player, they're totally different! So what interests you the most? Is it the result? Is it winning? Federer could play thirty years more because he just loves the game. He loves the bounce. He loves to make those little tricks. And it's effective as well. I recognise that.'

You're really not a serve-and-volley kind of guy yourself, are you?

'I really love that Federer way of playing. To have such control that you can trick a goalkeeper, trick the opponent. Like Federer's drop volleys, the little disguised lob. To be able to do something like that, yeah ... to do something that others don't do or don't understand or are not capable of doing. That's my interest; not following, but creating your own thing.'

So all this comes from yourself? You're not doing stuff you've seen on television.

'Oh, I'm doing that as well. You see a lot of things on television. Like watching Hoddle. After one World Cup – at least I think it was a World Cup – Marcel and I would be in the hallway kicking our soft foam ball. Maybe I'd head the ball and it would be a goal and I'd celebrate with my hands in the air shouting like this: *"Graaa-zi-aaaaaaniiii!"* Yeah! [*Laughs*] I loved that. [It turns out this was the 1982 World Cup, where Dennis and Marcel, who was four years older, took a shine to Francesco Graziani, mainly on account of his thrillingly Italian name and the exuberant way he celebrated his goal against Cameroon. Graziani had run off, clenched fists raised, leaping and shouting for joy. Dennis and Marcel copied him every chance they got, yelling Graziani's name as the TV commentator had done.]

'And Maradona. I loved seeing him, too. Of course, later, when I was at Ajax, I'd see Cruyff and Van Basten doing all sorts of things and you wouldn't exactly copy it, but you'd sort of file it away and think: "That's interesting."'

Did you stand out in your street games? Were you playing in an original way then?

'No, no. I'd be doing quite normal things. I mean I'm probably better than other kids, but it's not like I'm there at that age. I'm a bit quicker than the others. I can control the ball. I can go past someone – light feet, quick feet, that sort of stuff.'

What position did you play?

'Striker. And I scored plenty of goals because I had a good kick. I often scored free-kicks above the heads of the small goalkeepers. They were too short to reach! And when I was nine or ten I used to like scoring direct from corners. I mean it wasn't on a full-sized pitch, but later even on a full-pitch I enjoyed that. And, remember, thirty years ago we played a lot eleven v eleven on full-sized pitches. It wasn't like now where the kids play on reduced-size pitches. The idea was: "If you can play proper football, you can play on a proper pitch."

'So, yeah, I was quite a conventional player back then. The main thing was my pace. I could go past my defender, or a pass would be played behind the full-back and I could beat him that way. Quite conventional skills, really. But I was inventive in scoring goals, like lobbing the goalkeeper. I always liked that. Always with a thought, not just hit it but thinking: "What can I do?" But even with the lobs it wasn't an invention of mine. I'd seen that on TV. I think Cruyff scored a famous one against Haarlem in his first game back at Ajax, didn't he? And Glenn Hoddle did a famous one. We even had a word for it in Dutch: *stiftje*. It's like a wedge shot in golf with the clubface open ... and it drops over the goalkeeper. I got a lot of pleasure from those shots. It's fun, but it's also effective. I got upset when people complained about me only doing it "the nice way". I said, "No, it's the *best* way. There's a lot of space above the goalkeeper."

'I was lucky because in my generation, where I lived, there were a lot of boys my age. Out of school, all the time it was: "Come on, let's play football." I always had about five or six boys playing football with me. It's the classic way of street football, isn't it? But my brother Marcel didn't have that because there were only girls at his age. So for him it was completely different. He had no one his age to play with. So he had to play either with me and my friends or with Ronald, who's older. So when people ask me: "How did you become a professional football player?" maybe that's one of the reasons. Ronald was like me in school as well. If he got nine out of ten, he was never pleased with that. He'd say, "What did I do wrong? Why didn't I get a ten?" I was like that. And that's why I like what Wenger said about being a perfectionist: "He wants to strive for perfection." Even if I don't reach it, I can be happy as long as I'm striving for it. You're taking small steps all the time, improving, moving on.

So you had quite an old-fashioned childhood, really? No video games, not many cars about. You were like the generation of '74 who grew up playing football on empty streets after the war.

'Yeah, in those days when you had a holiday, you didn't go abroad. You stayed [at home] and played. I think my generation was the last that had that. Later, it was a different kind of street football which took place in the "courts", like a basketball court with a high fence around it. The Surinamese guys had those; there were competitions between courts in different neighbourhoods around Amsterdam and that's how they learned.'

And how was it when you got to Ajax?

'Very different from now. It's one of the things we talk about as coaches. At that time, we had the strict shouting coaches who'd take you through an exercise you had to try to copy. Almost like a military thing. I had one trainer called Bormann. He was a nice guy, but he had a real military air about him. That was for two years.

Then we had Dirk de Groot, who was really strict; there'd be a lot of shouting and you'd be a little bit scared, like "Oh no, I'm going to get *him*". [*Laughs*] But he was a lovely guy as well. And in the A Juniors we had Cor van der Hart, with his hoarse voice. Also a nice guy, but very strict. And sometimes we had Tonny Bruins Slot [Cruyff's assistant]. So the discussion we have now is "So how did you become a good player then?" If you look at the coaches we have now, they're so different. They all have their badges, and they are all very sympathetic and know exactly how to play football and what kind of exercises you should do, and for how many minutes, and the distances between the goals, and where the cones should be where you're playing positional games. And they know not to play too long – one and a half hours maximum. They all know exactly how *everything* should be done. Maybe that's the problem. We never had that sort of attention, so we were more self-taught. Even with all the shouting, you just created your own thing.

'Sometimes we even played pickup games like we were on the street. You know: sixteen guys, and the two captains play *poting*, which is like scissors, paper, stone but with the feet, and whoever wins that gets first pick. So one captain picks the best player, then the other one makes his pick, and so on. This is really true! This is how we made teams! And then we'd play a game. This is thirty years ago. We're in the Ajax Youth, but it's like the street. And one of the coaches is supervising, but more like a referee. "This is a goal, that's a foul . . ." Not at all like now. Nowadays the coach stops the game and says: "Hey, guy, if you've got the ball here, where do you have to be now?" and shows the player everything. For us it was much more like it was in Cruyff's time. It was really quite free for you to teach yourself. There's no shouting or military guys any more, but it's more strict in the football sense. Everyone is a head coach, everyone is a manager, everyone has their badges, and everything is done by the book. Is it too much? Probably. Everything is done for the kids now. They're picked up from school by mini-vans. The food is there, the teaching is there. Everything. "OK, guys, we're going to do the warm-up. Do two laps now. OK, now you're going to do this, now you're going to do that ..." How can they develop themselves if everything is done for them? We've got players in the first team now who've come through the Youth and are used to playing a certain style and doing certain things. And as soon as it's a little bit different it's: "Oh no! I don't know what to do!" You see them looking at the bench to find out what they should do.

'It's really a problem. You can see the difference with Luis Suarez when he was here [at Ajax]. Of course, maybe you wouldn't agree with the things he did, but he was always trying to create something, always thinking: "How can I get the best out of this situation? Do I have to pull the shirt of the defender to get in front of him? Do I get out of position to control the ball?" His mind is always busy thinking. And sometimes he steps on someone's foot or he uses his hand. Silly things. But the idea in his head is not bad. And he's very creative. So that's one of the things we try to do with the training now in the Youth – give players the chance to develop themselves into creative, special, unique individuals. We can't copy what we had in the past. Somehow we have to find a different way, so the players who come into the first team are creative again, can think for themselves, can make a difference, basically. Be special. Be unique. That's what we want. You can't be unique if you do the same thing as the ten other players. You have to find that uniqueness in yourself.'

2

JOHAN

'HE WOULD NEVER say it himself, but he *is* Dutch football,' says Dennis. He is talking about the key mentor of his career. Johan Cruyff spotted Dennis's talent when he was in the Ajax Youth team, then played Yoda to his Luke Skywalker and guided him to higher things, often in surprising and mysterious ways. Cruyff has done the same for others, too, of course, influencing most of the great talents of modern Dutch football (and plenty of Spanish and Danish ones, too). More importantly, says Dennis, he shaped the footballing mindset of the nation.

'All the Dutch players who are adventurers – and most of us are – get it a bit from Johan. That's his personality and philosophy and it became the Dutch way of playing. Of course, we adjust to the country or the club where we are. But we still have the Dutch mentality. We want to be someone, to do something our way. We're the kind of people who say: "I know what I'm talking about, and I know what I want, and I see what I can do." That can be seen as a bit arrogant, but it's not really. Cruyff is the biggest one in that. He's not arrogant. He just knows what he's talking about. Maybe it's a Dutch thing, or an Amsterdam thing as well, but Johan really was the biggest influence. Because his career was extreme, he was a pioneer. He's been there – *really* been there – and he's done it all. And no one did it before he did. He was fantastic as a player and fantastic as a coach, so we listen to him.'

For many years the relationship between Cruyff and Bergkamp was that of master and pupil. These days they are on a more equal footing. In 2010, Johan persuaded Dennis to join him in what became an extraordinary and controversial coup by ex-players which seized control at Ajax. Football had never seen anything quite like it. As we shall see in Chapter 21, they succeeded and now work closely together, restructuring the club and its youth system in order for it once more to be the envy of the world. Dennis: 'We didn't see each other much for a very long time, and then suddenly we were meeting very frequently. That changed things. When he was my manager, I used the formal *u* [like *vous* in French]. For me he was always "Mr Cruyff". But when you work together and fight side-by-side for the same cause and everyone around you calls him "Johan", then you inevitably try that yourself, too. It was peculiar for me, because I still even address my mother as *u*. Suddenly, I heard myself calling him "Johan". I was startled. But it has become increasingly normal. I wouldn't say Cruyff and I are now friends, but he has certainly become Johan for me.'

It used to be said that Marco van Basten was the closest thing Cruyff had to an anointed successor. These days, along with Pep Guardiola, his most esteemed protégé from Barcelona, Bergkamp probably fits the bill. The pair first met one afternoon after Johan had returned to Ajax as a player after eight years away in Spain and the USA. Dennis was playing for the Under-14s at the old Youth academy ground behind the stadium when Johan suddenly appeared and took over from the trainer during shooting practice. Dennis was awestruck: 'That really does something to you. I felt an even stronger urge to prove myself. I had a powerful sense that I really had to perform at that moment.'

* * *

WAS CRUYFF YOUR *idol?*

Dennis: 'I wouldn't put it that way. I didn't have any idols. Cruyff was just one of the best footballers in the world, light-years ahead of us.' It still seems to work that way. When former top players like Frank de Boer and Dennis lead training sessions, members of the current Ajax first time seem to try a little harder, keen to impress their predecessors.

Later, when he was your coach, Johan must have taught you a lot. What sort of things would he tell you?

'Actually we didn't talk a great deal. Just a few words here and there, in passing, on the way to the pitch. That was enough. I still need only a few words from Johan. He had to speak much more to others, he had to give them instructions. He knew what to expect from me, he knew I was a quiet, modest lad, but I was daring on the pitch. He gave me a lot of confidence by just saying: "Do what you're good at." It's similar to Wenger, who never said: "Do this, do that." With Johan it was more like: "What you did in the Youth, just do the same here, and the players behind you will help you, as well. Jan Wouters and Frank Rijkaard will help you." When we did a circle drill, for example, he'd tell other people to make more space or move to the left or right, but he never had comments for me, and that gave me the sense that I was doing well. It's been like that throughout my career. None of my managers had to tell me to change the way I play.'

*

THE CONCEPT OF A reticent Cruyff is hard to imagine. As a kid at Ajax in the mid-1960s, he drove older team-mates to distraction by offering unwanted advice on what they were doing wrong. What annoyed them most was having to admit he was usually right. Nicknamed 'Jopie', Cruyff went on to become the chattiest and bossiest of captains at Ajax, Barcelona and the Dutch national team, forever pointing, shouting, cajoling and giving detailed instructions to everyone, including referees. Thanks to his frequent appearances on radio and television, Cruyff became perhaps the most quoted Dutchman ever. He once explained why he didn't believe in religion: 'In Spain all twenty-two players make the sign of the cross before they enter the pitch – if it worked all matches would end in a draw'. Cruyff not only loves to talk, he developed a language of his own. In Holland, he is almost as well known now for his paradoxical, Yogi Berra-like axioms and left-field *aperçus* as for his football: 'Coincidence is logical' ... 'Before I make a mistake, I don't make that mistake' ... 'Sometimes something's got to happen before something is going to happen' ... 'Every disadvantage has its advantage'. But perhaps his most revealing line came at the end of a combative TV interview: 'If I'd wanted you to understand, I'd have explained it better.'

Dennis and Johan were always on the same wavelength: like Dick Halloran and his grandmother in *The Shining*, they seemed to be able to have entire conversations without ever opening their mouths.

Cruyff's coaching methods were unusual: a provocative, high-wire style based in part on the 'conflict model' he learned from his own guru, Rinus Michels. Michels used to raise energy and adrenaline levels among his players by provoking an argument. Cruyff, for complex psychological reasons linked perhaps to the early death of his father, also seemed to believe that adversity stimulated learning. As coach, he often needled and criticised his best players about their technique or attitude, expecting to get a creative, positive response. Being ordinary was never acceptable. Cruyff was relentless in his demand for improvement and excellence. Dennis observes: 'He is very instinctive. He really sees a lot of things, and, yes, he's got a dominating character as well, an urge to control things. But that's Total Football. You want to see everything, and Johan does see everything. If you are a Total Footballer, you can't be just doing your own thing. You have to have the whole picture on the pitch and outside as well.'

Likewise, Cruyff admired Dennis's skills and intelligence: 'Bergkamp is one of those people I have a special football relationship with. He belongs to a group of special guys, with Van Basten, Van't Schip and Rijkaard. Intelligent guys. And that's what it's all about, because you play football with your head, and your legs are there to help you. If you don't use your head, using your feet won't be sufficient. Why does a player have to chase the ball? Because he started running too late. You have to pay attention, use your brain and find the right position. If you get to the ball late, it means you chose the wrong position. Bergkamp was never late.'

That very appreciation of his qualities meant the maestro felt entitled to play mind games with the youngster – for his own benefit. Cruyff explains: 'We wanted to promote Dennis, but he had to toughen up a bit first.' As a teenager Dennis was technically and tactically good enough to reach the A1s, the highest junior side. But his trainers considered him too timid for the first team. One afternoon Cruyff's assistant, Tonny Bruins Slot, gave Dennis the bad news: he was to be demoted to the A2s for a month because of his 'lack of motivation'. Furthermore, he would not play in his normal right-wing position there but as a full-back. Dennis was bewildered. 'I didn't get it. Lack of motivation? Perhaps my game didn't look like I was working flat out, but I was.' The blow hit hard, and he never forgot the humiliation. 'It must have really affected me.

Later I often wondered: did Cruyff do it on purpose? Did he want to provoke me?'

Cruyff laughs. That was indeed the strategy. 'Yes, of course we did that to provoke Dennis. We didn't demote him because of any shortcoming and it also had nothing to do with his attitude. It was just to boost his resilience. If you put a good player in a lower team, he has to play against but also *alongside* less talented players. The game is more physical and that makes it harder for him. We also made it more difficult by playing him in a different position. If you play someone like Bergkamp at right-back with a right-winger in front of him who does nothing to help defend, then he experiences first-hand what it's like for the guy behind him when he's the winger and lets his man get away. He really learns from that. Or you play him as a centre-forward and make sure he keeps receiving high crosses from the wings. Then he really has to stick his little head where it hurts. That makes him tougher.'

Cruyff also wanted to see how Bergkamp would react to being the best player in an ordinary team. 'When you're the best player you have more time, and if you have more time you need to use it wisely, helping other players, talking to them, coaching them, leading them.'

Dennis served his time in the A2s, then returned to the A1s. Then came another shock. On 13 December 1986, at half-time in a game against Amsterdam club DWS, his coach brusquely informed him: 'I'm taking you off.' Dennis was upset because he knew he was playing well. Then, grinning, the coach added: 'I'm taking you off because tomorrow you're in the first team.'

Dennis had been 12 years old when Cruyff returned from semi-retirement to play for Ajax in 1981. The nation's greatest-ever player had become rich with Barcelona, then lost all his money in a scam involving a pig farm. Confounding those who doubted his ability to stage a comeback, he scored a brilliant lobbed goal in his first match back, then began a revolution whose consequences for world football are still being felt. The Dutch game at the time was in a sorry state. The Total Football generation had faded away after the 1978 World Cup. Holland were thoroughly outplayed by the Germans at the 1980 Euros and would fail even to qualify for the next three major tournaments. A dreary new 'realism' (a.k.a. defensive football) took hold across the Netherlands, and at Ajax the lessons and doctrines of spatially sophisticated football had been so thoroughly forgotten that the great young hope of the day was the Brazilian-style individualist Gerald Vanenburg, a classic dribbler of the very old school.

As colleague and teacher, Cruyff now galvanised a generation and reignited the fire of what we now call 'the Dutch style'. Cruyff was a huge influence on young Dutch players at Ajax like Frank Rijkaard, Marco van Basten, Sonny Silooy, John van't Schip, and John Bosman. He also left his mark on the club's Danes, Jan Molby, Soren Lerby and Jesper Olsen, helping to set the fuse for the remarkable 'Danish Dynamite' team which played Total Football at the 1986 World Cup. At the end of the 1982–83 season, Ajax chairman Ton Harmsen declined to renew Cruyff's playing contract because he thought the maestro was 'too old' to perform well enough to pull big crowds to justify his salary. Furious, Cruyff signed for rivals Feyenoord and won them the Double in his only season there (passing on his wisdom and attitude to his young team-mate Ruud Gullit into the bargain). Harmsen vowed that Cruyff would 'never set foot in here again'. Having made his point, Cruyff finally hung up his boots at the end of the 1983-84 season and retired to his house in the village of Vinkeveen, south of Amsterdam. Restless, he was soon looking for a way into management, preferably with Ajax, the only club in Holland he cared about. That the club already had a rather good coach, Aad de Mos, the chairman hated him, and Cruyff didn't even have a coaching

badge (as Dutch FA rules said he must) were the merest of difficulties. His two best mates in the team, Van't Schip and Van
Basten, agitated on Cruyff's behalf, undermined de Mos and he
was finally sacked. The media was on Cruyff's side, too, and
Harmsen was forced to appoint him as manager in 1985. To get
round Dutch FA regulations, Cruyff was called 'technical director'.
A model for Ajax takeovers, to be put into effect again nearly 30
years later, had been established.

While Dennis was patiently working his way through the youth
ranks, Johan went straight into revolutionary mode, quickly building a dazzling new version of the old Total Football, or, as he puts
it now, 'working according to my own philosophy'. And what is
that? 'Throwing the opposition into chaos. That's football. If you
get past your man, you throw the opposition into chaos. Creating a
one-man advantage using positional play has the same effect. If you
don't get past your man, if you don't get that extra man advantage,
then the opposition stays organised and nothing happens. The one-
man advantage *is* Ajax football.'

Highlights of some of the games Ajax played at that time are on
YouTube: treat yourself by looking them up. To say that Cruyff got
his team playing 4-3-3 would be to miss the point. What counted
was not the formation but the state of mind. His daring young side
pressed, passed and moved in beguiling patterns high up the field.
Rijkaard, Ronald Koeman, Van't Schip and Van Basten were impe-
rious. Silky veteran Arnold Muhren, lured from Manchester
United, rarely misplaced a pass, and goalkeeper Stanley Menzo
played so far from his line he sometimes seemed to be an auxiliary
midfielder. In Cruyff's first season, Ajax scored 120 goals, Van
Basten getting 37 of them in just 26 games. The team had off days
as well, of course, but when they were good they were spectacular.
A couple of years earlier Van Basten had led an 8-2 demolition of
Feyenoord. Now rugby-esque scorelines – 9-0, 8-1, 6-0 – became

routine against lesser teams. After his first season, when technical midfielders Koeman and Gerald Vanenburg followed the money to PSV, Cruyff counter-intuitively replaced them with two gnarly defenders, Danny Blind and Jan Wouters. Having revamped the Ajax Youth system, he also promoted youngsters like Aron Winter and the Witschge brothers, Robbie and Richard. The team, thus stabilised, played even better than before.

This was the Ajax into which Dennis, still at school, would now be thrown. He describes himself as 'pleasantly nervous', as his parents drive him to the stadium in their little Datsun Cherry for his first game against Roda. Dennis's mum tells the security guy that the kid in the back seat will play in the first team. The security guy has never heard of him and only lets him through after a conversation on his walkie-talkie. Inside, Dennis is soothed by the calm of the players' lounge where Frank Rijkaard welcomes him and cracks some jokes. Dennis just watches and takes it all in. Then Cruyff arrives. 'He's a pretty small guy but his presence was enormous,' Dennis remembers. 'You felt a personality enter the room. He didn't speak to me. That came later. Everyone wished me a good time, including "Auntie Sien" the bar lady.' Soon the game is about to start and Dennis takes his place beside Cruyff in the dugout. 'Nice to see you here,' says the great man. 'Take a good look around, taste the atmosphere, enjoy it.'

'There you are, in the stadium, sitting next to Cruyff. But I wasn't scared, not at all. The only one thing I wanted was to get on the pitch. I was sure Cruyff wouldn't have brought me out there for nothing. I thought, "After half-time he's going to bring me on."' In the 66th minute, he does. Dennis, aged 17 years and seven months (the same age as Cruyff on his debut 22 years earlier), trots on wearing number 16 and takes his place on the right-wing. 'I wasn't a bundle of nerves. I was just excited.' There are just 11,000 people in the stadium: barely half full. His parents, having bought their own rather expensive tickets, are sitting in the Reynolds Stand, on Dennis's side of the pitch. Marcel, nervously standing near the F-Side, tells one of the regulars: 'I think that's my little brother warming up right now.' Dennis remembers every detail. 'I went onto the pitch and I loved it: the grass, the atmosphere in the ground, being able to join such a great squad, the encouragement from the other players, especially Rijkaard. And I had Wouters behind me, which was reassuring. Right away I saw I was faster than my opponent, so I thought: "OK, I have options here: my advantage is speed and I'm going to use it." I really wasn't thinking: "Oh my God, I'm playing for Ajax!" I just felt good, totally natural.' Ajax won 2-0. Afterwards, in the dressing room, Rijkaard came over and asked Dennis how old he was. 'Seventeen? Then you've got a golden future ahead of you.'

A few weeks later – after the Dutch winter break – Dennis started a match for the first time and made an even greater impression, ruining Haarlem full-back Luc Nijholt's day and even scoring in a 6-0 win. Faced with a more experienced opponent whose main tactic was the sliding tackle, Dennis devised a simple counter-measure. 'I thought: "A little chip, that's the solution." When Nijholt came at me, I lobbed the ball over him and I'd beaten him. I was free to make the cross. Wingers played a more simple game back then. You weren't expected to get in the box and try to shoot. You had to stay wide, feel the chalk of the touchline under your boots. Your job was to stretch their defence, get past your man at speed and cross the ball.'

Bergkamp was soon playing regularly, but the toughening up process continued. 'We used all sorts of sneaky little methods,' admits Cruyff. 'For example, we told Dennis [during free-kicks] to stand in the wall, on the outside, so he'd have to coordinate with the keeper. We wanted to see how he would manage that, and how he'd react to free-kicks. Would he turn his shoulder in, put his arm in front of his face? Dennis learned quickly. You really didn't need to work hard to make him tougher or more cunning. And he had a sense of responsibility. He understood he was playing with other people's money. At that time income was based on match bonuses and Dennis felt he shared responsibility for the salary of older players, guys with families to support. He was a well-mannered kid but knew exactly what was expected of him on the pitch. Others took longer to get it. Rijkaard, for example, was a bit slower on the uptake. But Bergkamp was smart.'

Dennis was also learning from his team-mates, especially the peerless Van Basten. 'I paid attention to absolutely everything. I watched how Marco and Frank worked, but also how all the players and trainers interacted, the dynamics in the dressing room, the players' attitude to me, the relationship between me and the trainers. I noticed everything. And in the same way that I'd watch Hoddle on TV, I'd observe Van Basten in training, seeing what I could borrow from him. I liked the way he could accelerate. He'd drag the ball past his opponent with the outside of his boot and then accelerate, leaving his man for dead. He was very good at that. Marco was a killer, a real goal-scorer, always at the front of the attack, whereas I was more of an incoming striker. If records had been kept they'd show how often Marco scored from ten yards or less. For me it was from about fifteen yards.

'Marco was more ruthless than I was. At Arsenal, Ian Wright was like that too, but Marco did it all with great elegance. He could find every inch of the goal, and he had that sharpness in his shot. A short quick flick of the foot – *bang!* I had that as well. And he had a characteristic way of running with his feet a short distance apart which was also like me. Later, when he had problems with his ankle, his posture sagged a bit whereas I stood straighter. But the way we ran and the way we leaned forward as we sprinted away, were similar. It was a way of running that enabled us to get away very fast, faster than our opponents. It was something that just came naturally. I didn't learn to run like that at the athletics club. There they told me: "You run beautifully, very naturally."'

Because he was still a pupil at the St Nicolaas Lyceum (Louis van Gaal's old school, too, thanks to one of Cruyff's 'logical coincidences'), Dennis could train with the first team only on Saturdays. During the week he worked with the reserve team whose sessions were arranged to fit in with school hours. 'We weren't so much training the reserves as using the reserves to train Dennis,' Cruyff explains. 'The trainers knew their job was to work on his shortcomings.'

Juggling school and top-level football became increasingly difficult. When a biology test prevented Dennis travelling with the team to Malmo for a Cup Winners' Cup quarter-final, he made his own way but had to sit out the match on the subs' bench. Four days later, in the return leg, came his breakthrough performance. In the first match, the Swedes, coached by future England manager Roy Hodgson, had unnerved Ajax with their fierce, hard-running game and won 1-0. For the return, Dennis would have to face the experienced Swedish international full-back Torbjörn Persson. Before the match, Bruins Slot presented his dossiers. Dennis was surprised. 'He knew everything about the other team. He'd say: "That defender is semi-professional, his day job is a postman, he's got two kids called such and such, he's left-footed and he likes to go forward ..." Frankly, it went in one ear and came out the other. I didn't really have any use for that. My attitude was more like: "We'll see how it goes, I'm just going to play my game and trust my speed."' Cruyff's approach was more basic still. He told Dennis: 'That defender is an old fart, he's useless and slow, you're better than he is.'

It was yet another psychological ploy. Cruyff: 'I always told my strikers: "You're better than the other guy." I wanted Bergkamp to forget all about the stadium, the TV cameras, the European trophy and focus on beating his man. "Two things can happen," I said to him. "Either you get past him and then he won't dare go forward any more, or you don't get past him and then he'll forget about you and run forward whenever he fancies. But then I'll tell the others: Pass everything to Bergkamp because his defender has abandoned him. So either way it's good." That's how I presented it, but of course I was always taking a risk. It was a gamble, but it usually paid off.' Dennis did as instructed and gave Persson a torrid night, bringing the crowd to their feet and setting up chance after chance as Ajax won a tumultuous match 3-1. But there was no time to celebrate – Dennis had to be up early next morning for his maths class.

* * *

IT MUST HAVE BEEN weird for you. One minute you're a star playing in front of thousands of screaming fans. The next you're in a classroom. How did you cope?

Dennis: 'It was very strange. You can't be big-headed, of course. That's not even *allowed* in Holland! "You're playing European games? Yeah? So what?" Of course, you've got some jealous people, but most of them were positive. After the game, a TV camera crew was allowed into the classroom to watch my reaction to the semi-final draw, which was live, so they could ask me: "How do you feel about that?" So the draw happens and they say: "OK, Dennis, now how do you feel about the draw?" and I say: "Well, it's OK, I don't mind."'

Getting in some practice for all the in-depth interviews of your later career?

'Exactly! But it was all good stuff. And for the people at school it wasn't like it was a surprise. I'd been in that class, and in the Ajax Youth for four or five years already, so they understood the situation. And being at Ajax is already a big thing. So they knew it was coming. And to have a professional footballer in the school was something nice for them as well, something for them to talk about.'

Dennis was surprised by the lasting impact of his performance against the Swedes. 'For years afterwards, people kept talking about it: "Wow, Dennis, I remember how you drove that left-back nuts." For me, too, it was such a thrill: playing in the first team in that stadium, coming out of the dressing room, walking down the tiled corridor, seeing the other team coming from the opposite direction. Studs clicking on the tiles, picking up the flowers which we took onto the pitch and threw to the crowd. Seeing the red and white nets in the goals, the wonderful, white Derby Star ball. The huge pitch which was usually immaculate with the grass neatly cropped, then the murmuring of the crowd, sometimes whistling, and the surging noise when I get the ball . . .'

As it turned out, the semi-final draw was indeed OK. Ajax beat Real Zaragoza comfortably. Next stop would be Athens for the club's first European final since the glory days of the early seventies. Their opponents were the East Germans of Lokomotive Leipzig, whose most colourful contribution in the final turned out to be their bright yellow shirts. Dennis, given special leave of absence from school, flew with the squad to Athens. 'That trip made a huge impression on me. For example, when we arrived in Greece, Van Basten came and sat next to me on the coach and started talking about the match bonus. I think it was 17,500 guilders. Maybe it was even 25,000, but it meant nothing to me. I wasn't thinking about money at all. I said something like: "OK" but I was thinking: "Who cares about that anyway?"'

He also had another chance to observe Cruyff's fascinating mind at work. In Athens, Danny Blind injured himself running on the beach, leaving the team without an experienced full-back. Cruyff calmly picked one of the youngest players in the squad, Frank

Verlaat, telling the older players nearby to cover him in case he got into trouble. 'Everyone was panicking because we'd lost Danny, but Cruyff didn't bat an eyelid. Whenever something went wrong, it actually seemed to interest him. I think it gave him a kick. I was like that as well. I never panicked when circumstances suddenly changed. It just made me think about how to solve the problem. I liked the challenge of getting out of my comfort zone and adapting.'

In the event, Verlaat coped just fine and Ajax won a rather dreary game 1-0, thanks to a Van Basten header, his last goal before he left to join Ruud Gullit at AC Milan. Dennis came on as a substitute in the second half but remembers little. 'I remember Marco's great goal, but that's about it. I think I set up one attack, but suddenly it was all over and we had won the Cup. There was a party in the hotel afterwards, but I was quite calm. I didn't really stop to think how special it was. Now I think: "I had just won a European trophy."'

Before the start of the 1987-88 season Dennis signed for Ajax as a professional. His physiotherapy studies would continue for another year, but football now took priority. Meanwhile, Cruyff was losing his footing on the high wire. To fill the void left by Van Basten's departure, Cruyff had recruited Frank Stapleton, Arnold Muhren's former team-mate at Manchester United, which proved to be a big mistake. Stapleton, a strong and clever centre-forward in his day, was chronically injured. While Ajax struggled in the league, Cruyff argued with his players and the club. He demanded that the team grow up fast and wanted the club to be run more professionally, in a more American style. Harmsen fumed: 'Cruyff doesn't know how to listen.' Cruyff accused the club of amateurism. Team unity began to unravel. By mid-September, Ajax had lost three games. Then they lost their new captain when Frank Rijkaard stormed out, shouting at Cruyff: 'Stop your constant complaining!' Unlike Van Basten and Van't Schip, who didn't mind being criticised, Rijkaard had had enough. He then vanished, turning up only later in the season at Real Zaragoza before playing in Euro '88 and then signing for Milan. Around Christmas time, Harmsen publicly denied having agreed earlier in the season to extend Cruyff's contract. Cruyff was livid. A few days later, at the beginning of January 1988, he told Harmsen he wanted to quit. If it was a bluff, it backfired. The board accepted his resignation. Suddenly, Cruyff's reign was over.

As a coach, Cruyff went on to greater things, moving back to Barcelona, building their Dream Team, winning them the European Cup (with Koeman scoring the winning goal), teaching Pep Guardiola everything he knew, and setting up Barca's Youth academy, La Masia, to run on Ajax-like lines. Ton Harmsen's folly ultimately cost Holland the 2010 World Cup final when a Spain team full of Cruyffian footballers, playing explicitly Cruyffian football, beat a Holland side dominated by players from an Ajax team that had fallen below his exacting standards. But, as we shall see, Dennis and Johan were a long way from being finished with each other, either.

Johan's admiration for Dennis never dimmed and is particularly strong now they are helping to run Ajax together. 'Dennis is a guy with a helicopter view. He sees everything and he keeps things in balance, because he's in balance himself. You can't pressurise Dennis Bergkamp. No matter how loudly people around him shout, he always remains calm and thinks. And because Dennis is able to think broadly, he sees connections. He is a truly decent and amiable man – until he gets angry. Then you see genuine anger, but also intelligence. Then his comments are incredibly incisive, even hurtful, but always well considered. So when someone like that becomes prominent within an organisation, maybe even the most prominent individual, it makes sense. It happens automatically.'

Meanwhile, the older he gets, the more Cruyff-like Dennis seems to become. 'I'm really fond of Johan, even though I certainly don't always agree with him. But the discussions are always about details, never about principles. We never disagree about principles.' Their relationship is pleasant rather than close, but Dennis is not the least bothered by the suggestion that he has grown to be like his mentor. 'That's not a problematic observation,' he says with a smile. 'Sometimes I notice we have very similar thoughts. I don't know if that's because Johan influenced me when I was young or if we are just similar in nature.'

Have you ever deliberately tried to imitate Cruyff?

Dennis: 'Do me a favour, please! Imitating someone else is really not my style. And anyway, Johan would see through that immediately.'

But you don't like fighting with people as he does?

'Yeah, I can understand when people say that he is always looking for conflict. That's probably in his character. Conflict is what he wants, that's what he needs. And when things are smooth, he's always looking for another thing . . . Yeah, he likes it. But I understand him. I know where he is coming from. That's probably where we're different. I prefer things to be smooth.'

3

LOUIS, LOUIS

I T IS NEARLY MIDNIGHT and smoke from flares among the tens of thousands of raucous fans hangs over the Leidseplein. It's a May night in 1992 and Ajax have just won the UEFA Cup but their star player is absent. Having played wonderfully throughout the tournament, Dennis actually slept through most of tonight's final against Torino, laid low by flu and a high fever. On the crowded balcony of the Stadsschouwburg theatre, with his players and the giant silver trophy, bullish and jubilant young manager Louis van Gaal has something to say. He grabs the microphone and pushes through to the balcony railings. Louis wants to tell the crowd just who they should thank for tonight's triumph: 'ONE MAN!' he shouts, jabbing at the night sky with his forefinger as if proclaiming the arrival of the Messiah. 'ONE MAN!' He is now leaning so far forward he seems certain to fall into the throng. He pauses for effect. Then he screams out the name: 'DENNIS B-E-R-G-K-A-M-P!!!!' The crowd roars. Louis roars. Every child, woman and man in the ecstatic gathering chants the young star's name in unison.

Van Gaal would never speak so emotionally in public about Dennis again, but that night the two seemed an unbreakable double act. In just six months in charge of the club, Van Gaal, the intense former teacher with a face like an Easter Island statue, had turned his collection of prospects into a whirlwind of a team. Ajax had whipped through the UEFA tournament with a delicious variant of the traditional Ajax game: crisp and creative, quick and daring, and splendidly organised. And Dennis had become the main man.

The UEFA Cup triumph was all the more impressive for coming after a period of astonishing instability. In ancient Rome, AD 69, the so-called Year of Four Emperors, was considered the acme of political chaos. Between 1989 and 1991 Ajax had nine coaches – *nine!* – in a bewildering series of combinations. 'I forget the sequence,' says Dennis, 'but there really were a lot of coaches in a short time!' When Johan Cruyff walked out in January 1988 he was replaced by a triumvirate of Bobby Haarms, Barry Hulshoff and Spitz Kohn. They, in turn, were ditched for German physiotherapist Kurt Linder ('the worst coach I ever had!' Dennis remembers). He lasted just three months before Spitz Kohn (again) and Louis van Gaal (in a junior capacity) paved the way for Leo Beenhakker, who jumped ship for Real Madrid after a season and a half.

On top of all that, before Van Gaal finally took the managerial reins in late 1991, Ton Harmsen, the chairman who had clashed so bitterly with Cruyff, was forced from the club by a combination of fan outrage and media derision. A few months later he suffered a stroke. Furthermore, the club was not only convulsed by a tax scandal but had been banned from Europe for a year because a hooligan fan had speared a rival goalkeeper with a metal rod ripped from the F-Side terraces. Meanwhile, the players had suffered enough tactical turbulence to sink a navy. Dennis's formative football years involved being bounced around between positions and roles. 'Yeah, it was quite an interesting period,' he says equably. 'But I learned a lot from it, and from all those coaches. Good or bad, I really just learned a lot.'

Under Cruyff, Dennis had reached the first team, played in a European final and established himself as a right-winger. In a side bristling with stars like Frank Rijkaard, Marco van Basten and Jan Wouters, he more than held his own. Then the simmering feud with Harmsen boiled over and Cruyff departed. Departed, that is, without a word of farewell. Indeed, he and Dennis had no contact for the next three and a half years. 'I would have expected a phone call from Johan, a few encouraging words, some reassurance like: "Keep calm, things will work out for the best." But maybe he intentionally didn't call because he thought I needed to manage on my own. And that's what I did. I never experienced it as a trauma.' Meanwhile, with its three new bosses, the team continued in muddled fashion through the 1987-88 season but managed to reach the Cup Winners' Cup final again, but lost to Mechelen, a Belgian team managed by yet another former Ajax coach, Aad de Mos. Dennis played in most games, scoring occasionally but more often using his speed on the wing to get past opposition full-backs and deliver precise crosses.

Kurt Linder's arrival at the beginning of the following season was more problematic, because he was the man chosen by Harmsen to roll back the Cruyff revolution. Cruyff, as always, had created a team for attack, and fielded bafflingly fluid formations: 4-3-3, 3-4-3, even 3-3-4. Along with other football conservatives in the Netherlands, Harmsen regarded Cruyff as brilliant but essentially unreliable. What was needed now, the chairman felt sure, was discipline and defensive solidity. Hence his approach to Linder, a German who had coached Ajax briefly in the early eighties. The two men were skiing buddies and although Linder had retired from football to run a clinic in Switzerland, Harmsen persuaded him to return to bring some order to Amsterdam.

'Linder was an obvious outsider,' says Dennis. 'He didn't

understand the culture of Ajax at all. The young players challenged him and the older ones were tactically superior to him. As Amsterdammers, we liked to bluff, show off, be cheeky, boast. If you're a coach, you have two ways to deal with that. Either you can be like that yourself – and do it better than the players – or be aloof and come down hard when the squad plays up.' Linder did neither and was soon being openly mocked in training sessions. Nor was he a match for his sophisticated players, three of whom had just played under the great Rinus Michels and won Euro '88 with the Dutch national team. From the start, captain Jan Wouters emerged as the tactical leader. 'During matches Jan would give detailed instructions. He'd say things like: "You, two yards to the right. You, to the left and you drop back." If Linder tried to say something, Jan would get really annoyed and tell him to back off and Linder would just say: "OK, do it your way." It was extremely embarrassing.' Even so, Linder still had enough power to kick Bergkamp out of the team. 'He played four-four-two without a right-winger, which was my position. So he demoted me, just like that, without a word.'

Actually, Linder used four words. Dispatching both Dennis and the future Barcelona star Richard Witschge to the Youth team, he informed the lower-level coach: 'Those two are useless.' The coach in question was Louis van Gaal. And he saw things differently. Dennis was demoralised, but Van Gaal saw potential. He had a feeling Dennis might be playing in the wrong position. So, instead of the winger's number 7, he handed him the number 10 shirt. Dennis's experimental new position would be in the centre of the team as a second striker working just behind the centre-forward. Van Gaal encouraged Dennis to think strategically. As his performance in a youth tournament in Volendam demonstrated, the switch electrified him. Dennis was now able to deploy all the quickness of his brain as well as of his feet. He began to move astutely between the lines, sprayed clever passes, confused opponents with sudden positional manoeuvres and scored goals. He was crowned the best player of the tournament. Rather more importantly, he had discovered his destiny. Looking back, he sees this as one of the key moments of his career; as important as being picked for the first time by Cruyff and winning a place three years later in the national team under Rinus Michels.

To the relief of everyone – including Linder himself – his reign lasted just three months. He was replaced by Kohn and Van Gaal. Notionally, the latter was the junior partner but in practice he called most of the shots, and Dennis was central to his ambitious plans. Dennis was sensational in his evolving role as free man behind a centre-forward and two wingers. He set a new national record by scoring in ten consecutive matches, and so original was his new position there wasn't even a name for it. Eventually, the press came up with *schaduwspits*. Shadow striker. Dennis had found the role of his life. 'I suddenly felt completely free in my game. I could use my two-footedness and show I could score goals. Everything I had learned playing for the juniors and what the fans didn't yet know about me, could manifest itself in that position. Being the number ten gave me that wonderful tension again. It was new, it was exciting. I didn't hesitate for a moment, wondering where I should run to. It was all automatic. Suddenly, something amazing happened to me.'

Ajax only narrowly missed out on the league title. The new board now handed Leo Beenhakker the job and Dennis came down to earth with a bump. Bizarre as it seems in retrospect, Beenhakker was not convinced by Dennis and thought three other candidates might be better in the number 10 slot: Wim Jonk, Ron Willems and Ronald de Boer. Dennis found himself offered other roles, none of which suited him so well: centre-forward, left-winger, deeper-lying central-midfielder, substitute. 'I was demoted and I really struggled with that because I felt I'd earned my place. I had more or less created my own position in the team: the "Bergkamp position". Then along comes a different manager with other ideas and he wants to show everyone that there's another way of doing things, namely his way. Managers want to enforce their style because they think in terms of power. Kohn and Van Gaal approached me together during a training session and said: "If anyone asks you who put you in the number ten position, then you know what to say, right? That was us, we did that." That made me wonder: "What's all this about?" Managers want to impress because they crave recognition. That's especially true of Van Gaal and it was already the case back then.'

Beenhakker was amiable, but Dennis's plight was in some ways worse than it had been under Linder. 'At least I could understand why Linder dropped me. If you're playing four-four two and you think Bergkamp is purely a right-winger, then Bergkamp has to go. But for Beenhakker the issue was my football skills. He just didn't think I was good enough.' Beenhakker denies this and says he was just trying to win the league, which he duly did. But he thought too little of Dennis, then aged 20, to take him to the World Cup in Italy. (In fact, Dennis had a lucky escape: the Dutch stars had wanted Cruyff as coach. In Italy, instead of concentrating on football, they spent most of their time fighting with each other, with Beenhakker and with the Dutch FA. Holland, who should have won the tournament, came home without winning a match.)

Meanwhile, Dennis spent the summer more productively. On his return to Ajax, Beenhakker was astonished: 'I was confronted with a completely transformed Bergkamp. Dennis was self-confident. He had a defiant attitude, as if he was saying: "Come on then, I'll show you what I'm made of." It sometimes happens to young players that they suddenly grow a lot in just a few weeks. During that summer he changed himself from a youngster into a man. It had nothing to do with me.'

Dennis doesn't remember the period in detail. 'He said that? If he noticed, then it must have been something. I was hurt the season before. If the coach is not happy, if he's not playing you, you think: "OK it has to be different now." Something would have happened with me at some point. I think I worked a bit harder, did some running, got into a different mindset, got into an extra gear. I'm sure that must have happened. But when I look back now through my career, and at other players as well, sometimes you just find a certain balance within yourself, or your body or your life or something like that.'

Whatever triggered the change, there was now no doubt: Dennis was the best number 10. And he began to develop a remarkable understanding with team-mates. These relationships foreshadowed later ones with Ian Wright, Nicolas Anelka, Patrick Kluivert and Thierry Henry. Dennis's movement and the almost unearthly precision of his finishing began to mesh with Wim Jonk's genius for long, defence-opening passes. Spectacular goals began to flow. Scarcely less productive was the partnership with Swedish centreforward Stefan Pettersson whose selfless running made space for Dennis's rapier thrusts from deep. Dennis and his colleagues were developing most of this by themselves and Beenhakker was mesmerised. As he said at the time: 'The timing of Bergkamp's sprints, his ability to score, all the time quickly turning in limited space ... it's all equally amazing.' Even so, he thought Dennis was still too modest. 'He doesn't manifest himself enough in the group. As a person he's the ideal son-in-law, slightly reticent, very wellmannered. These are wonderful traits – but not necessarily for a professional footballer. It's like he needs to develop two personalities: Bergkamp off the pitch and Bergkamp on the pitch. These two will have to converge.'

Finally, Beenhakker was lured back to Spain and Van Gaal got his chance with the first team. Dennis remembers: 'Everything became more intense. We talked a lot about things like taking positions, and every game was evaluated in detail afterwards. Louis always had his little notebook with him in which he wrote down all sorts of stuff. He constantly emphasised what was important, what we needed to learn and practise. He brought structure to the way we worked and gave us clarity. At that point in my career I really liked that.' The team became more Total, rarely conceding possession and pressing with ever-greater energy. After the winter break, Ajax began to fly. In a 7-0 win over Twente, Dennis scored a sublime hat-trick and Louis van Gaal was moved to tears by the beauty of his young team. In the league, a more conventional PSV side built around the singular genius of Romario was outpointing them. But all Europe began to notice Dennis's starring role in a series of dominating UEFA Cup performances, not least against Osvaldo Bagnoli's Genoa. (We shall meet Bagnoli again shortly.)

'You could really sense there was a new generation emerging. Van Gaal made us even more eager and ambitious. Our game was innovative, attractive to watch and enjoyable to play. If we slipped up, we didn't give up. We kept bouncing back because we stuck to his philosophy that the team is more important than any individual player. "If everyone adheres to the agreements we make as a team, success will inevitably follow," Louis said time and again. It gave us the stability we needed.'

Van Gaal also encouraged Dennis to think critically and creatively about every aspect of the game. 'We trained meticulously. Every detail, shooting, passing, everything had to improve. And everything became more tactical. Where should you run and why? "Think, guys," Van Gaal would say. "Consider every move you make." He gave us pointers, but during matches you had to do it yourself. He constantly hammered home that you had to be aware of everything you were doing. Every action had to have a purpose. I focused on what I was good at: being decisive. I thought a lot about tactics, about the position of defenders and about finding the opponent's weak spots. I began to choose more intelligent positions by communicating more with the players around me. If a midfielder was marking me, I would play as far forward as possible, forcing my man to play between his defenders to make him uncomfortable. And if the player marking me was a defender, I would drop back to the midfield so he would feel out of place. I really loved approaching football that way, analysing my position like that. I was completely obsessed with being decisive. I was always watching my opponents, paying attention to details, observing the situation on the pitch. I constantly watched for opportunities to win the ball. All I needed was the slightest chance and I would rush at it.'

If this is beginning to sound like 'Louis, I think this is the beginning of a beautiful friendship', it shouldn't. Football is not the movies. A rift was coming between coach and star, and their second season would make it manifest. Part of the problem was Van Gaal's sheer intensity. 'We were young and keen to learn, but if we'd been together for five years, I don't think Van Gaal's fanatical approach would have worked.' And Dennis was beginning to assert his independence. 'We discussed things, but ultimately I did what I thought best. That might sound presumptuous, but even then I was more developed as a player than Van Gaal was as a manager. I just knew, instinctively, where I needed to be to be decisive. Let's say Van Gaal tells me: "Move ten yards back to be in a better defensive position, Dennis." I'd say: "I'd prefer not to, Coach, because if we win the ball I'll have to make up those ten yards at a sprint, and that will cost me that little bit of extra energy I need to be decisive."'

Dennis was also thinking of his next step. He had started learning Italian via a correspondence course a year earlier and, after the UEFA Cup win, Europe's top clubs began wooing him aggressively. Dennis eventually agreed to join Inter. Wim Jonk would go, too. A future issue of conflict was that the deal was signed on a Friday night in The Hague, 36 hours before a crucial league match at PSV on the Sunday afternoon. Van Gaal was desperate to win the championship, and regarded the Inter business a distraction. The match – on Valentine's Day – went badly. In the first 45 minutes, Ajax played brilliantly and Dennis scored one of his greatest goals yet. Seen now, it looks like a prototype of his winning strike against Argentina in the World Cup six years later. Sprinting at the PSV defence, he perfectly controls a high 50-metre pass from Frank de Boer with his knee (his *knee*!), then chips the goalkeeper from a narrow angle. It was hardly Dennis's fault that a minute later a defensive blunder gave PSV a soft equaliser. Even Romario later admitted that the 1-1 half-time score was a 'bizarre' reflection of the balance of play. After the break, however, Ajax tired and PSV, despite having a man sent off, won 2-1. Ajax dropped to fourth in the table and Van Gaal was apoplectic.

Twenty-four hours later, the Inter deal was made public, as Dennis and Wim attended a press conference in Gouda. They then immediately returned to work. In their mind the entire business had been done to avoid harming Ajax. They posed for one public-ity picture in Inter shirts, then said they would give no interviews to the Italian media until after the season; the players' only concern was to finish on a high note, by winning trophies. Dennis and Wim's agent, Rob Jansen, joked that while his boys would be mil-lionaires Ajax would become multi-millionaires (Inter paid about ten million guilders for Jonk and 30 million for Bergkamp – the largest amounts ever paid for Dutch players).

In the last four months of the season, Ajax were maddening, one week crushing eventual champions Feyenoord 5-0, the next drop-ping points to minnows like MVV Maastricht. In the UEFA Cup, two mistakes by goalkeeper Stanley Menzo cost Ajax a tie against Auxerre and Van Gaal revealed his ruthless side: Menzo was dropped and permanently replaced by youngster Edwin van der Sar. In another match, winger Bryan Roy failed to follow Van Gaal's instructions to the letter – and was promptly shipped off to Foggia.

As the chances of glory receded, Van Gaal appeared to take out his frustrations on Bergkamp and Jonk, blaming them for the PSV defeat. Even now, this rankles. Dennis: 'His criticism of me and Wim was unjustified. I did everything I could that season to win the title with Ajax. I was totally committed to that. While Rob Jansen was negotiating with Inter, there was only one thing on my mind: the match against PSV. I wanted to win it. Yes, I had to go to The Hague on the Friday night to confirm the agreement, but I had everything under control. I took it easy on the Saturday and went to bed early. I more than made up for one late night. Van Gaal insinuated that my attitude changed after I signed for Inter. It's just not true. Every match I wanted to perform better than the previous one. I always had that same drive, to be the best player on the field, to win. That didn't change. Louis really should have known better.'

At the beginning of May, Ajax lost 1-0 to little Willem II, ending their title hopes. Twenty minutes into the second half, Van Gaal replaced his star striker with mediocre defender Johnny Hansen. As he walked off, Dennis looked daggers at Louis and jerked his head as if to say: 'What the hell are you doing?' A TV microphone caught Van Gaal's non-answer: 'I'll tell you tomorrow.' When tomorrow came, Van Gaal claimed the substitution was tactical 'because Bergkamp wasn't in the game. Or rather, he wasn't in the game *again*. Dennis is a sophisticated talent, but at the moment he seems to be blocked.' Dennis reflects now: 'It was obvious what he was doing. It was my last Ajax season and I'd hit my ceiling in Holland. I needed to go but somehow I felt he needed to keep me in my place, to say: "You're nothing special, you're just one of the team." In that game, it was really a silly decision. I was top scorer in Holland. There was almost half an hour to go. We could have saved that game. But he wanted to make a statement.

'Towards the end, I had the feeling that Ajax resented the fact that I was leaving. That puzzled and disappointed me. Before the

[1992-93] winter break I'd already announced – well in advance – that this would be my last season. I gave Ajax plenty of time to prepare for my departure and the club earned a huge amount of money from my sale. What more could they have asked for? It's normal procedure at Ajax for a home-grown player who has performed well for a while in the first team to be sold off for a lot of money.'

* * *

IT SEEMS STRANGE that your football relationship with Van Gaal can be so productive – yet there's tension. And even though your football relationship with Leo Beenhakker was much less creative, you still like and get on well with him.

Dennis: 'I couldn't get angry at Beenhakker. I still can't. Leo is a great guy, with his clever comments and his ability to manage a group. He has great rapport with star players, but he's also friendly with the reserves. He's more suited than anyone else to a team that includes big names. He's a real people manager. That's the main difference between him and Louis. Leo has a lot of wisdom and he knows how to manipulate the media, too. I enjoyed working with him, even though we didn't agree about me being number ten. Damn, that was my position! But I enjoyed training every day. Leo always had something nice to say and I admired the way he could correct or encourage players by taking them aside and just saying a few words.'

Van Gaal was all smiles when, after the final league match of the 1992-93 season, fans at De Meer gave Dennis and Wim an emotional send-off with a fireworks display. A few days later, though, when Dennis played his last-ever competitive game for Ajax, he revealed his feelings. Scoring in the Dutch Cup final against Heerenveen, he celebrated with an atypical snarl and clenched fist – gestures that spoke of his anger and frustration.

And that, between the two men, was that. The match turned out to be the last time Dennis would ever play for Louis. Their paths as player and coach never crossed again. By the time Van Gaal became national coach in 2000, Bergkamp had retired from *oranje*. More recently, the two men were on opposite sides during the civil war at Ajax that followed the coup of 2011. Dennis was Cruyff's closest ally, while Louis was the candidate of the anti-Cruyffists. Van Gaal is now national coach once more. When asked for an interview for this book he declined via his press officer, who said that everything Louis wanted to say about Dennis was in his 2009 book *Van Gaal: Biography and Vision*. There he mentions Dennis only to disparage him, claiming that Ajax were only able to win the Dutch title and the Champions League because Bergkamp left: 'It's not nice to say so, but [Jari] Litmanen as number 10 was an improvement on Bergkamp. Thanks to him the team became more balanced.'

It's an odd and ungenerous remark. Bergkamp and Litmanen were very different players, operating in different roles at a different time and with different colleagues. In any case, Van Gaal has elsewhere acknowledged that it was the return of Frank Rijkaard, first in midfield, later in central defence, which truly stabilised his side that went on to become European Champions in 1995.

* * *

Is there bad blood between you and Van Gaal?

Dennis: 'It's OK between us. It would be too strong to say that I don't get along with Louis. Looking back, I'd say I had him as a coach at just the right time. If I'd stayed another season, things would have become difficult. It would have been a war, actually. But it's not a big problem.'

You basically respect him?

'Of course.'

Your difficulties weren't like the ones you had at Inter with Ottavio Bianchi?

'Oh no! It was nothing anywhere near that. And you have to remember, Louis has always wanted fantastic football. Ajax football. He would never admit it, but the football he wants is like the football Cruyff wants, and Wenger ... It's just their methods are different. Cruyff's coaching is based on what he was like as a player: adventurous, spectacular, attacking. Johan relies on instinct and skills, he doesn't analyse much. Van Gaal is more didactic. He gives his players assignments which they have to carry out in order for the system to work. And the system is sacred. Wenger is somewhere in between. His nickname is "The Professor". He's good at tactics, but he's even better at creating balance in his team. Wenger doesn't think in terms of systems. He thinks in terms of players, intelligent players, and he allows them to determine the system on the pitch. And, like Cruyff, he loves technical players, guys who can play instinctively.'

As Van Gaal showed in the mid-nineties at Ajax and a decade later at AZ Alkmaar, his forte is working with young players who still have everything to prove and with teams who still have everything to win. It's tougher for him when his players are less obedient. At Barcelona he clashed with Rivaldo. At Bayern he fell out with with Luca Toni and Franck Ribéry. And, five years after winning the 1995 Champions League with his young Ajax disciples, the same players were no longer willing to follow his orders blindly in the Dutch national team. Their experience with bigger clubs abroad had made them more independent.

Dennis: 'For Van Gaal all players are equal. For him there's no such thing as big names, because everyone serves the team and the system – *his system*. By contrast, Cruyff relied on exceptional players, on individualists, because they were the ones who could decide a match. He stimulated his great players and challenged them, even by creating conflict if necessary. Johan himself was the greatest player of all and the other players served him, but that would be unthinkable in a team led by Van Gaal. Even for the greatest players, the team has to take precedence. But imagine you have ten mediocre painters and you also have Rembrandt. Are you going to tell Rembrandt he's really no better than the others? Or are you going to make him feel special and let him *be* special, so he can create his most beautiful works of art? Wenger is different again. He keeps his distance and goes out of his way to avoid creating conflicts. His calmness, seriousness, professionalism and intelligence all rub off on the group. That's how he makes sure everyone behaves professionally and the big players are team players. At the same time, he lets them do their own thing, which gives them the freedom to be great.' And, of course, the Rembrandt of Dutch football was Johan Cruyff.

When Van Gaal first started out as a young trainer under Cruyff, the two football men who grew up near each other in east Amsterdam understood and were intrigued by each other. But that changed. Differences in character gradually drove Louis and Johan unimaginably far apart. A reconciliation between two forceful and stubborn personalities seems impossible, particular after the coup and counter-coup at Ajax during 2011.

Philosophically, the key difference may be that while Van Gaal advocates the same football as Cruyff, he remains convinced that his players need him to play it. If football is physical chess, then Louis sees himself as the grandmaster and his players as pawns. Cruyff, by contrast, aims to educate intelligent, talented players to become independent-minded individuals who will then instinctively make the right choices and collaborate efficiently with team-mates. In other words, while Louis sees the role of the manager as supreme, Johan wants to develop footballers who make the manager superfluous.

Dennis entirely prefers Cruyff's approach and is in turn precisely the kind of player Cruyff holds up as an example. Indeed, the whole Cruyffian plan at Ajax now – as Johan might put it – is to create new generations of Dennis Bergkamps.

4

INTERMEZZO

I. The Religious War

SIGNING FOR ONE of Italy's biggest clubs seemed the smart move. But Dennis's decision to join Internazionale in 1993 plunged him into a whirlpool of confusion and stress. He became a victim of broken promises and cultural misunderstandings, fell out with his coach, found himself mocked both by his own fans and by the Italian press and was even dubbed 'strange and solitary' by his striking partner, Ruben Sosa. By the end, his experience of football in Italy turned so bleak that Dennis considered retiring early. But what was it precisely that made the two years at San Siro difficult? 'We were in the middle of a religious war,' explains Tommaso Pellizzari, renowned sports writer of Milan's main newspaper, *Corriere della Sera*. Dennis had unwittingly stepped into the middle of a battle between Italy's future and its past.

The immediate cause of conflict was one that outsiders might consider a minor doctrinal matter. But since Italian football is dominated by tactics, the issue was profound. It was this: should Italian teams stick to their traditional man-marking methods or follow the example of coaches elsewhere and switch to zonal defence? Beneath this technical issue lay a philosophical question: was defensive football really superior to the attacking game? And lurking deeper still was the yet more complex issue of identity. Should Italians continue to be Italian? Or should they try to become Dutch?

The seeds of strife had been planted in the mid-1980s when an emerging media tycoon called Silvio Berlusconi, owner of AC Milan, the lesser of Milan's big two football clubs, began to take an interest in the ideas and methods of an obscure young coach called Arrigo Sacchi, then at little Parma in Serie B. Sacchi himself had been incubating heretical ideas since his youth. The official creed of Italian football had long been defensive security. The country's footballing greatness had been built on *catenaccio*, the 'door-bolt' system whose key feature was a belt-and-braces approach to stopping other teams from scoring. The strategy was to build an impregnable fortress in central defence, with two midfielders shielding two man-markers and a free man, the *libero*, sweeping behind. Writer Gianni Brera may have claimed that perfection in football was a 0-0 game in which neither defence made a mistake. But even the dourest defensive coaches preferred to deploy at least one free-spirited attacker whose job was to grab a goal so the rest of the team could defend the lead.

Many foreign observers were appalled by the Italian approach, which was rooted in their historical sense of weakness. (One notable exception was Stanley Kubrick: he preferred the dark neuroses of Italian football to the 'simplistic' pleasures of the Dutch or Brazilians.) It should be noted that defensive football had not always been the Italian way. In the 1930s, teams representing Mussolini's Italy had won two World Cups with a style based on the

WM formation of Herbert Chapman's Arsenal. But, much as Total Football became the official creed of the Netherlands, so post-war Italy turned devoutly Catenaccist. The system made the two Milan clubs, Inter and AC Milan, into European champions in the 1960s. Italian defenders were recognised as the best in the world; and *catenaccio* had proved time and again that it worked. Only now it didn't.

As a young man, Arrigo Sacchi had worked as a salesman for his father's shoe factory but his real passion was football. Despite the prevailing orthodoxies, he was instinctively drawn to attacking teams like Pele's Brazil and the great Hungarian and Real Madrid sides of the 1950s. But the style with which he fell most deeply in love was Dutch Total Football. In the early 1970s, as the golden Ajax of Cruyff and Johan Neeskens approached perfection and won the European Cup three years in a row, Sacchi found himself visiting Amsterdam with his father on business. While his dad attended trade fairs, Sacchi headed to the Middenweg to watch and learn from the great Ajax team's training sessions.

Sacchi was not the only Italian to be enchanted by the Dutch. In 1972, Ternana, a small team from Umbria, reached Serie A with an Italianate version of Total Football dubbed the *gioco corto* (short game). Ternana's coach Corrado Viciani recited Camus to his players and drilled them to previously unimaginable levels of fitness. And when Ajax played Inter in the 1972 European Cup final, Viciani appeared on TV to declare that, for the good of Italy, Inter should lose by three or four goals: 'The Dutch play real football, but in Italy managers are interested in playing defensively, in playing horrible and un-aesthetic football.' In the event, Ajax outclassed Inter, but only won 2-0, and the defeat, like Ajax's 1-0 victory over Juventus in the following year's final, failed to shake fundamental Italian faith in their 'horrible' – but still rather successful – style.

Meanwhile, Sacchi had turned his back on the shoe business and gone into coaching, starting with his local team and working his way up to Parma. Central to his vision was the abolition of man-markers and *liberos*. Instead, he deployed 'The Zone', a flexible four-man defence moulded to play as part of a fluid, compact Dutch-style formation which pressed high up the field. His defenders, midfielders and attackers were required to move as one unit and concentrate on offence. At a time when most Italian teams trained only once a day, Sacchi insisted on two sessions, so his players ran further and faster than anyone else. Silvio Berlusconi recognised the potential of this kind of entertaining football and in 1987, after Parma had beaten Milan in two Cup games, he recruited Sacchi. To help him, he went on to buy the three greatest Cruyff protégés of the day: Ruud Gullit, Marco van Basten and Frank Rijkaard became the three most important players in the Italian league. Thus was born 'Il Grande Milan', one of the great teams of history. Sacchi's Italo-Dutch fusion swept all before it, and in the process thoroughly eclipsed neighbours Inter, which remained a bastion of the old ways under coach Giovanni Trapattoni, a veteran of the glory days of *catenaccio*.

In the six years leading up to Dennis's arrival in the city, then, the two Milan football clubs were locked in a theological as well as tribal conflict. And the contest became embarrassingly one-sided. Pellizzari, a lifelong Inter fan, recalls the shock of witnessing Milan's era-defining destruction of a great Real Madrid side in 1989. 'People remember the second leg, when Milan won five-nil, but the one-one away draw was more astonishing to us. For the first time we saw an Italian team go to Madrid and play as if they were in the San Siro. Milan went to Madrid and attacked! Traditionalists said, "No, we cannot play this way because we are Italians." It was even seen as a betrayal of our identity. Trapattoni and Inter represented this view.' Even when dour Inter won the *scudetto* in 1989, they were promptly overshadowed by Milan's dazzling 4-0 victory in the European Cup final.

In light of what happened to Dennis at Inter, it's worth stressing that even Sacchi's revolution almost failed before it started. In his first months, the Milan old guard were suspicious and defenders like Franco Baresi and Mauro Tassotti found it difficult to understand what was being asked of them. In the autumn of 1987, when Milan were knocked out of the UEFA Cup and lost a league game at home to Fiorentina, the atmosphere turned mutinous. 'Everybody thought Sacchi was finished, but then Berlusconi made his famous intervention. He goes to the dressing room and says to the players: "I want you to know that Sacchi is the trainer for this year and also for next year. As for you guys, I don't know." Then everything changed.'

Italians in general, and Italian trainers in particular, are cynical, Pellizzari observes. They rarely think about aesthetics and care only about results. 'The real revolution of Sacchi was not that The Zone game looked good but that it *worked*. Sacchi showed you can win this way. That's why one of our great football writers, Mario Sconcerti, says that Sacchi is for Italian football what Kant is for philosophy: there is before Sacchi and after Sacchi. He changed us and all Italian coaches now are his heirs. Actually, I don't think Sacchi invented anything. He borrowed it from Holland. But he is treated as if he was the inventor because nobody imagined we could play this way in Italy before.' Even so, there is still resistance to Total Football. 'Earlier this year a journalist called Michele Dalai wrote a book about why he hates Barcelona's football. It was called *Against Tiki-Taka* and it did quite well. He doesn't like Barça's passing, pressing and attacking. He calls that "masturbation football". He wants to score one goal, then defend.'

Meanwhile, back in the early 1990s, Inter were in trouble. After Trapattoni left for Juventus in 1991, Inter president Ernesto Pellegrini, painfully aware of the superiority of Milan, tried to replicate Berlusconi's revolution. He lighted upon Corrado Orrico, another philosophical coach, who had brought attacking football to Lucchese in Serie B. But Orrico was no Sacchi, and the Inter old guard, not least key defenders Giuseppe Bergomi and Riccardo Ferri, were unimpressed. Orrico failed and was replaced by the veteran Osvaldo Bagnoli, a much-loved, old-fashioned coach best-known for winning the championship with outsiders Verona in 1985.

By the time Dennis Bergkamp had decided to leave Ajax and half of Europe and all the top Italian clubs wanted him, the picture had shifted once more. Sacchi was now running the Italian national team and his successor Fabio Capello, while keeping most of Sacchi's tactics and squad, had made Milan less flamboyant but impossible to beat. Between May 1991 and March 1993 Capello's team pre-emptively eclipsed Arsenal's Invincibles by going a staggering 58 games without defeat. By the beginning of the 1993-94 season, though, their Dutch trio was no more. Ageing Ruud Gullit had fallen out of favour and gone to Sampdoria, Rijkaard had returned to Ajax, and Van Basten's career was nearing its premature end because of his injured ankle. Pellegrini spotted an opportunity. Inter had finished the 1992-93 season second to champions Milan. Surely a sprinkling of magic from the Netherlands would be enough to win back the title? Inter went a-wooing and soon Dennis Bergkamp and Wim Jonk were posing for photographers in their new black and blue shirts. The Italian press hailed the signings as a *nerazzurro* masterstroke.

* * *

OF ALL THE GIN JOINTS in all the towns in all the world, Dennis, you walk Inter theirs?! You were the hottest young talent in Europe! Everyone wanted you! You could have gone to Barcelona, or Milan, or Juventus. Yet you picked the world headquarters of defensive football. It's still hard to understand.

Dennis: 'Well, promises were made and it felt like the right move. I think there's been a thread running through my life which is that I've made a lot of big decisions on feeling, on instinct. And that was one of them. And, you know, maybe it was the right decision in the end. I didn't enjoy it, but I learned a lot at Inter. It was the making of me in a way. I would never have had the career I did at Arsenal if I hadn't been there. You mentioned that I could have gone to Barcelona. Well, yes, I sort of knew Johan [Cruyff] wanted me to go there. He would drop hints about it. But he never said anything directly, so I was like "OK, if you don't ask ..." Anyway, at that time Spain had the rule of only four foreign players for each club, and Romario, Koeman and Hristo Stoichkov were already at Barcelona so I'd have been the fourth one. But that wasn't really why I chose Inter. For a long time my heart was set on Italy because it was absolutely the best football country then. Italy, Italy, Italy ... it's all I was thinking about.

'In the end, it came down to a choice between Juventus and Inter. My agent and my brother were talking to Juve and phoned me from Turin and said: "Dennis, we really don't have a good feeling." I said: "Well, you two guys are my eyes and ears so I believe you, I trust you." So I chose Inter.'

Didn't you think to ask the AC Milan Dutch guys for advice? You were close enough to Rijkaard and Van Basten from Ajax and Gullit from the national team ...

'I didn't feel I could pick up the phone and call them. More importantly, I didn't want to. I was thinking: "I can go for the comfortable options of Milan, or Barcelona, or I can make my own adventure." I wanted to do something new, go somewhere no one from Ajax had been. Guys like Johan and Frank and Marco want to let you make your own decisions. They want to help you, but if you want to make the decision yourself, that's better, even if it's the wrong decision.'

So you follow your intuition. You go to Inter and the rest is ... well, just misery, isn't it?

'Not only. I really loved the country. And my personal life couldn't have been better. We'd [Henrita and I] just got married and it felt like a long honeymoon. We had a beautiful house outside Milan, in a small town called Civate looking over a lake. Brilliant! The guy I rented the house off was fantastic, a real Inter fan. He'd sold pots and pans out of his own garage and built up the business to be a big company. I like those success stories of people who work hard for their money. And we saw that house and loved it. Later we asked him why he hadn't given the house to his daughter. And he said: "I don't want to give it to that son-in-law!" [*Laughs*] We had a good feeling with each other. He was really normal and he talked about Inter in a nice way. He was very frustrated with their way of playing as well, so we bonded a little bit. And I remember we had to make up a contract for the rent, and he said: "No, no, you fill in the figure." Crazy! We had another agreement as well. He had an old Ferrari in his garage, which I admired because I like cars. So he said: "If you score twenty goals, you can have it." That was at the beginning of the first season. I thought: "I've just come from Holland with twenty-five goals, yeah, I think I can do that here." I never got near the car, of course. No chance!'

The first season wasn't so bad. You scored some good goals and lots of penalties and everyone says you were the best player in the UEFA Cup. But you weren't exactly surrounded by love.

'Yeah, in the first season we won the UEFA Cup, though the stadium was never full and no one seemed to think those games meant much. But yeah, generally, it was ... You know, many times I said to my wife: "We should have done it the other way around, first England and then Italy. That would have worked better." As it was, I went from the comfort zone of Ajax, which is all playful, lots of creativity, warmth and young people to this boring, business-like atmosphere. Suddenly it's a nine-to-five job and all the players are walking around with long faces. I'd say: "Come on, let's have a good game today!" and they'd say: "No let's get a *result* today." It was so difficult because you *see* the space, you see the things you can do, and you see the quality in the team. But nobody wants to play the way I want to play. Nobody wants to follow you and I was too young to create something. And I think I turned into myself as well, a little.'

You mentioned promises. What promises?

'This was very important for me. Before we signed, the Inter president Ernesto Pellegrini came to meet us in Holland and promised to change the way Inter played. He said they wanted attacking football, to be like the Milan of Sacchi. And that's why they wanted to buy us, me and Wim Jonk. That's what he said! And I believed him. So, at the beginning of the first season we tried pressing. That's what they'd promised. They felt like Arsenal did two years later: "We need to change." But we played two pre-season games with the pressing and we were all over the place. That's normal because you've had a really different culture in the club. We didn't know where to run. And we had a coach, Bagnoli, who for thirty years played in a certain style. He can't change. Maybe if they'd got a young coach in from Europe, or a strong coach like a Sacchi, it might have been different.'

Your second season with Inter was just awful. The fans turned hostile, the media were hostile and you were injured a lot and ended up scoring just two goals. And you had a coach you came to loathe: Ottavio Bianchi.

'Yes, the first year was quite OK. The second was really difficult with the new coach Bianchi.'

Wasn't Bianchi the coach of Napoli when Maradona was there?

'Yes, he did mention that a few times ... every *hour*. I'll just give one example of what he was like. He had an assistant coach who was a few years older. When we had a double training session, while the players rested Bianchi would play tennis with the assistant. To get to the court they had to walk from the training ground, past the dressing rooms and across two pitches. Well, I was brought up to show respect for people who are older than me. I look out the window and see Bianchi with his phone in his hand, walking out in front, and his assistant, who is much older, walking behind carrying the rackets, and four bottles of water and a bag . . . He's got all this heavy stuff. He's walking like this, carrying everything! And Bianchi is walking in front carrying nothing! Well, you lose my respect. That's it. It's gone. Maybe it's supposed to be like that in Italy. But I can't have that.'

The relationship with Bianchi became increasingly strained, especially after Dennis returned to Holland over the winter break to get treatment for a groin injury. (Bianchi wanted him to stay in Italy; Dennis was frustrated by the failure of Italian doctors and physios to help him.) In February, Bianchi called Dennis into his office. 'He was really strong, attacking me: I didn't give enough, didn't bring enough to the team, I had to work harder. And then he mentioned something about respect. And I realised: "That's it, we're going to have to part ways." I said: "Listen, I really don't have respect for you. I've got respect for my dad, but I don't have respect for you. The things you have done . . ." (I had in mind the tennis thing, and the talking about Maradona, and what I saw as his arrogance and lack of respect for other people) ". . . so don't talk to me about respect. I've got respect for the people I should have respect for." Well, that's the end of the relationship, isn't it? You know me. It takes a lot for me to get to that point, to say those sorts of things. But I'd really had enough from him.'

So who should we talk to from your Inter days?

'Well, in the team, the people I was closest to were Massimo Paganin and Paolo Tramezzani.'

But they were very junior. Maybe we should find people you didn't get on with, like Ruben Sosa.

'Get their side of the story, you mean? That could be interesting. We need an opinion, don't we?'

They could be hostile. They could say: 'Dennis was rubbish, his attitude was wrong, he should have done this and that . . .'

'I don't mind, as long as I get a chance to react.'

You can react all you like. It's your book!

'In that case, yes, you could get comments, but not silly ones. If you want honest opinions, you'll more likely get them from someone like Bagnoli. He's serious and intelligent. Yes, it might be interesting. I sort of know what they expected from me and what they wanted. But there is my truth, too. They have their truth and I have mine. Maybe they can come together somehow.'

II. Their Truth

OSVALDO BAGNOLI, THE coach of Dennis's first year at Inter is 78 years old now and lives in Verona. He is puzzled that Dennis is interested to hear his point of view. 'I'm surprised he remembers me. I was with him for less than a year.'

What do you remember about Dennis Bergkamp?

Bagnoli: 'Oh, a *bravo ragazzo*! A good guy who maybe couldn't find his way in Milan and that's probably why he didn't play to his level.'

Couldn't find his way in football or culturally?

'I think even he cannot answer this question because it is very difficult to say. I remember for example his problems with planes. He didn't want to travel by plane. I was the same. I didn't like travelling by plane either, but I did it. But somehow this was Dennis's way of being: "I don't like it. I don't do it."'

Before Dennis and Wim Jonk joined the club, the president promised

them that Inter would change and play attacking football like AC Milan.
You were the coach, so Pellegrini must have discussed this with you …

'No. I never heard about this and never talked about it. Every Wednesday I used to go to dinner at his house, but there was never anything like that.'

When he appointed you as coach, did Pellegrini give you targets or instructions like 'win the scudetto' or 'play like Milan'?

'I think I was chosen by Inter because at that time I was fifty-six or fifty-seven years old and I had a reputation as a man with a lot of experience who was very calm, so I could work in an atmosphere of a club which had not won for a long time. I had won a *scudetto* with Verona so they thought I could run a difficult situation. But nobody asked me to win something, because it was very difficult in those years. Inter was not a winning team. In my first season we came second. That was a good year. But in the second year I was sacked twelve games from the end of the season, and in the twelve games after I left Inter won just one point. They were at risk of being relegated.'

So Pellegrini never asked you to change the playing style?

'No, there was nothing like that. But sometimes his wife asked me to write things down. Later, I found out she was an expert on handwriting and she studied my way of writing my signature. I don't exclude the possibility that my sacking depended on my signature! I'm the kind of trainer who is very loyal to the club, loyal to the firm. That's how I was in my nine years with Verona and with Genoa, too. I always had a very good relationship with the people of the club. So it happened that we might discuss about a player. Is this one or that one better than another? But I always used to accept with no problem all the choices of the club. In the case of Bergkamp, he was chosen by the club. I didn't know anything about the fact that they were trying to buy him. He arrived and for me it was OK.'

At Verona you were known as a rather attacking coach. But at Inter you used the classic Italian defensive style. What was your approach?

'I was never a trainer who imposed my way of playing. Usually, I went to the players and said to them: "How do you prefer to play?" And then I tried to organise the team after having talked with the players.'

Didn't you ask Bergkamp?

'I really don't remember. It was twenty years ago. I remember there was a problem with the language, and I also remember studying him, trying to best understand his way of playing.'

One of your ex-players, Riccardo Ferri, said your ideal was to reach goal with just three or four passes? That wouldn't fit Dennis's passing game at all . . .

'Three or four passes? But it is obviously true! I used to say to the players: the fewer passes you make the better it is. I don't like tick-tock football. I used to say even to the goalkeeper: if you have the ball and you see the forward is free then give him the ball. Throw the ball down there. If it is possible to do this, then do it. But if it's not possible then we can also do the short game, the passing game, with possession of the ball because you can't always do only one thing. So these things were also for Bergkamp. For us, he was a number ten in the offensive sense, though that doesn't mean that he doesn't come back to defend.'

So Dennis was isolated up front?

'When I was a player I was an attacking midfielder. So it was one of my principles of the game: it is totally useless if you have a forward up there on his own without the team moving altogether forward. If the forward is up there on his own, alone, you always lose the ball.'

But that was Dennis's experience! He was on his own with just one other attacker, usually Ruben Sosa, and it was two attackers against five defenders!

'I don't remember if this way of playing was successful or not in the sense you are asking. But I am quite sure that Dennis must have been used to playing with two forwards in Holland.'

No. At Ajax, as the number 10, he had three other forwards and mid-fielders and defenders supporting the attack as well. When you say 'the team moving altogether forward' maybe that means something different in Italy?

'That's possible but I repeat: in my first season we finished second.'

But Dennis wasn't in that team. He only came in your second season.

'Maybe. I don't remember. But it is important to remember that in those years the idea was still very strong that the first thing is to use the counter-attack. That is why you have to remember the different numbers.'

What about Dennis's relationship with Ruben Sosa? It was so bad it was in the papers.

'Generally speaking, I must say there is a great difference between reality and words, and even more between reality and words twenty years later. I really don't remember. When I was sacked I don't have any memory of me having problems with players or players having problems with each other. But I do remember Dennis never felt quite comfortable and never created a good relationship ... actually neither a good relationship nor bad. I was not the kind of trainer who went to the players and said: "Please help these guys." But I had the impression that the other guys didn't help him. I've been a player myself, so I know those kind of dynamics in the dressing room. But my impression was not that there was bad will against Bergkamp. It is that maybe people thought that he was like this, so they left him alone. Maybe they respected this way of being, because they thought he was like this, because he preferred to be like this. Maybe that is what the other players thought. That's why they didn't accept him as leader.'

Actually things weren't quite as bad as Bagnoli remembered in

1994, after he was sacked. During the last 11 league games, under Giampiero Marini, Inter lost seven games but won twice and avoided relegation by just one point. On the other hand, Inter also won the UEFA Cup, playing a more attacking style, and Dennis was the star and top scorer with eight goals. When we told Wim Jonk what Bagnoli had said, he was quite impressed. He thought his comments were 'sincere and open-hearted'. Wim also said: 'I felt at the time that that was how it was, that no one had spoken to [Bagnoli] about a different playing style. Could we have done anything? Should we have demanded to speak with the trainer? Looking back, yes, we should have done that. But at the time we thought: if Inter spend so much money for two players, then surely they have a good idea, a purpose, a plan? But there was no plan. Fear reigned at Inter. There was quite a lot of quality in that team and it definitely would have been possible to put us on a different path.' Wim reckons it was the older players who thought differently about football to the younger generation. 'So Dennis and I were suspended between two worlds: the Italian football traditionalists and the modernists.'

WHAT DO YOU RECKON to all that, Dennis?

Dennis: 'I think Wim is right.'

He says the power in the team lay more with senior players like Bergomi and Ferri.

'He's right about that, too. What did they say?'

* * *

BEPPE BERGOMI IS AN impressive, elegant guy. And the defender is still a legend for the Inter fans. He won the World Cup aged 19. He played for Inter for 20 years. And now he works as a TV commentator most famous for getting emotional at the end of the 2006 World Cup semi-final. Italy had just scored two late goals to beat Germany and reach the final in Berlin. He shouted: *Andiamo a Berlino!!* ('We're going to Berlin!'). It's like Kenneth Wolstenholme in 1966 or Jack van Gelder going crazy when Bergkamp scored against Argentina.

Bergomi lives in an apartment near the San Siro. When you see how everything in his home is arranged, you realise that elegance is quite important to him ...

WHY DID IT GO SO badly for Dennis at Inter?

Bergomi: 'It's relative. He was very young when he came to us, but he made a *grande prestazione* in the 1993-94 UEFA Cup. He was fundamental to our success in that. So it is only partially true that it went badly. In the UEFA Cup, he was a really good player and scored seven or eight goals. Also, he was not really well-accepted in the team. The team didn't help him. But we did recognise his qualities.'

Pellegrini promised Dennis that Inter would change its playing style to attack ...

'I don't know what was in the mind of the president or the coach. Everyone in Italy at that time was trying to copy the strategy of Milan, but they couldn't because it was really a switch of strategy in the Italian philosophy of football. We tried to change but basically we couldn't do it. So we went back to what we knew. Before Bagnoli we had had five years of Trapattoni and one year of Orrico. [In 1991] Orrico had wanted to try to copy Milan and it was a complete failure. And with Bagnoli we returned to the style of Trapattoni.'

Tell us about Orrico.

'He couldn't really experiment because in Italy this change of strategy needs time, and after one year he didn't get results so he quit. One year is not enough time to change strategy. Orrico arrived,

I think, with the idea of changing everything. But his idea was three-two-three-two, like before the Second World War! And his experience was limited to Serie B. And this double WM formation was a really old-fashioned way of playing football, like Vittorio Pozzo. We played this way in two games before the championship started and we were even failing to beat Serie C teams. In Italy you don't have time for this! Either your strategy is successful immediately or it's a failure. And Orrico was not at the high level of Sacchi. I didn't realise when I was playing, but now I have studied it and realise the problem was that he was not teaching us how to do it.'

There must have been a culture shock for Dennis coming from Ajax – how do you compare him to the three Germans Inter had before Dennis arrived?

'I think when a big champion arrives, he has to adapt. He has to bring his qualities and dispose them to the team, like Matthaus, Brehme and Klinsmann did. And it was not easy. Matthaus and Trapattoni fought with each other constantly. They were two very strong, difficult characters! [*slams fist*] Matthaus wanted to be more attacking. They argued about that. And when Trapattoni said: "OK, go forward," Matthaus went further back! But Matthaus had a different mentality. He came and said: "OK, tomorrow we are going to win" and they did. Dennis didn't have that mentality. I know at Ajax the game is for pleasure and fun. I followed Dennis's career from when he was young. It's very difficult when you bring someone out of that climate ... you see it also with other players, like Seedorf. He had a troubled career at first at Sampdoria, but later went to Madrid, and came back to Italy with Milan and was a great success. But it took him time to adapt. After Ajax it is particularly difficult. You're very young, with a very different mentality and you need *patience*. And Inter was not patient enough with Dennis, because Inter had not won for many years and they kept changing strategy every year. They wanted immediate results.'

So although it's a culture clash there was actually quite a small differ-ence between Dennis succeeding and failing? Did some of the fault lie with him?

'No. He could have done better, of course. But the club was not patient and Dennis was not patient, either. To repeat: during the UEFA Cup Dennis was extraordinary, and I recognise that absolutely he was the best player. I really remember that. He left a very strong impression, it was a really good sign for Inter. But in my opinion the problem was he couldn't – they couldn't – transmit all his qualities to the team.

'Dennis's big difficulties were from a human perspective because probably he couldn't stand the pressures on him. The media pressure ... It's difficult to come to another culture. So we went to eat together. We hung out together and I tried and the club tried to help him acclimatise, and also to help [Wim] Jonk. Though Jonk is a different character, easier, more relaxed and humorous.'

Dennis is quite introvert when he doesn't know people, but he's really funny and mischievous and open when he feels comfortable. At Arsenal he was the practical joker of the team.

Bergomi [raises his famous eyebrows in astonishment]: 'But I think Dennis could have done more to adapt, to become more Italian. With the qualities he had he could have done more. For example, later, when Ronaldo came, our trainer was Gigi Simoni and we came back again to the real Italian system: *catenaccio* with a *libero* behind, which was me, and Ronaldo on his own in attack. But we won because Ronaldo adapted to the Italian system.'

Ronaldo was a dribbler with lots of tricks – that wasn't Dennis's game at all.

'Ronaldo was everything.'

Dennis wasn't interested in playing that way.

'No, that is clear. Ronaldo can be solo. Dennis is a team player who needed the others. Ronaldo didn't. We won the UEFA Cup in ninety-eight with him. And we did that with a really traditional old Italian system.'

What was your opinion of Ottavio Bianchi?

'There was a conflict, and from my point of view Dennis's criticisms are fair. But in Italy it is really important to get the result. And Bianchi was successful. As long as there is the result you can behave pretty much in any way you like.'

What Dennis didn't like was that Bianchi treated other people disrespectfully.

'Yes, and Dennis is completely correct and fair. This type of behaviour is not OK in Italy, either. It's not simple. Ultimately, Dennis could have managed that relationship better. And during that season I now understand Bianchi could have behaved better. Probably without going to play tennis during lunch. He should have taken second training.'

He delegated that?

'Yes, he left the second training to the assistant. But Bianchi was a really strong character, and not an easy person everywhere. Generally, towards people who worked for him, he was not a nice boss. But I can't say for sure about the things Dennis saw.'

What about talking about Maradona all the time?

'Well, Bianchi did talk a lot about Maradona. But then the other players in the team were curious, so sometimes they asked him. As to the other part, in my opinion Napoli became big because of Maradona, not because of Bianchi! That's clear.'

Why did Dennis do so much better in England?

'In England they weren't used to seeing players of great technical quality like Bergkamp or Zola. The English league was very physical but there was little technical quality. So they were happy to have these technical players who gave a completely new interpretation, a new perspective of football. [But] in Italy, the football has always been really technical and tactical. [In the eighties and nineties] we had players like Maradona, Careca, Van Basten, Gullit, Vialli, Mancini ... all great champions. So it was not such a surprise to see someone like Dennis. In Italy, Zola was not a *baronetto* at all. When he was in Italy they didn't even let him play! In Italy he was considered ordinary, but in England he was "extraordinary".'

DO YOU WANT TO react to any of that, Dennis?
'First I'd rather hear what Riccardo Ferri has to say'.
He was critical of Inter – and critical of you.
'No problem. Let's have it!'

* * *

RICCARDO FERRI WAS unmoved by Bergkamp's tale of broken promises.
In Holland a promise is a promise ...
Ferri: 'And ...? Look, it happens all over the world! People made me promises all the time, and never kept them. Life doesn't stop because you are disappointed. I had the same disappointment with Pellegrini when he promised I could go to Napoli and then I had to go to Sampdoria.'
So it's just part of football everywhere?
'It's part of *life*! I think it's Dennis's problem. I mean, if my son gets disappointed about something, I say: "OK, but it's not the end of the world."'
But Dennis's criticisms of Inter were much stronger.
'It's really absurd that the club promised [Dennis] this, because in the short amount of time, in my opinion, it was not possible to change completely the playing style of the club with only two players! Bagnoli was a great coach, but he could never be *trasformista*. But the biggest problem was that Inter wanted to compete with

Milan, but they tried to do it too fast, and without building the structure. They just wanted very quick results.

'I would have been willing to change, but it couldn't be done quickly. You need interpreters, teachers and you need two or three years. But in Italy this is not possible because you have to have results immediately. Everything is short term.'

There were also financial problems ...

'At that time, we were very much in the shadow of Milan and we had less money. It was Pellegrini v Berlusconi, so whereas we had a squad of fourteen, Milan had twenty-two top-class players. They had a much bigger squad. That's very important. We had thirteen or fourteen good players, but the rest of the squad was basically kids like Tramezzani and Paganin. Milan had much more. Even after Gullit and Van Basten left, they had Savicevic, Boban, Papin, Massaro ...

'But the real problem was that there was no *project*. Milan had a project, but at Inter this never existed. Inter had no concept. At Inter the idea was just "buy great players" ... and they gave no thought to how these stars actually functioned. At Milan the players fitted with the philosophy of Arrigo Sacchi: Tassotti, Baresi, Maldini, Costacurta, Gullit, Van Basten, Rijkaard ... they all fitted his idea of pressing and playing an attacking game. So Milan bought players in service of the concept, of their zone tactics. But Inter didn't do that at all! Bergkamp was a talent, a great talent. But there was never a structure around him that would bring out his qualities. The whole idea was a bad one! Bergkamp was a great prospect. But he was not Ronaldo or Maradona, players who could create something on their own. They could make the difference in the Italian championship. Dennis could not.

'Every year Inter bought one great player like a Rummenigge. That was Pellegrini's "philosophy": buy one star per year to fight against Milan! But this was not part of a strategy. Inter is still like this. Still without much means and still without a project. They still have the same idea of buying stars without knowing how they will play together. Look at the three years since Mourinho. When Inter beat Bayern [in the 2010 Champions League final], Inter was far above Bayern. Since then Inter has spent 140 million euros and where are they? Nowhere in the league and not in the Champions League. Failure! In the same period Bayern spent 135 million euros – that's five million less. And now Bayern are the best in Europe. So, in three years: disaster for Inter! It's exactly like when Dennis was here. [Inter's president, Massimo] Moratti has never had a project, though Jose Mourinho and Roberto Mancini created their own projects. They were trainers who led. So you have this pattern: no vision, no leadership from Moratti, especially since [Giacinto] Facchetti died.'

And where does Dennis fit in all this?

'The fans were expecting Dennis to be like Van Basten. But if Van Basten had come to Inter and Dennis had gone to Milan, it would have been the other way around. Dennis would have been a star at Milan and Van Basten would have failed at Inter. He would have done no better than Dennis in that period.'

But you also think Dennis was too young, introverted and anti-social to become the big player he should have been. Sosa called him 'strange and solitary' in the press.

'Ha ha! But it's true! It's not an insult. Ruben Sosa is a Latin American guy, and Dennis is from the north. Not a Viking, but, you know, *really* from the north. Like Jonk as well. Dennis found a nice house, and he wanted to be there with his wife. We used to invite Dennis and his wife, and Jonk and his wife or girlfriend: "Hey, come and eat with us! Come have dinner with us!" But they never came. Never! Never! Never! We had a nice boat and we invited them, but Dennis was just at home in Civate. We found him rather cold. Everyone in the team tried, but he was quite cold. He didn't socialise with us. Sosa was the exact opposite. He was very warm, and friendly, *simpatia,* you know? Funny and friendly, eating with us, singing, dancing ... we would all go over to his and have dinner, and sing songs, but always without Dennis. Dennis and Jonk never came. Actually, I roomed with Jonk for a while. I'm friendly and talkative and for some reason they always put me with these introverts!'

On the field how did Sosa and Dennis get on?

'Tactically, I remember he and Ruben Sosa were not suited to each other. Dennis needed a different sort of player. Ruben Sosa was very technical but interested only in the conclusion. He'd dribble, go forward and shoot at goal. He was an individualist. Bergkamp needed collaborators ... *Boom! Boom! Boom!* ... people to play quick passes with. There was not really a collaboration in passing the ball. It wasn't a passing team, because Bagnoli wanted to be in front of goal within three or four passes. Fast. And Dennis is much more about passes. [At Inter] it was very different from the possession game of Ajax which is slow ... *largo!* ... *doom* ... *dooooom* ... *dovoom* [*mimes extreme boredom*] ... Slow passing ... *doooom* ... *dooooom* ... *doom.* I don't want to criticise Dennis or say that Ruben Sosa was perfect. Not at all. But Dennis was an introvert, in his private life and on the field the same.

'Matthaus, Klinsmann and Brehme were very sociable, friendly, outgoing, and Gullit was like that too, even Rijkaard a bit, though Van Basten was not. I played with Gullit at Sampdoria. Lovely man. I got close to him.'

So, for you, Dennis mainly had a 'personality problem'?

'Yes, yes, yes.'

What about the fans and the media?

'They were cruel and harsh with Dennis, but I blame the club. The club created too many expectations, and the media and fans automatically followed this. The club said: "With Dennis we will win." They put all the responsibility on him. That's why the press attacked him. It was a mistake. The fans are conditioned by the club and the media. They were expecting Dennis to be like Van Basten. But Van Basten had a team behind him.'

At the beginning of Dennis's second season you left and went to Sampdoria and later played with another Dutchman from Ajax, Clarence Seedorf.

'A great guy!'

What was the difference between them?

'Clarence also was young. And he had trouble with [coach Sven-Goran] Eriksson who made him play on the right wing when he wanted to be in the centre. But he had a different personality to Dennis. Very different. His character was better adapted to Italy. I was a really good friend of Clarence. I helped him to find a place to stay, and to buy a car. They wanted to trick him when he was buying a car. Genoa, eh? Bastards! It was not a good deal at all. And Clarence's mum and sister came to see him training. They'd sit in their car by the side of the field eating huge tubs of chips ... and his mum was a huge woman ... without even getting out of the car! What we are discussing here is the difference between the top, *top* level and the merely outstanding. That's the difference. Dennis was a big player, but not an outstanding one. With a different mentality and a different character, he could have been top *top*.'

At Arsenal he was. They loved and admired him. The French guys at Arsenal who played in their national team said Dennis was equal to or better than Zidane.

'Well, he was faster than Zidane. But Zidane was more open-minded. Dennis was a top player technically, but his character was not. He was too quiet. Too closed. Narrow-minded. Not like Zidane.'

Closed culturally, or as an individual?

'I don't know. But he had everything to be a top, *top* player like Zidane. But he needed to be stronger, more open-minded.'

Yet in London Dennis is seen as this sort of great philosopher king who opens the English culture. He unlocks and opens the door to something much bigger. He changes English football! He gives it another vision.

'Yes, OK. In England. But not here. And in the Holland national team, how was he?'

Great.

'No. Normal. A normal player.'

All through the 1990s Holland are great and strong. Then Dennis retires in 2000, and Holland go straight down.

'OK, but for me I don't remember him being decisive. When I think of Holland and I think of the decisive players, I think of Koeman, Seedorf ... Cruyff years ago. Bergkamp? No. Not like Zidane. He should have been decisive because he had the same talent as Zidane. Dennis was not as decisive for Holland as he was for Arsenal.'

Well, Holland should have won the World Cup in 1998 and Euro 2000. They were the best team in both.

'They needed different players, with different talents. Dennis had to be a bigger star, like Zidane was for France. Zidane was the dominant player at Juventus, Real Madrid, France. Wherever he played he dominated. Always. Always the leader, the obvious leader. But Dennis ... the difference is that Zidane led more and was more ... manifested than Dennis. But Dennis Bergkamp has very great qualities.'

The old Arsenal players said the fans, media, even the TV couldn't see everything Dennis did. He didn't draw attention to himself, but for them he was absolutely the technical leader. You couldn't even see the perfection of his passes, for example. They weren't just good but perfect. The curve, the timing, the pace ... every pass a 'caviar', as Thierry Henry said. Perfect.

'Yes, yes Dennis was technically brilliant. His quality is not for discussion. Extraordinary! Extraordinary! But his personality was problematic.'

III. My Truth

OK, DENNIS. THOSE *are their truths. What are yours?*

Dennis: 'Well, I thought a lot of the comments from Bergomi and even more from Ferri were fantastic. And Bagnoli ... that was unbelievable because he didn't say anything interesting, which I thought was *really* interesting! I mean, how can a guy in his position have nothing to say?'

It could be shyness.

'Being shy doesn't mean you don't have an opinion. As a coach you have to stand for something. Maybe it showed he wasn't really important at Inter. Maybe that says it all. It sounds as if he had no power at all, no philosophy, no input with the style of football, no memory or knowledge of what the plan was with me.'

But Bagnoli was a much-loved, old-fashioned, decent Milanese guy from the 1950s. And everyone loved him. They loved that he'd won the league with little Verona a few years before.

'No doubt about it. I remember my first impression of him. I'm quite good at first impressions. And when I met him I thought immediately: "I've got respect for you." I'm sure he was fantastic with Verona, and he played a certain style. OK, I didn't see that at Inter, but I understood that about him. And he's a decent man. He doesn't harm anyone. He probably doesn't make players better, but he doesn't make a problem with them, either. Like Tommaso [Pellizzari] says, he was just *there*. I think maybe that half year we had together just wasn't enough time. He says the same about me. But when you asked him: "Did you have to play pressing?" or "Did Pellegrini tell you something?" and he says:

"No" or "I can't remember" – well, I think that tells you a lot. This was probably the biggest job he ever had. So he must know every detail.

'By the way, I liked what Tommaso said earlier about the 'religious war'. I didn't understand it like that then, but I think he's put his finger on it. The question was: did Inter want to change? I don't think so. It's fantastic the way Bergomi and Ferri talk, but you can tell they didn't want to change. Now they say it would have been a good idea, but back then I think they saw change as a threat. If we play with an extra striker or one man more in midfield, does that mean we play with one defender less? Probably. They're not so keen on that. And what Ferri said about there being "no project" ... that really got to the point! Tommaso backed him up on that. Yes, I think that was exactly the problem!

'I must say I'm quite touched that Bergomi talks about my *grande prestazione* in the UEFA Cup, when I scored a lot of goals. Coming from an experienced Italian player like him, it means something. And he confirms what I said about Bianchi who really wasn't a good guy. But when he talks about the difference between England and Italy, it reminded me of Arsene's words about how players should serve the game. My feeling was, and sometimes still is, that in Italy they think football *is* Serie A! They think their league and players *are* the game and everyone else has to serve them. Every now and then they do make changes, like with Sacchi. But fundamentally Italian football hasn't changed in all these years, and that's their problem.

'In a way, Inter looked like Arsenal did. Both teams with a strong, settled "old" base of defenders, and both on the verge of change. But you need strong characters within the club and help from the media. At Arsenal, the experienced players were willing to try to change. They were curious about what I could bring. [Vice-chairman] David Dein was there, Wenger came and yes, then I could make the difference with help from quality players. At Inter, they all sat back and looked at me. And taking me out to dinner is not helping me!

'I found it so interesting about that guy who hates Barcelona football and even now just wants his team to score one goal and defend. I don't think it was a joke. I think there may be a lot of people in Italy who think that way. Bagnoli says "tick, tock, tick, tock" because he thinks that sort of passing is boring. I think: "What are you watching?" But they've seen it, and they still don't like it. If that's what they feel, well, you can't do anything. It's the end of the conversation. It's their opinion. Not all Italians think that way. But in general, I think Italian footballers are happy to do what they do. And they'll always get to finals. They'll always win trophies because there's enough talent there. Football is their culture. Football is their thing. They do it very well.'

Like Italian food? In London and Amsterdam and even Paris, you can go into a supermarket and buy food from all over the world. In an Italian supermarket you can buy food from all over ... Italy.

'They don't want to change. They like their food. It's great food. And they like their football. Why should they change? It's not in their genes to embrace change. You never hear people saying: "Oh, I love to watch Italian football now! They made such big steps!" It didn't happen. In England it happened with the Premier League. It happened in Spain, of course. It happened in Germany. Holland is developing all the time. That's the Dutch thing: always change. It's different now than it was with Michels. Cruyff is different. Van Gaal is different. It's always evolving, and I think that's the good thing about it. In football, you have to evolve, you have to create new things. In Italy, I feel, they'd rather stick to their old stuff, than really make ... I mean, look at what happened with Sacchi. There's a four, five-year Sacchi thing. "Oh wow, oh fantastic" ... and all of a sudden straight back again. It didn't last. Bianchi tries it for a couple of games pre-season – *boom!* – straightaway back. You mentioned they tried it a few times but they're not comfortable with it, whereas in Holland, we're not comfortable with conservative football. "This is what we've always done, so we're going to keep doing it ..." No. We always want to improve.

'And the other point that really struck me, was the way they kept saying I was not being social. It's very, very strange! Ferri said I was not open-minded. Well, I played with quite a few strikers and they were all different, and I could play with them all, so ... not open-minded? I'm open-minded enough to come to a different country ...'

They admitted you had problems with Ruben Sosa.

'Yes, but even with him it's not like a hate thing. It's more like: "Jeez, come on man, look around you! I'm there as well." He was the only player that I thought: "I can't make you better in this way and you're certainly not making me a better player, and you're not helping your team."'

Did you try to talk about it with him?

'No, because, remember, I was twenty-four. My career had just started. In Holland it was fantastic, but you're in second or third gear, you're just cruising in a way. Of course you're doing your best, but it's a playful thing, it goes by itself. Then – *bang!* – they expect you to click immediately at Inter and immediately lead a team with guys like Bergomi who've done everything! "OK, you're leader now."'

Did they say that?

'Then, no. But it shows now in the way they speak. And look at their criticism: "He should have been the leader, but wasn't the leader because he didn't invite us for dinner! He didn't sing with us!" I mean ... come on! You're trying to adjust to the culture, and they expect you to lead straightaway?'

If you'd known how it worked ... if Bergomi had said: 'Forget Holland, here it's serious, and this is what we expect ...' Did you never have that kind of conversation?

'Actually I did. Once. In my first season. We were on a plane – but I was OK with that at the time – and it was a really good conversation. I think Davide Fontolan was there. He was a good guy. A strong character, funny as well. And the Paganin brothers, Massimo and Antonio, were there. And Ferri. And Wim Jonk, too. And some of them were sitting next to me and others were leaning over from the seats in front and we spoke in English and in Italian, mostly Italian, about what was expected. For the first time, I went: "Wait a minute, I'm part of this." They were opening up. They said: "Try to be a little bit different, you know? Run a bit more. Start with that. We don't expect you to score three goals a game, but put some working effort in there." I was still in Ajax mode. I thought my role was to make a difference. Give me the ball, and I'll do something. But they said – and it was one of the things I took to England later – "first work one hundred per cent and then get to football". It was a different way of thinking.

At Ajax I could miss a chance, and it's no problem because I'll get another one, and another, and another. The team is so well-organised, the patterns are known. You know where the wingers are, and the midfielders. Everyone knows what to do. But at Inter, I'd look at the team sheet and not understand a thing! Is that four-four-two? Is it four-five-one? Is it four-three-three? It was not clear to me. And no one explained it! And if I don't know that, how can I lead? "Oh, we're going to follow him." But what am I doing? I'm up front with Ruben Sosa, and every game we play against five defenders. Sometimes one of our midfielders comes up, too. Great! Now we've got three up front. But where am I running? Where are my lines? What am I doing with the other striker? If I've got no relationship ... In all the other teams I played in, if I make a certain run, I know how the others will react. But here ...'

So it's not just a problem with Sosa?

'It's with the whole team! Either the system helps you, or the players help you, or a coach tells you how you're going to play. But I had none of that. I was just, "OK we're going to play." And I have my striking partner, which could be Pancev or Schillaci or Sosa and I'll be adjusting to my partner because that's my personality. But what am I adjusting *to*? If he gets the ball, and I make my run, will I get it? From Sosa probably not.'

Ferri says Sosa's only idea – and he was great at it – was to get the ball, turn, dribble and shoot.

'And I can't blame him. In private, he's not a bad guy, but as a player, I thought: "Wait a minute, you're killing the team!" But he probably didn't know anything else.'

He scored 20 goals the season before.

'Right. So who am I to criticise? But I'm coming from a place where everything is based on a system and patterns, and on playing creative attacking football ... I was adjusting, but they want me to lead! Where do you want me to lead? How?

'In Italy they see Bagnoli as an "attacking coach", but when he explains his idea of attacking you see how different it is to mine. He says he wants two or three passes, then a shot on goal. That's not attacking, that's counter-attacking football. And that's always based on: "First get your defence right, win the ball, and then you go." Ask any Dutch guy, "What is attacking football?" and he'll say "Dominating, playing in the other team's half." They're totally different things. No one told me. *No one told me!* So when I signed my contract, Pellegrini and Piero Boschi [Inter general manager] said: "Yeah, yeah we're going to change this all around. We're going to attack, we want to play pressing." Maybe they just had a different idea of what pressing is.'

But they'd seen Sacchi's Milan playing. And so had you. Didn't Louis van Gaal take you all to Barcelona to see them beat Steaua Bucharest in the European Cup final in 1989? That's reckoned to be one of the greatest performances ever. What did you make of it?

'Yeah, we sat with Milan fans behind one of the goals. And we were fans of Milan, too, that night. But you recognised it, you recognised the football. "Oh yeah, I know how this goes and why ..." You had Marco in the centre and Ruud Gullit operating from the side, mostly from the right. Right-half, wing, that sort of area. And Rijkaard in the middle, controlling the midfield with another guy, and on the left side, I think it was Donadoni. So there's already three strikers and a midfielder coming as well. Hey! I know what this is ...'

You're noticing that it's Dutch Total Football but with an Italian flavour? Like the great Barcelona of Guardiola but with a Spanish-Catalan flavour, and Arsenal is the same with an English-French flavour?

'Right. It was interesting, too, what Tommaso said about how Baresi and the defenders changed when Sacchi came. They were uncomfortable, then Sacchi taught them and then Berlusconi came in and said, "I don't care what you think, this is how we're doing it." Pellegrini never did that. It's very difficult to put your finger on the difference between Milan and Cruyff, or between Italian football and English football, but when I think of Cruyff, what he always says is "it's about distances". It's the space between players. Sacchi used to train with ropes, and shadow playing, with eleven against zero. We did that with Arsene as well. It's all about distances. So you learn that if your left-winger moves to make an attack, your right-back must also move. If everyone's got a twenty-yard rope tied to the next player, tied to the next one, tied to the next one, and so on ... it's like a framework or grid moving all over the field all the time. He moves there, so this one automatically comes in, and you go back, and you go forward ... When he ran one way, the whole team, in their positions, ran too. He went to the left, so we went to the left. It was all based on keeping the distances correct. If I'm near the other team's penalty area, when I look back I'll see Tony and

Bouldy [Tony Adams and Steve Bould] on the halfway line. The gaps should be quite small, maybe twenty or twenty-five yards between the lines.

But at Inter I'd be up there with Sosa and let's say two midfielders have joined the attack as well ... I look back and my defenders and the other midfielders are still deep in their own half! There's a huge space between us and it's *dead* space! It's killing me. It's killing the team, because when you lose the ball, you've lost four players who were in attack because all the rest are just sitting back waiting for the opponent to come. Now, in my opinion, that's not pressing football! It's not dominating football like Barcelona, like Milan, like Arsenal, because in those teams as soon as you lose the ball, you win it back again – in their half – as soon as possible. Or, if you can't win it in three or five seconds, then you come back in position and make the compact thing, again with the correct distances between the players. Attacking, the distance is maybe twenty-five yards on average. Defensively, it should be closer, about ten or fifteen. That's so important. At Inter I always thought, "I'm on an island here!" How am I supposed to teach them all that at the age of twenty-four? Pellegrini doesn't understand this, obviously. And no one has said a word to Bagnoli. He's the one who's supposed to be teaching us in training! If they don't even tell him ... no chance!'

Wim Jonk says it was Bianchi, in the second season, who tried pressing. After two games it was 'Enough of that! It doesn't work! Back in defence!'

'Yes, I think Bianchi had more authority, more of a philosophy of, "Oh, I'm going to try this."'

But you never forced the issue with Bagnoli?

'It's difficult to explain why. We were just married, we're having an extended honeymoon. I've got a new house. I've got my own car instead of a leased car. I'm trying to adjust to a different country ... I've got a hundred things new in my life on a personal level. Then

I've got another two hundred things different on a football level! I wasn't ready. I'm still thinking, OK I'm a good player, but I'm learning. When I moved to Inter I thought I was moving to a team with experienced players, a team that will give me a solid basis, and I can give them something extra. That's how it was later when I moved to Arsenal. Inter had experienced players, but they wouldn't or couldn't change, go for something new. When I moved to Arsenal, it was different, like I wanted: experienced players with an open mind, willing to follow me ...'

Inter's idea of a good player and your idea of a good player are different, aren't they? They're thinking traditionally: the job of the forward is to produce something from nothing. Give him the ball and he'll score somehow. We're not sure how, but he'll find a way, it's his job.

'A big part of it, and I kept telling them this, is they wanted me to adjust. I'd say: "You've got a good player, everyone would agree with that, but how are you going to use that talent?" That's what I do now as a coach. You think: "How can I get the best I can out of that player?" That doesn't just mean he has to adapt to the others. They have to adapt to him as well. In the UEFA Cup – Bergomi said it – I scored eight goals. I was a "fantastic" player. So surely he should be thinking: "What's he doing that's different? Can I help him?" Helping is not "I've got an idea – I'll take him out to dinner!" That's their own weakness, I believe. "We don't really know what it is, so we'll blame him, because he doesn't socialise!"'

You didn't socialise much at Arsenal either.

'No, but does it happen in football? You go out with players you feel comfortable with. I'm not going out to dinner because it might help me in my football career. No! I'm going out to dinner in my private life, because I enjoy it. And at that stage, in my first year, fairly or otherwise, I couldn't say Ferri was necessarily my type of guy, you know? So, do we hang out with each other? No, you stick with Wim because you know him. I really don't understand this idea that that would solve the football problem. I know the idea that a team of friends is a successful team. But it's not true. At Arsenal some years, you bonded with more players than other years. But come on! At Inter you have to sort out the football first – that's where the problem is! And it's a deep problem, a problem of different philosophies. Look at how they trained the goalkeepers. They trained very hard, but separately. Then they come and join the rest of the team. I need shooting practice, but the goalkeepers are so tired they only try to save one shot in four. That doesn't help me! In Holland the idea is: score as many goals as possible, do everything to make the attack better. In Italy the most important is the goalkeeper. If he keeps a clean sheet, you can't lose. For me, it was really mind-blowing sometimes. I'd think, Jeez, I want to do some finishing, and we've got a goalkeeper who doesn't make an effort. How can I improve my shooting? They say, "Yeah, but come on, he's been working hard all day."'

I guess it comes down to this idea that they see the striker is an individualist. Ferri said it very strongly that you're not a Ronaldo. They wanted you to be like him. When Van der Sar went to Juventus he had to stop playing like a Dutch goalkeeper. They made him stick on his line like an Italian. He went along with that and felt later that he'd betrayed his principles. He felt he should have said: 'Actually I'm not doing that, I think my way is better.' He had to come to England, to Fulham, to find himself again. After you left, Ronaldo arrived. He was happy to play catenaccio style as the lone striker. He adapted and they loved him for it. You never did that. You could have tried to be Italian, like Ronaldo, be a dribbler. You could have thought of that as adding some skills. But you seemed to see it more as losing something, not developing your art as you needed to, or not fulfilling your destiny or something. Any thoughts?

'I need other players around me. That's when I become a good player, because I need them to perform like me, and I need them to be moving for me. I did learn from the Italian league. At home the vibe is more playful: "Oh look how good I am, I can do this . . . and even this!" And in Italy it's more a job. You've got one chance, and you've got to make sure you score that goal. I learned a lot from that. I learned what professional football is. They do two training sessions a day. You come in at nine, you rest there in the middle of the day and train again in the afternoon. Every minute of the day, you're a football player. That's what I learned there, but I would never do different than what I'm good at. I'm not a dribbler, so I'm not going to dribble. After that conversation on the plane, I understood they wanted me to run around more, work harder. No problem. I can do that. It didn't help, though. I still wanted to make a difference, to score a goal or make a fantastic pass. But I've got no one around me. I'm frustrated, but they just didn't care. If I was working for the team, making space, making runs, they were happy. I could do that easily, but it wouldn't win games. It wouldn't make me a better player. But they'd expect it of me. OK. I'll do that. I'm open-minded.'

But would it actually have damaged you, trying to play their way? Would you have lost something in your game? Or added something?

'It wasn't my strength, but I was willing to put that in my game, and later it helped me. That sort of stuff helped me in England, where I was one hundred per cent in the game every time. I became more business-like in winning the ball, or scoring goals, or finishing or passing. I learned the mentality: this pass has to be right, because you really only have one chance. Or this shot has to be on target . . . that sort of stuff. That's what I learned in Italy, but I would not have accepted them making that my game, running around. With all due respect to Italian strikers, most of them – not all of them – are just working for the team in the four-four-two system. Just running, holding the ball, passing, getting into the box. It's similar to some English strikers as well, but I've never felt that to be my game. If I'd made the decision: "OK, I'm going to adapt to Italian football," I would have been a lesser player. I would have been there longer, and they would have been happier with me. But I would never have been the player I became in the end.'

You stuck to your vision?

'No. It was more a feeling. What was I comfortable with? I thought: "This is not me." How do you want to play football? How do you approach football? What do you feel happy – or happier – with? What can you do? It comes down to my intention of being a better player today than yesterday, and always looking for possibilities and opportunities. I was looking for quality instead of quantity. Higher and higher. OK, I can do this for twenty years, and at a certain pace. If I just do what they expect of me, I will be appreciated, but I will be one of . . . many. And in my mind, I want to be different. That's why I made the choice for Inter instead of other teams. Other teams would have been easier. I don't want it easy. At Milan, they would have understood immediately. I could have followed Marco, but I wouldn't make a name for myself. I didn't want to be a follower. I didn't want to be "the new Van Basten" or "the new player from Cruyff" at Barcelona. I wanted to follow my own path, my own way. I wanted to be Dennis Bergkamp, basically.'

5

PLAYER POWER

DEMOCRATIC TENDENCIES in the Dutch national team have sometimes helped Dennis's career. At other times they have blighted it.

Of all the football-loving nations, the Netherlands probably has the most complex pattern of power relationships between coaches and players. Notoriously, as during the 1990 World Cup and the European Championships of 1996 and 2012, the tendency to form cliques and argue about everything from tactics to money has turned toxic. At other times, though, Dutch democracy has proved a strength. In 1974 and 1988, for example, groups of talented, sophisticated, strong-willed players created spectacular football precisely by taking responsibility and finding ways to work together more effectively than anything an autocratic coach could have imposed.

In 1990, at the dawn of Dennis's decade in an orange shirt, both aspects were visible. During the summer, at the Italy World Cup, a combination of feuding superstars, an unwanted coach and intransigent suits at the KNVB (the Dutch FA), produced nothing but poison. The team of Van Basten, Gullit, Rijkaard, Koeman, Wouters, Van Breukelen and Van't Schip – then all at their peak – couldn't even beat Egypt and came home in disgrace after falling to the Germans. A few months later, however, the picture changed. Soon after Dennis made his debut as a substitute in a friendly against Italy in Palermo, player power reared its head again. But this time it worked more productively.

Dennis's first full match, partnering Marco van Basten in a two-man attack, came in October 1990 against Portugal in a European Championships qualifier. The Dutch, confused by their coach's tactics, lost 1-0. The coach in question, holding the job for the third time in his brilliant career, was the great Rinus Michels. In his glory years in the late sixties and early seventies, he had invented Total Football with Ajax and transferred it to the Dutch national team (or rather he had *co-invented* it with his players, the most important being Johan Cruyff). Now aged 62 and soon to be named FIFA's 'Coach of the Century', Michels had mellowed and now favoured a variant of the 4-4-2 system in vogue all over Europe. It certainly had its merits and, under Michels, Holland had won Euro '88 with it. Having returned to the job after the Italy World Cup fiasco, he was unconvinced by Dennis's performance against the Portuguese and decided to replace him for the next game, against Greece, with big former PSV man Wim Kieft, an English-style centre-forward now playing for Bordeaux. Michels had even promised Kieft his place.

One problem was that the Dutch media didn't approve of the tactics. Much more importantly, neither did Marco van Basten. During training, whenever a move failed or a pass went astray, the greatest striker on the planet made a show of shaking his head to demonstrate his contempt for Michels's plan of attack. Van Basten urged Michels to play the Ajax 4-3-3 using two wingers and Dennis

as number 10. Michels's nicknames – 'The Bull', 'The General' –
convey the impression that he was no pushover. Indeed, by Dutch
standards he was considered a fearsome disciplinarian. But this
being the nation where player power was more or less invented, he
was both open to ideas and keen to avoid a damaging clash with his
biggest star. Michels therefore asked his squad which tactic they
would prefer. At the Kievit Hotel in Wassenaar, a wealthy suburb
of The Hague, a players' meeting was convened. By Dutch tradition, senior players tend to influence such gatherings and, as the
meeting turned into a clash between Ajax 4-3-3-ers and PSV
4-4-2-ists, Ajax's former and current club captains Van Basten and
Jan Wouters held sway, the PSV contingent was outnumbered and
several young Ajax players even mocked Kieft as a 'tree trunk'.
When the meeting voted to adopt 4-3-3, Kieft stormed out.

In the match that followed, Dennis played well and scored his
first international goal (with a header, strangely enough). Holland
won 2-0. According to Dennis: 'That game was important, both for
the team and for me. We chose the Ajax approach and it worked
from the start. It was great and really important for my self-
confidence. I was in a phase then when I was becoming more of a
determining player, more dominant. Only a short time before, I'd
been struggling with feelings of resentment about being constantly
in and out of the Ajax team. I solved it myself, by working
extremely hard to improve my form. Yes, that's possible. You can
work your way to form by making sure you stay fit and in a good
rhythm, and by going the extra mile, like practising your shooting
after training has finished. And you have to stay positive.'

Dennis's career in *oranje* had begun in earnest, and he now
mingled with established greats, observing Michels at close quar-
ters and playing alongside 'The Milan Three', all still at the height
of their powers. Michels tended to delegate training sessions to his
protégé, Dick Advocaat. 'Dick trained us while Michels wandered

along the touchline. Now and then he would walk on to the pitch to speak to a player. His match analyses were interesting and compelling. You listened to him because he was a great personality. Being selected by Michels was very special. To me, he was an imposing figure, a real presence. I was impressed and had great respect for him.'

Training and playing with Marco van Basten, Ruud Gullit and Frank Rijkaard isn't bad either. 'I really enjoyed testing myself against the Milan guys. At first you think: "Wow, it's amazing to be on the pitch with players like these." But after a while it's more like: "Wait a minute, I can keep up with them and that means I can make giant steps too." When that happens, you're already on your way to playing abroad. At first I shared with Marco, but the lads from Milan soon got their own rooms because that's what they were used to at their club. It didn't bother me, I liked having a room to myself too. When I was seventeen, Marco was already a sensation, but he didn't act like a star. With the national team it was like it had been at Ajax. I got along really well with him. He thought of himself as completely normal, you could have a laugh with him, too, and he had a really good, sharp sense of humour. Even when he became a star at Milan, he didn't think he was different, but I thought he was pretty special.'

Holland cantered through qualification and by June 1992 Dennis was on his was to his first big tournament, the European Championships in Sweden. 'I wasn't nervous, there was hardly any pressure. I was just curious. I thought to myself: "Let's see what this is all about." I didn't feel as if we absolutely had to win, and I wasn't even sure whether we were capable of winning. I knew we had a good team with a mix of younger and older players. I was just focused on enjoying myself, learning and gaining experience. I really enjoyed tournaments: the whole thing, including the tension. It didn't disturb me. I played five major international tournaments, and I must say I loved all of them. I was always able to focus well, always ate, drank, rested well, trained regularly. It was all good. I never felt out of place at any tournament.'

His job was different in the national team. At Ajax, Dennis was used to being served by Stefan Pettersson. In *oranje* he was to serve Van Basten. Holland's first two group games were disappointing, their attack was sputtering and Marco wasn't scoring. A goal by Dennis beat Scotland but reviews back home were hostile after the 0-0 draw with the post-Soviet, pre-Russia team know as CIS (Commonwealth of Independent States). Qualification for the semi-final depended on beating the Germans.

The greatest rivalry in European football was in its most bitter phase. The Dutch had never got over the trauma of losing the 1974 World Cup final. Beating the Germans in the semi-final of Euro '88 had salved the wound somewhat. But the last time the teams had met – in the World Cup second round match in Milan – the Germans had triumphed once again. Poisonously attached to such matches were all the complex Dutch feelings about the Nazi invasion and occupation during the Second World War. Now the two best teams in the world – the reigning European and World Champions – clashed amid the low, wide, orange-dominated spaces of the Ullevi Stadium in Gothenburg. Dennis: 'It was my biggest game so far. The atmosphere was very charged. The media attention, the pressure, everything was more intense than anything I had experienced. And the Germans had some great players ... Kohler, Brehme, Effenberg, Möller, Klinsmann, Riedle ...'

Against the old enemy, everything suddenly clicked. The Dutch, playing with passion, focus and precision, blew away their rivals with one of the era's great international performances. The Germans appeared prosaic and had no answer to mesmeric Dutch movement, technique and imagination. Total Football seemed reborn in the 3-1 triumph, and Dennis scored Holland's memorable third, benefiting from a moment of Van Basten brilliance. As Aron Winter hared up the wing, Van Basten made a lethal-looking run to the near post, yet had the awareness to notice that Bergkamp was better placed behind. As Van Basten ran he also pointed behind him. 'I saw Marco pointing and I saw Aron understood his hint. As Marco sprinted to the near post, I automatically rushed to fill the space he'd created. Nowadays, most teams play with their midfield pointing backwards, precisely to catch the opponent's most advanced midfielder. But that wasn't the case then, and you knew you'd find space in the middle when the centre-forward pulled his marker away with him. Heading wasn't my specialty, but Aron's ball had just the right pace and, because I was moving at speed, all I had to do was touch the ball with my head. It was an amazing feeling.' It still looks an amazing goal, too. Holland topped the group, but Germany were second. The two teams would surely meet again in the final. All Holland had to do was beat Denmark, who were only in the competition by default, the winners of their qualification group, Yugoslavia, having collapsed into civil war and ceased to exist.

But four days later, the Dutch blew it. In the same stadium in which they had crushed the Germans, Holland played one of their worst games, drawing 2-2, then losing on penalties, Peter Schmeichel making the final decisive save from Van Basten's spot-kick. Observers at the time and historians since have attributed the Dutch defeat to arrogance and over-confidence, but Dennis denies this: 'We didn't underestimate Denmark. Not at all. We prepared for the semi-final exactly the same way we did for other games. We were completely focused on our next opponent. Nobody mentioned the final. Of course we celebrated after beating Germany, and it's logical that we slowed down a bit after that. But we came on to the pitch for the semi-final fully motivated and totally concentrated. We were all surprised that we suddenly couldn't perform at all. None of us knew what was going on. No, it wasn't hubris.'

Dennis, who scored the first goal of the match, also scored in the shootout: 'I never suffered from nerves anyway. I liked that pressure of having to take a penalty, of walking to the spot with the ball under your arm, feeling the tension but not seizing up. You know you're about to do something you've mastered. You're close to scoring a goal, all you have to do is execute a well-rehearsed routine.' Against Schmeichel he shoots to the left, at a saveable height but hard and wide. The side of the net bulges satisfactorily. Things will be different next time.

GETTING TO THE 1994 World Cup finals in the USA would prove much harder than expected. Holland and England, drawn in the same group, were both expected to qualify comfortably. But little Norway, coached by Egil Olsen, a disciple of the English long-ball theorist Charles Reep, usurped them both. For a while, remarkably, Norway were ranked second in the world. Holland, now coached by Michels's former deputy Dick Advocaat, and England, under the hapless Graham Taylor, were condemned to play two epic matches against each other for second place. Dennis played a decisive role in both games.

The two countries had only recently become rivals. Cruyff's *totaalvoetbal* side had humiliated Don Revie's England in 1977, but that was a friendly. More recently, Van Basten had given the 22-year-old Tony Adams the run-around to score the hat-trick that knocked England out of Euro '88. Five years later, on a dank night at Wembley in April 1993, England raced to a two-goal lead but were forced to settle for 2-2 after a Dutch comeback. The turning point of the game was one of Dennis's most notable goals. In the 35th minute Jan Wouters lofts the ball towards the 'D' on the edge of the

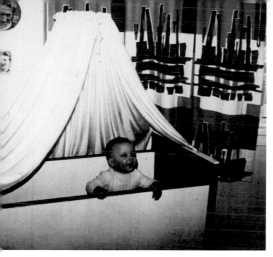

Denis Law – on wall – watches over baby Dennis, Amsterdam 1970.

Dennis outside the family home at James Rosskade (circa 1975).

On holiday in Drenthe. Dennis (in front) with older brothers Marcel, Wim, Ronald and TV actor Jantje Krol (in hat).

Lunch break for the Wilskracht (Willpower) D-Team (Dennis, centre, in blue tracksuit top with arms raised).

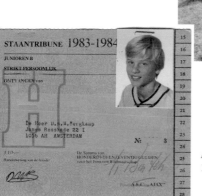

Ajax Youth season ticket for 1983-84 – Dennis, aged 14.

With his dad at a tournament in Belgium, 1983.

An early trademark lob as captain of the Ajax Under-15s, 1983.

The wooden Maradona carved and painted by Dennis in his arts and crafts class.

The 1985 Ajax A1 youth team with coach Cor van der Hart. Dennis stands fifth from left.

Celebrating winning
the Cup Winners' Cup
with fellow teenager
Frank Verlaat, Athens,
May 1987.

Dennis in his first
full league game for
Ajax, beating Haarlem
defender Luc Nijholt,
February 1987.

Dennis leaves the field
to a standing ovation
near the end of his
brilliant performance
against Malmo,
Amsterdam 1987.
Coach Johan Cruyff
gives him a pat on the
back. (Louis van de
Vuurst, Ajax)

Delight after scoring against Den Bosch, November 1988.

The Ajax bench after the sacking of Kurt Linder. From left, new coaches Spitz Kohn and Louis van Gaal, substitute Arnold Muhren and physio Pim van Dord. September 1988. (ANP)

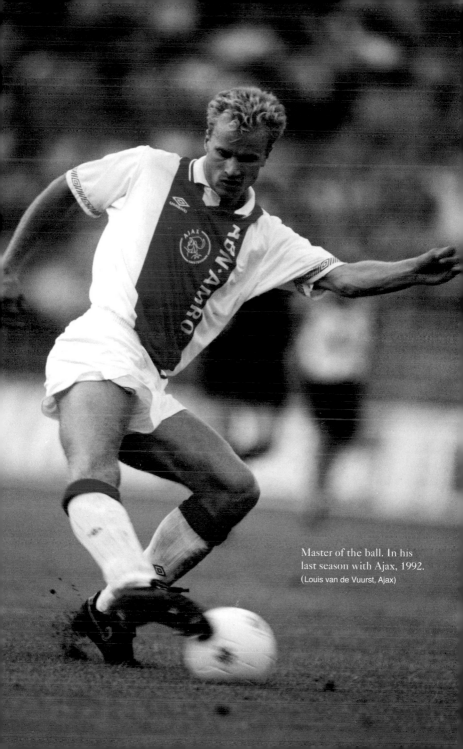

Master of the ball. In his
last season with Ajax, 1992.

(Louis van de Vuurst, Ajax)

Seventeen-year-old Dennis lifts his first major trophy, the Cup Winners' Cup, Athens, May 1987.

A header against Volendam, 1988. (ANP)

With former Ajax
team-mate Aron
Winter after Lazio–
Inter, Rome 1993.
(ANP)

Top-scorer of the tournament,
Dennis lifts the UEFA Cup,
San Siro, Milan, May 1994.
(Getty Images)

With Wim Jonk,
both holding their
UEFA Cup winners'
medals. (Getty Images)

Dennis with Arsene Wenger, pre-season 2004. (Stuart Macfarlane, Arsenal)

Dennis about to receive a red card for pushing Danny Cullip of Sheffield United in an FA Cup match, February 2005. Dennis was angered by Cullip's foul on Cesc Fabregas, who lies stricken in the background. (Stuart Macfarlane, Arsenal)

England penalty area. Adams gives chase but, with a burst of smooth acceleration, Bergkamp gets there first. 'It was over my head, thank you,' remembers Adams with a grimace. 'I'm still struggling to get to it even now. And it's still beating me. He's taken it *with one touch* and put it the other way ...' His voice trails off. Even by Bergkampian standards it's remarkable: an immaculately controlled reverse flick-lob that floats implausibly into the far corner while goalkeeper Chris Woods, rooted to the spot because he was expecting a shot to his near-post, can do no more than stare in wonder.

'Good thing it was only a friendly, eh?' says Adams. Sorry, Tony, but it was an incredibly important World Cup match. 'Oh shit!' Adams laughs and reflects on the cosmic injustice of it all: 'Forwards will always come out on top because they've got freedom. Freedom of the park! Nothing to lose! Nobody remembers their misses, but us *workers* at the back ... one little mistake and that's it! They never let you forget it!' On the Sky commentary, Martin Tyler gropes for a local angle: 'Bergkamp has stamped his class on the game! Dennis Bergkamp, named after Denis Law, a disciple of Glenn Hoddle, and he's bitten the British hand that guided him.' His colleague Andy Gray puts it more accurately: 'It's a fabulous goal.'

The decisive return in Rotterdam six months later has passed into legend as the game England lost because the German referee failed to send off Ronald Koeman in the second half for an obvious red-card foul on David Platt. Less well remembered is that Karl-Josef Assenmacher also blundered in England's favour in the first half, wrongly disallowing a Frank Rijkaard goal for offside. Koeman, minutes after his foul, chipped Holland's first goal from a free-kick. A few minutes later, Bergkamp skipped past Adams again to administer the *coup de grace*, shooting low from the edge of the area to beat another future team-mate, David Seaman. Many Englishmen still feel cheated, but Adams generously concedes that the result was fair: 'We were all over the place. And in their own backyard. It was too much for us. They were the better team.'

In any event, it would now be Holland's – and Dennis's – turn to suffer disappointments, traumas and a sense of being cheated. The build-up, yet again, was dominated by Cruyff. Would he lead the team in America? In 1990, the players had voted for Cruyff and been rebuffed by the KNVB, who had imposed Leo Beenhakker, the preferred candidate of Rinus Michels. This time everyone in the country seemed to want Johan: the public, the press, the players, the KNVB. Dick Advocaat said he would be perfectly happy to step aside. Yet somehow the negotiations failed. The KNVB said they'd reached a verbal agreement with Cruyff to take the job. Cruyff equivocated. Wearing the official KNVB blazer would be a problem because it carried the logo of Lotto and he preferred to wear his own brand, Cruyff Sports. The KNVB sent Johan offers by fax; Johan never saw them because he didn't know how to use his fax machine. Negotiations carried on through third parties. There was haggling over money. Finally, abruptly, the KNVB stopped negotiating. Both sides blamed each other.

On the very eve of the tournament, the Dutch talent for self-harm was revealed again. Van Basten, desperate to play, was simply too injured to join the team. Then Ruud Gullit announced at a press conference that he would not go to America. He refused to say why and promised to explain all later. Shocked Dutch fans were bereft. Some even burned their Gullit wigs. But the players responded with surprising indifference. Gullit had never been the most popular member of the team and now Dennis took the lead in declaring that the team could cope without him. To emphasise the point, two days later, Dennis scored the first and last goals in a 7-1 demolition of Hungary in a pre-tournament friendly.

Nearly 20 years later, Gullit still hasn't explained, but Dennis has his theory about why he walked out on the team. 'After 1990 Ruud wanted us to play more Italian-style football, with a large defensive block fronted by a pair of free strikers. But in 1990 Michels emphatically chose to play the Ajax system: four-three-three with a deep midfielder as shadow striker behind the centre-forward, or three-four-three with a diamond-shaped midfield. Advocaat maintained that. The structure was clear and he didn't want to abandon it just to please Gullit, especially not when we were already so far into preparing for the 1994 World Cup. The team was working well and everyone was happy with how it was going. When Ruud announced he was leaving, most of the lads responded in the same way. It was like: "If he wants to leave, let him leave. It's a shame, but we have enough self-confidence to continue the path we've chosen." In 1994 the generation of 1988 was becoming the generation of 1998, that of Frank and Ronald de Boer, Overmars, Jonk and Bergkamp. That sometimes led to conflicts, not on the pitch or in the dressing room, but in people's feelings. My own feeling was: "I'm taking over now because I'm growing to a higher level, my status is increasing. Hand over responsibility to me, I'll take it, I'm ready." That's what I was thinking, and that's how Frank de Boer and plenty of others were thinking as well.'

Holland stuttered in their next warm-up match – a 3-0 win over the Canadian national side in Toronto – but were taken aback to find themselves being hammered in the Dutch media for being 'boring'. In response, the team collectively decided to grant fewer interviews. 'I had just come off a difficult season in Italy, where I'd had to deal with a huge amount of criticism. I didn't want to deal with any more blabbering, especially before the World Cup finals had even started. "Get lost," I thought, and I wasn't the only one. So we decided to be a little less cooperative with the press. They didn't appreciate that of course, and they particularly went to town on me. For the first time I was no longer the ideal son-in-law, that nice, friendly guy.'

With temperatures in the mid-30s, the Dutch started the tournament slowly with a goalless draw against Belgium in Washington, and fortuitous 2-1 wins over both Saudi Arabia and Morocco in Orlando, with Dennis scoring against the Moroccans. The Dutch media was unsympathetic to their difficulties. As 31-year-old captain Ronald Koeman suffered in the heat, TV commentator Eddy Poelman mocked him: 'Our so-called world-class defender is playing like a fat old tart.'

Against Ireland, however, the team finally clicked and overwhelmed Jack Charlton's side with a terrific first half in Orlando. Dennis not only scored the first goal but also created a remarkable little vignette. The time-honoured method of flicking a ball on from a corner is to ram a high ball to a spot a few yards in front of the near post where a big man uses his head to alter the direction of the cross. On this occasion, Marc Overmars drilled his corner hard and low to the same position. Half-turning and with a velvety touch of his right foot, Dennis simultaneously drew the fierce pace out of the ball and lofted it like a hand-grenade to the penalty spot. Sadly, Ronald de Boer's bicycle kick went harmlessly wide, but Dennis had provided a delicious moment of invention.

So to Dallas where the Dutch faced Brazil in the quarter-final. In Britain the match was seen as an entertaining and sweet-natured classic, perhaps the best game of the tournament. For Dennis, however, the memory remains bitter. The BBC gave the game a showbiz build-up, using the opening credits of the TV show *Dallas* with the faces of JR, Bobby Ewing and Sue-Ellen replaced by the likes of Bergkamp, Bebeto, Romario and Rijkaard. In a goalless first half, Holland, shackled by fear, play a cramped and nervy game. In the second, after Brazil score twice, the Dutch throw caution to the wind and attack with passion. Dennis powers through for the first before Winter heads the equaliser from a corner. The momentum is now all orange, but a few minutes later Brazil earn a free-kick

30 yards from goal from which Branco fires home a spectacular winner. Afterwards Des Lynam beams. 'Well, we said it had potential, and it potentialled!'

In his *History of the World Cup*, Brian Glanville observes that absent friends might have made the difference: 'It's arguable, but had Gullit played instead of sulked, Holland might well have won their crucial game against Brazil ... and gone on to beat Italy [in the final].' What sticks in Dennis's mind is that Brazil's victory owed more than a little to the decisions of the Costa Rican referee Rodrigo Badilla and his linesmen from Bahrain and Iran. Romario, scorer of Brazil's first, looked offside and Branco grabbed the winner after pushing Overmars in the face; Badilla ignored that foul but blew for Jonk's retaliation a few strides later. 'Later, you wonder what all that was about. A referee from Costa Rica and linesmen from Iran and Bahrain? Why are they allowed to officiate at such a crucial match?' (Four years later, Holland would play Brazil again, this time in the semi-final, and this time with a referee from the United Arab Emirates and linesmen from Oman and Kuwait. Dennis: 'Pierre van Hooijdonk got a yellow card for diving when in fact his shirt was pulled in the penalty area. That makes you wonder what's going on. Twice we had to contend with debatable refereeing decisions when we were playing Brazil in the World Cup.')

Dennis was also frustrated by the lack of ambition and courage from his own side. After the game, coach Advocaat seemed satisfied. On the plane home from the States he told the Dutch press: 'We are one of the top eight teams in the world. Not bad.' Dennis: 'Dick Advocaat is one of the most ambitious people I've ever met and I had a good relationship with him. He was always completely committed, had tremendous drive and always strived to achieve maximum results. The World Cup was his first big tournament as manager ... but I thought we could have done better. After the

Brazil match it was as if he was relieved because we hadn't done too badly in the end. But he didn't accomplish the maximum achievable. We didn't play with enough guts. We were capable of more than we realised. As players, we were afraid we wouldn't measure up against Romario and Bebeto and allowed ourselves to be intimidated by the Brazilians' flair, bluff and arrogance. And Dick should have let us take more initiative sooner. The team was up to it. Overmars and Van Vossen were in great form, our attacks were effective and we had some seriously experienced players like Koeman, Wouters and Rijkaard. They knew how to respond when the Brazilians pushed the boundaries in terms of physical play and intimidation.'

The month in America was traumatic in other ways, too. Dennis had suffered through two air incidents. On one occasion the Dutch plane was forced to make an emergency landing after an alcoholic journalist travelling with the team became ill. On another a flight was four hours delayed because of a hoax bomb threat. And after the drama in Dallas, Dennis felt shattered. 'I was finished. I was exhausted, physically and mentally. I was angry at the referee and because I thought the team hadn't pushed itself as far as it could have done. That was something I often felt after defeats, especially when it meant elimination. I would think: "I did everything I could, I gave it my all, but can all the others say the same?"'

Soon after the World Cup Advocaat accepted a lucrative offer to manage PSV and Guus Hiddink, best-known for winning the 1988 European Cup with PSV, became manager of the national team. Once again, qualification for the next European Championship finals, to be held in England, proceeds uneasily. In June 1995, Dennis decided to stop flying. Fortunately, the next three major international tournaments would all be in Western Europe: after Euro '96, the World Cup would be in France and Euro 2000 would be shared between Holland and Belgium. Playing in the 2002 finals in Japan and Korea would be out of the question, of course, but since he planned to retire after Euro 2000 this wouldn't be an issue. Until then, Dennis's international career need barely suffer at all.

In any case, the problems thrown up by Euro '96 would be entirely different. Before the tournament started, Dennis began to sense tension within the squad. 'I was part of the players' committee and more and more of the black players wanted to join. At first I just thought: "Fine, come on in." But as the committee got bigger and bigger it made me uneasy. Why do so many guys suddenly want to be on the committee? It tells you something about how much they trust the committee. They hardly trust it at all.' Meanwhile, he noticed the black players separating themselves in various small ways. At mealtimes players had got into the habit of sitting at separate tables. Surinamese food was served at one, traditional Dutch fare at the other. On one occasion, Clarence Seedorf turned up late for lunch and when Danny Blind, by now the team captain, chided him, 'One-thirty is one-thirty,' Clarence shot back, 'I'll come to the table when it suits me.' The tension seemed to be related to internal strife at Ajax and Hiddink did not intervene.

In terms of the sheer quality of the squad offered, there was plenty of cause for optimism. The emerging generation of '94 had now been joined by a crop of brilliant youngsters like Patrick Kluivert and Seedorf, who played a big part in Ajax winning the 1995 Champions League. Ajax had reached the final in 1996, too, but lost on penalties to Juventus. In December, after a lackadaisical qualification campaign, the side had gelled splendidly and thumped the poor Irish (again) in the play-off. More than a few bookies installed the Dutch as favourites. Dennis was optimistic, too: 'It had been a difficult time for me. After the World Cup we spent a long time soul-searching. A lot happened, to me and to the Dutch team where a generational change was taking place. Patrick Kluivert was a rising star, and, after Inter, I'd rediscovered the pleasure of playing football again. There were times when I doubted myself and I wondered what might happen to me now that Kluivert had come on the scene. But the play-off against Ireland went so well, and playing behind Patrick I felt like the shadow striker I'd been behind Van Basten. Excellent! I was ready for the European Championships. We had a young, largely new team, but with quite a few lads from Ajax who had played in two Champions League finals. I thought: "Yeah, this could work."'

Holland's first group game, 0-0 against Scotland, was unimpressive but calm. Only during the second match, a 2-0 win over the Swiss at Anfield did things begin to unravel. Dennis and Jordi Cruyff (Johan's son) scored Holland's goals, but the real drama was on the subs' bench. Just 26 minutes into the match Hiddink withdrew Seedorf, who'd been booked 12 minutes earlier and had just escaped a second yellow. For Hiddink it was a case of looking after a player when he seemed certain to get sent off. Seedorf, however, interpreted his substitution as an insult and spent most of the rest of the game fuming about it with his friend Edgar Davids, who was also angry at being dropped. Later that evening, Davids was overheard telling a foreign journalist that 'Hiddink should stop sticking his head up other players' arses.' Davids was sure that Hiddink was favouring white players like Danny Blind and the De Boer brothers to the detriment of the black ones. Davids's remark made the news and Hiddink demanded to see him in private. When Davids refused to apologise, Hiddink angrily expelled him from the squad. Hiddink then called a team meeting in the hotel, said he'd noticed tensions among the players and then – amazing as it seems to non-Dutch eyes – told them to sort it out by themselves. 'Talk it through,' he said before leaving.

All hell broke loose. Seedorf, speaking on behalf of the *kabel* (cabal) of Surinamese players which included Davids, Patrick Kluivert and Michael Reiziger, brought up grievances from Ajax and claimed that Danny Blind and Ronald de Boer had too much influence with Hiddink. Seedorf, aged 20 at the time, also revealed that the reason he left Ajax for Sampdoria a year earlier was that he failed to secure the right-midfielder position which Louis van Gaal had promised him. Ronald de Boer had got the slot instead, proving that the De Boers wielded undue influence not only at Ajax but in the national team. Michael Reiziger spoke next to support Seedorf's allegations. He also said the black players at Ajax were treated as juniors. He gave details of their contracts to bear this out. Danny Blind, he revealed with bitterness, was earning six times as much as Patrick Kluivert.

Dennis recalls: 'I couldn't believe what was happening! It just exploded and the tone was really aggressive. There were three groups: one group consisting of Seedorf, Kluivert, Reiziger and [Winston] Bogarde were fighting with Blind and De Boer while the third, largest group, to which I belonged, just sat watching, open-mouthed.' Although the *kabel* were convinced the Ajax salary structure was racist, Dennis points out now that ethnicity was utterly irrelevant. As always, what counted at Ajax was seniority. Because Blind was 35 years old and the club captain, he would obviously be paid more than the 20-year-old Kluivert, who had been in the first team for less than two years. The *kabel* argued that since Ajax's Champions League successes were largely due to them, they should be rewarded accordingly. For the black players the key word was 'respect'. And Hiddink wasn't showing them respect either, because he didn't include them in the starting line-up.

For the rest of the squad, the key question was: 'What the hell does this Ajax nonsense have to do with us?' Dennis: 'There was a huge amount of frustration in the air. All sorts of major and minor issues were raised which they had taken with them from Ajax. It was just by chance that it hadn't escalated there yet. Or maybe it wasn't by chance and Van Gaal could have contained things.' The neutrals tried to calm the situation, with Dennis and Arthur Numan of PSV urging a truce. The most important intervention came from the most unexpected quarter: Barcelona winger Jordi, playing for Holland in his only major tournament. 'I'm an outsider here and I hardly know you,' he told the meeting. 'But I do know that we're here for something infinitely more important than your disagreement. We are here for a major tournament, we are here to perform at the European Championships. Let's do that and put your frustrations aside.'

Dennis was impressed. And so were others. The battling factions failed to resolve their dispute but, following Jordi's speech, they agreed to work together. 'Jordi was a newcomer,' says Dennis. 'I thought he was good in the group. We shared a room and we hit it off immediately. We're similar, with the same wry sense of humour and an attitude that says: "Who do you think you are?" When I made a cynical joke, Jordi immediately came back with one of his own. I thought he was a great guy.' Dennis ridicules the rumour that Jordi was only in the team to keep his father off Hiddink's back. 'That idea was ludicrous. As if Hiddink had anything to fear from Cruyff! Guus and Johan got on well together. No, Jordi was there on merit. He often played as a winger for Barcelona, and Overmars was injured so it was a logical choice.'

So everything would be fine now, wouldn't it? Not quite. Holland's team spirit was in tatters and their last group game would be at Wembley against an exuberant England who had just beaten Scotland. Not only would the hosts be pumped up with patriotic pride, they also had the indignities of 1988 and 1993 to avenge. Moreover, they had a coach, Terry Venables, who had a clear idea of how to dismantle the Dutch tactically. What followed was one of the great humiliations of Dutch football – and one of England's best nights in decades. The final score was 4-1. As England attacked with focused and (for once) tactically sophisticated aggression, the Dutch simply collapsed. There were two genuinely great goals as well. Alan Shearer's second goal (England's third) rounded off a move involving a Paul Gascoigne dribble and a brilliant lay-off by Teddy Sheringham. Holland's consolation goal followed an even more remarkable assist by Bergkamp, who controlled a drilled ball from Seedorf before hoisting a soft parabola-arced pass for Kluivert to score through Seaman's legs. Surprisingly, the goal was enough to send Holland through to the quarter-final against France. At Anfield Dennis had to come off with a second half injury and could only watch as Holland lost on penalties. At least, at the end of the Wembley drubbing, he had been able to exit with dignity, conjuring one of his great assists, then swapping shirts with Tony Adams.

Adams looks back: 'I played over three generations so, with Holland, Van Basten was my contemporary. I'd wanted to get revenge on him and he went and bloody retired! So when we beat Dennis's team in 1996 it felt like: "I'm getting revenge against the wrong people." I know the Dutch were in chaos, but take nothing away from us. I thought we played some great football and Teddy Sheringham was a fantastic number ten. You know, I'm an Englishman and sometimes we don't put ourselves forward enough. I'm patriotic. I love Dennis and I think he's a super player, but also I played with Teddy Sheringham who had a hell of a lot of talent in the same type of role.'

Hiddink, however, believes that disaster was caused not by English prowess but by Dutch in-fighting. He had pleaded with his players to come to their senses: 'Think about how privileged you are to be acting on this stage. Put everything aside for this.' But against England many of the players were still clearly thinking about problems with each other. 'I felt like I was on a runaway train that I couldn't stop as we raced past every station.' Ultimately, though, there was a silver lining because 'all that shit' had come out during the tournament and he would now be free to clear the decks and make a fresh start.

Dennis saw it differently: 'I was really fed up. When the trouble really broke out, I knew right away that we had no more hope of winning. I thought: this is hopeless, it's impossible. It was a terrible tournament. Everyone seemed relieved after that group discussion, but the mistrust ran too deep. The discussion came too late. If that whole issue had come out into the open before the tournament, we might have been able to genuinely solve it and find our rhythm. But that was no longer possible.'

The one bright moment was his assist for Kluivert's goal. 'The way I did that was becoming typical of my game at Arsenal. That action meant a lot to me. After Inter I had kind of lost my way and at Arsenal I rediscovered my love of football, but it wasn't immediately obvious what my role should be. I scored, but I assisted too. Slowly but surely I was assisting more than I was scoring. Patrick's goal confirmed that I was developing that way in the national team, too.' The negatives, however, far outweighed that single plus. 'It was my third tournament and I thought: "What if this is it, and my final tournament is ruined by this kind of unprofessional, selfish behaviour?" It was just awful.'

6

TURBULENCE

'ANNOYINGLY OFTEN,' SAYS DENNIS, 'I was told I should *do something* about it. People would say: "You can take a course to cure it, you know?" That really pissed me off.'

Dennis's aversion to flying began to develop in the summer of 1994. After his stressful first season at Inter, his World Cup campaign had been arduous and ended in disappointment in the heat of Dallas. In the aftermath of Holland's 3-2 quarter-final defeat, he says: 'I was exhausted and stayed exhausted. It wasn't unusual for me to be dead-tired after a match, but usually I recovered pretty quickly. Not this time. I was really wasted. I went to the hotel with Henrita, but things only got worse there. I started trembling, I felt unwell and I was extremely nervous about the flight home. Something was really wrong with me for a while, and my head was out of kilter too. I was panicking. I had been through a difficult first year in Italy. It had taken a lot out of me, both physically and mentally. Then straight afterwards the World Cup and an intense quarter-final in the heat.'

His legs felt like lead. In fact, everything about him felt heavy, including his arms and his head. Somehow he dragged himself onto the plane for Amsterdam. 'I was still in a panic but it got better once the plane was cruising above the clouds. I was fine for the rest of the flight.' But while the panic abated, his body had not recovered. 'When we got home I slept for two whole days, that's how tired I was. Then we rushed to go on holiday. We quickly booked a house in the south of France, but when we got there I was still extremely tired and morose. Usually, holidays are a time to wind down and recharge your batteries. But not this time. I wasn't able to enjoy anything. Not the beach, not the sea. And I couldn't settle down in that house, either.'

Dennis was worried about having to play football again soon and called Inter to ask if he could join pre-season training a little later. Ottavio Bianchi wouldn't hear of it. No exceptions would be made for Dennis. 'I said: "Look, Coach, I'm sorry, I really need more time." But Bianchi demanded that I turn up at the club for pre-season. He said he would take into account that I was still recovering from the World Cup.

'It was absurd. From the day I went on holiday to the first training session at Inter was just ten days! At Arsenal, Wenger always said four weeks' rest is the absolute minimum. Those four weeks were sacred for him.'

When Dennis reported back for duty at Inter after his brief – and useless – holiday, he was given a medical check-up and then driven up into the Dolomite mountains near Madonna di Campiglio. Wim Jonk, who was also exhausted after the World Cup and had tried to extend his leave, came too.

'Wim and I were supposed to be gradually eased back to fitness so we could rejoin the group. But after three days we were already expected to train with the others at full throttle. It was really tough up there in the mountains. We were pushed to the limit. We weren't allowed to gradually recover our strength and it was awful. Right there I got this horrible premonition that the coming season was doomed to failure.'

As soon as he returned from the mountains, Dennis was obliged to fly again. Inter almost always travelled to away games by air and, for domestic flights, used small propeller planes. Dennis recalls: 'They were those nasty little planes that stay in the clouds and shake all the time. When you looked out all you could see was white or grey. And inside there was hardly any space. It was so cramped it made me claustrophobic. You had absolutely no room to move and you just sat there shaking the entire trip. It made me feel so awful and I began to develop such an aversion to it that it suddenly dawned on me: "I don't want to do this any more." It got so bad I would look up at the sky during away games to see what the weather was like. Were there any clouds coming? Sometimes I was preoccupied by the flight home while I was playing football. It was hell. The last straw was when we had an away game against Fiorentina. I saw that boneshaker with its propellers standing on the runway and I broke out in a cold sweat. And sure enough, it was another disastrous flight. When we finally landed I called Henrita: "Where are you? Can you come and pick me up? I don't want to do this any more." She drove down to Florence and brought me back.'

Dennis doesn't recall the details – suppressing them, perhaps – but he must have flown a few more times with Inter after that Florence experience. Maybe he went by car or train to Naples for his last Italian league game? Dennis: 'That's highly unlikely. I probably gritted my teeth one last time. I have a vague memory of that, yes. But I know one thing for certain: I never flew again after that day.' He briefly considered flying with the Dutch national team in June 1995 for the European Championship qualifier against Belarus in Minsk. 'I went to the Dutch headquarters at Noordwijk to prepare, but I didn't sleep at all that night. I just lay there sweating until I finally said to myself: "I can't cope with this, so I'm not going to do it." That's when I took the decision.' At a meeting with team doctor Frits Kessel and manager Guus Hiddink, Dennis explained his feelings and said: 'I'm not flying any more.'

Uttering that one little sentence brought tremendous relief. 'It's weird, but it was as if I had regained my freedom. Once again I was able to play football without any inhibitions, and I could concentrate on a wonderful new career at Arsenal.' His announcement that he would stay on the ground in future was generally met with acceptance and understanding. But not from everyone. To those who suggested he take a course to cure his fear of flying, Dennis responds: 'I know what flying is! I've flown countless times in large planes, small ones, tiny ones. At Ajax, I once flew in a minuscule little plane over Mount Etna near Naples when we got into a terrible air pocket ... In terms of flying, I've seen and done it all and I'm simply not flying again. Ever.'

His agent Rob Jansen, responded just the way Dennis had hoped. 'He accepted it right away. He said: "If that's how it is, Dennis, then so be it." He didn't say: "Don't you realise what you're doing? That this is disastrous for your career? That it's going to cost you dearly?" No, he responded like a member of the family rather than like someone who only wanted to use me to earn money. That confirmed for me that I was in good hands with him. And it did cost me. In talks with Arsenal, if I said a million, they automatically deducted a hundred grand "because you don't fly". And I accepted that.'

It wasn't an issue at home, either. Henrita: 'I never pushed him. I never thought: "I've got to get him over this." Mind you, I did always think he would overcome his fear. Not by taking a course or something, but just spontaneously. After all, it started that way, too. It didn't go away, but it did turn out to be something we could live with without too much trouble. You know, when he said he wasn't going to fly any more, he calmed down. That calmness is worth a lot more than winning a few hours of travel time by flying. Our eldest, Estelle, loves flying. It doesn't bother Dennis. He's very realistic about it: "You're able to do something I can no longer do. So be it." It doesn't limit him, it's not a handicap. Dennis lets us do our thing. He takes us to the airport and picks us up again. No problem. For us it isn't an issue. If it is for the outside world, well, that's their problem.'

7

PAGES 301 AND 302

IN THE SUMMER OF 1995 Dennis made another important decision. 'I'd planned to be in Italy for at least four years, maybe six. But at the end of the second year I decided: "This is not the place to be."' Dennis's agent went to [Inter president Massimo] Moratti and told him that Dennis wished to keep developing as a player, so the club should either recruit a new coach and different players or allow Dennis to leave. Moratti said that was impossible and he would stick with Bianchi as coach. Dennis responded: 'OK, that's it. We're still friends, no problem. But let's shake hands and I'll go.'

'Looking back, I think I was really quite broken. The World Cup in America had been exhausting the year before and I think my problem with flying was because of that period. It was stopping me from enjoying football, so I had to make a decision either to go into therapy for months or years, or just play football and go a different way. And by the summer of ninety-five I had a lot of doubts in my mind. What kind of footballer am I? Do I still want a career? Do I want to stop at twenty-eight? Because after Inter I'm just fed up with this, I really don't enjoy this any more. And then in June I went to England and I felt straightaway the quietness. I thought: this is good. It's not all about football. You train, you play, and after the final whistle you talk a little bit about the game but then you can just be yourself: private. And that's what I needed.'

Was there anywhere else you could have gone? Arsenal wasn't as big then as it is now.

'There were several options. Germany was in the picture as well, but I just couldn't see myself there. The thought of playing for Bayern, it just ... didn't fit. And after Italy, Spain didn't fit either. My mind was set on England. Man United weren't interested and I wasn't going to go to somewhere like Newcastle or Liverpool because of the travelling from Holland. Spurs was mentioned, and that had been Hoddle's team, but even then I considered Arsenal to be a bit above Spurs. I'm not sure why. So I went back to Holland and Rob [Jansen, my agent] went to London. He already knew people at Arsenal because of Glenn Helder and Jan Wouters, who nearly went to Arsenal as well. The funny thing is, I really didn't know anything about Arsenal's reputation at the time for playing 'boring' football [under George Graham]. I'd seen a big article about the club in *Voetbal International*, the Dutch magazine, and it sounded good. They seemed to have a settled, stable team, with a lot of players of a certain age. I thought it would be easier for me to come into a team like that. I just had a good feeling about them. They had players who had authority: Tony Adams and the two full-backs [Lee Dixon and Nigel Winterburn] always played, they also had John Jensen at that time, Ian Wright, Paul Merson. This was not a collection of strangers. Eight or nine of these guys always played. I thought: "That suits me."

'They had done well in Europe, too: they'd won the Cup Winners' Cup in 1994 then been in the final again the following year. For clubs in Holland, doing well in Europe meant getting past the quarter-finals. So I thought: "Yeah, it's a big club, it's in London, and it's the way I want to play football. And Highbury is known for being a nice ground as well. Let's see what happens." I never expected to be there eleven years! Not at all! To tell you the truth, when I was at Inter I was thinking of playing until I was about twenty-eight and then going back to Holland. Just take a few years in England ... But it all changed once I was in London.

'The main thing for me was to move forward and get away from Italy. And it was my own adventure again, like when I chose Inter instead of Milan or Barcelona. I thought: "I'm the sort of player you don't see at Arsenal, so maybe I can show people this is my way of playing." Glenn Hoddle had stood out in this league and my way was similar to his way. I knew you could have space in England. So after a week, I made the decision and at the end of June I went with my wife to England for the first time, in the Channel Tunnel.

'When I arrived the contract talks were still going on, and the medical had to be done. We stayed in the Four Seasons Hotel and Gary Lewin [the Arsenal chief physio] picked us up and took us to the stadium. He was unbelievable the way he helped me in my first season. He sorted out everything, he was always friendly, jolly and funny, and he knew everything about the club. And then I saw Highbury for the first time ... *wow*! This was football! I loved all the houses around it, then you turn the corner and there's the stadium! That's not Dutch, nor Italian; you don't see it in Europe. It's just typically English. And you see the Marble Halls of course.

'So I remember coming up the stairs and then I met my agent. My brother Wim was there as well. And I saw in the room two people from Inter who were finalising the deal. It struck me: "I'm a thing you buy and sell. I'm a commodity." It was a strange feeling. Then I go up the stairs and I hear there's probably going to be a press conference. They are just talking about money and this and that. And then that was all done, and they opened the doors to the pitch. Nature! The grass! It was perfect. As soon as I saw the pitch, I thought: "This is fantastic!" Then it's the press conference with Bruce Rioch and David Dein and they're showing a little videotape with some of my moments, with goals and assists, and the music in the background is "This is The One" by The Stone Roses.'

'Immerse me in your splendour / All the plans that I have made . . .'

'Really? I didn't know the words. But it was a good song, and my moments on the video were good, too. It was kind of nice. Then we went on to the pitch for the famous photoshoot of course, with the shirt, with Bruce, and I remember I had to stand on a little wooden plank because the head groundsman Steve Braddock wouldn't let me stand on the grass! I thought: "I like this better than Inter." At Inter, they put you on a pedestal and I wasn't ready for that. I didn't have that status and it didn't fit my character. Straightaway in England it felt more normal. And it wasn't like Holland, where no one is allowed to be higher than anyone else because "we're all the same". England is in between, I think. It's a nice balance. Instantly, I felt: "I'm appreciated here, they're really happy that I came." But at that time it was a bit strange because I really didn't know what kind of player I was. How would I fit into the world's top hundred players?'

You didn't think you might be near the top?

'Not at all. Not *at all*! OK, I thought, I'm a good player, I'd done well at Ajax. But Ajax is Ajax. Ajax is Holland, and in my mind Holland is not rated in the world like England, Spain, Italy or Germany. I thought: "The normal person in the street probably doesn't even know me."

'Then we get back to the hotel. The deal's done, and we're in our room relaxing. As normal, I look up the sports headlines on teletext. We get the BBC in Holland so I know about Ceefax. I call up Page 301 and I'm shocked. The first two lines are in huge letters: "BERGKAMP JOINS ARSENAL." For the first time it hits me: "*Woah!* What's going on here?" I'm in this big country. I'm in London. I'm in this huge strange city where they drive on the left and . . . I'm on teletext. Me! They must rate me here, they still expect me to be like Van Basten or Gullit. I don't think of myself like that. Quickly, I go to Page 302, the football page, and there it is in more detail: "DUTCH STRIKER GOES FOR £7.5 MIL-LION." It was the first time it really hit what people expected of me. I looked at Henrita: "This is amazing! I have to step up." After Italy I had so many doubts. So many. Even when I played well, I always had to defend myself. And now you are in a hotel room and you see that. Physically it does something to you. Through your spine you get a feeling and you get a little bit emotional as well. And you look at your wife and your wife looks at you and you feel: "Wow, this is unbelievable!"

So DENNIS HAS signed for Arsenal, seen himself on Ceefax. He now sets off to drive home via the Channel Tunnel – and promptly gets lost. 'I wouldn't say *lost*. Not lost. We just took the long way because we made a mistake with the map. We're on the M25 and come to . . . is it the Maidstone turn-off? We made a mistake and ended up going the wrong way along the M25 south of London.

'We needed petrol so we pulled into a garage. You know how it is in a garage. There were two petrol pumps, one in front and one behind, and when I arrive the only free space is the one behind. But the car in front has just paid. As I'm filling my car, he drives off. Then another car comes up behind and they're like: "Jeez! Why didn't this idiot drive through to the next space?" I can see a lot of movement in that car. The guy is really angry and as he drives past me and goes into the space ahead, I can see him still gesticulating and talking to his wife ...'

The angry man from the other car recalls: 'I was driving home to Croydon, and I remember there'd been talk that Dennis Bergkamp might sign for Arsenal. "I hope it's true. God, I hope it's true!" Anyway, I had to stop for petrol at the Clacket Lane Services [on the M25] and there was this big foreign BMW 7-Series parked on the wrong side of the pump. My first thought was: "Who is this fool?" I mean, who'd put their car in a fucking stupid place like that? So I get out of my car to tell him what I think of his parking, and he gets out of his car ... and it's Dennis Bergkamp! I literally *screamed*! He's being Zen-Master calm, and I'm screaming because I've been praying that it's true that Dennis Bergkamp is going to sign for Arsenal ... and *here he is*!'

* * *

DENNIS TAKES UP the story: 'He's shouting: "Debbie! Debbie!! Look! It's Dennis Bergkamp!" And then he runs over to me and gives me a big hug. I was quite cool and down to earth, you know, but he was so happy to see me I thought: "Jeez, I feel welcome!" Think about it. It was during the holidays. The season hasn't started yet. And it was south of London in a place I wasn't supposed to be. How many people live in London? Seven million? And I've just run into Ian Wright, who is going to be my striking partner for the next few years ... If we'd met at the training ground or a petrol station near the training ground or near the stadium or something, OK. But in the middle of nowhere? On the day I signed? It was amazing at the time and it gets more amazing when I think about it now. What are the odds? It was meant to be! It was like a love story. Well, not a love story but ...'

There was another surprise in store. For Ian, the pleasure of playing alongside a footballer he hugely admired was soon doubled by the delight of rooming with his new friend. On their first night together, Dennis is in the bathroom getting ready for bed. The door swings open, Dennis walks into the room and Ian is shocked: 'I'd never seen a footballer wearing pyjamas before! Normally a player will have nothing on. And Dennis comes out in full pyjamas! That stands out more than anything else. It was so lovely. PYJAMAS!! It was so sweet, and so family and so genuinely the right thing to do. He did that all the time with me. I'm not sure if I went out and bought pyjamas because I wanted to copy him. I don't think I did but I certainly thought of it. Did he tell you he used to make fun of me for talking in my sleep?'

Dennis: 'Really? I don't usually wear pyjamas, so I'm wondering why I did. It's probably from my time in Italy.

Ian also said you made fun of him because he sleep-talked.

'With Ian you never know if he's making fun or if it's true. One night I remember, in the hotel, I was reading a book, and he was falling asleep, like normal. Suddenly he gets out of bed and goes "Hello." Is he making fun of me? "Hello?" He walks to the door, and listens at the door and goes "Urgh! Urgh!" and makes other weird noises, and then returns to his bed, looks around and goes to sleep. And his eyes were open the whole time. It was really strange.'

DENNIS BERGKAMP HAS been playing for Arsenal for a month and after seven games still hasn't scored. Because of his experience in Italy, he's not reading the newspapers. He hears, though, that the *Sun* is running a competition to see which of North London's hapless new signings will be the first to break their duck. Will it be the modestly heralded Chris Armstrong at Spurs or Dennis? Three days previously, when Arsenal played at Hartlepool in the League

Cup, Tony Adams scored two goals, Ian Wright one, Dennis none. The *Independent*'s reporter put it as gently as possible: 'Arsenal supporters are beginning to view a goal by Dennis Bergkamp in much the same light as a small child regards Christmas: they know it is coming, it is just the wait that is unbearable.' The next match is at home to Southampton.

Dennis: 'At that time the away fans would be singing: "*What a waste of money!*" when I missed a chance. I thought: "Wait a minute! [*laughs*] You can't say that!" But I kind of enjoyed it. It was funny and I could understand. I was also a bit upset with myself for not scoring. I only realised later that the tabloids made a huge thing out of it, which was lucky because that would otherwise have become a big thing on my mind. Against West Ham, I think, I missed two or three really good chances which I should have scored from, and I had a feeling that it affected our fans as well, in that there was a little bit of "hmmm..." in the crowd. They didn't want to boo me or anything but they were like: "What's wrong?" At Inter they would boo for sure, and Ajax fans are very critical as well. They'll boo you when it's nil-nil at half time. So I was expecting it. But the Arsenal fans stayed calm and that sticks in my mind. I think my problem was that I was still in Italy mode. I expected it to be tougher in England. I was getting much more space but I was still thinking: "I'll just lay the ball off here..." It wasn't a lack of confidence. It was more that my focus wasn't really on scoring goals any more. In Italy you have to look more for penalties and free-kicks around the box or a deflected shot. And of course, it shouldn't be taking me seven games to adjust. But I'd started with the idea it would take a few months to get used to things. Then I realised I had to speed things up. "OK, this is all good, I feel great on that pitch. I'm enjoying football again. It's fantastic here. I have to be patient but also positive." People hadn't said things directly. They'd come up to me and go: "You're doing well, but..." I knew what they meant. I was feeling the same thing myself. In training the players couldn't help making little comments. They appreciate you, they think you're a fantastic player and a nice person ... but they expect you to do something. And there had been an interview with Alan Sugar saying something to the effect that foreign players only come here for the money. I thought: "You can't take six months [to score]. You have to step up now ..."'

Ian Wright remembers: 'When Dennis started at Arsenal he didn't start great. There were murmurs from the fans and I remember him getting stick from a player from Hartlepool. This player from fucking Hartlepool was saying stuff to Dennis! I kind of took it personally myself. Dennis was playing well, but for some reason goalies were making saves against him or whatever. And the next game was against Southampton at Highbury. In the first half I remember Glenn Helder crossing it, and the ball comes a long way, and I see Dennis winding up ...'

Dennis takes up the story. 'What I remember most is that I didn't want to take any risk. It sounds a bit strange, because it's a difficult technique to hit a volley from a cross like that. You've got to get the timing right. How can I explain it? If you'd scored a hat-trick already, you'd try to hit it in the top right corner, or get a little bit of swerve on it, maybe, or hit it a little bit faster. You'd try to ... *add* something, be more creative. But now the idea was: "Be solid, just get the foot against the ball and see what happens." Just get it on target. The ball can easily end up in the goalkeeper's hands, but that's better than hitting it into the crowd. So, no risk whatsoever! Do it safe! And, yeah, it was far enough in the corner that the goalkeeper couldn't reach it. I did hit it solid. It had pace. It was good enough.'

As Highbury erupts, Dennis, in an ecstasy of relief, wheels away, arms spread and leaps in celebration. 'The way the crowd reacted was more than I could have imagined. I wouldn't say it was typically English but the way they celebrated, all jumping up and hands in the air together ... it's not explosive like that anywhere else. That moment was the start of the relationship with the Arsenal crowd. They'd been patient with me, and I didn't know why because they didn't know me. Maybe they saw something in the games leading up to that goal? It must be something like that because I seemed to have built up a lot of credit very quickly. Maybe they saw some moves or a pass, an assist or whatever. But they didn't know me. They didn't know my character and now they were giving this! The warmth was incredible. I'd only been here for one and a half months. After that goal we never lost that relationship.'

Then you scored again. And the second was even better.

'Well, that was like, "OK, now we start!" It felt like fifty kilos had been taken off my back [after that first goal]. I got the ball just over the halfway line, and I saw a lot of space in front of me. My whole game in England was filled with space. Between the lines, of course, I could play with that and create my own space with little tricks. So I have the ball. First I go to the right of the defender to get in the cross. I'm planning to cross the ball, then I realise, "I've got enough space to get forward here and shoot." First, I have to get the defender out of the way, so I take him across. I've never been a dribbler. It's just not my thing. So I shift to my left and then turn right. You cut into the space on the right, because you can see you have to make that move to get the shot. It's still thirty yards out but you're so confident. You know as well that when you take the ball from the left to the right, the ball will be rolling when you meet it. That's going to give it some speed, so when you hit it, in the end it will turn. It will curve to the right. I mean it starts left and then turns to the right, because of that little move you've done with the ball just before you hit it. So you don't aim for the corner of the goal but in the middle. You have to start it left ... it's something you've calculated many times before, so now you know what to do, though you don't know how much exactly it's going to swerve. Then it goes in like that, away from the goalkeeper ... and there's that explosion of the crowd again! That was so nice. When I look at that goal now, it seems to go much faster than I thought. In my mind everything happened slower. But certainly, from that day everything changed.'

8

BRUCE

Somewhere in a parallel universe where Bruce Rioch was not sacked after his one rather successful season as Arsenal manager, the following things happened: Arsenal's new boss built on the signings of David Platt and Dennis Bergkamp to create an attacking team which changed the club's reputation for boring football. Ian Wright was 'offloaded' to Glenn Hoddle's Chelsea in late 1996, but his replacement Alan Shearer turned out to be a classic centre-forward in the Highbury tradition of Ted Drake and Tommy Lawton, benefiting from the presence of Bergkamp, new Portuguese midfielder Rui Costa and winger Marc Overmars, bought from Ajax to provide 'ammunition' from the wing. Arsenal's surprising blend of English and continental talent won plenty of admirers. Meanwhile, Manchester United cemented their status as the most successful team in English history, winning the league in 1998, 2002 and 2004.

Actually, Rioch might have done worse – or much better. 'Bruce could quite easily have been where Arsene Wenger is today,' says Tony Adams. 'Quite easily. Different time, different place. But I really let him down. And so did Merse [Paul Merson]. And I've said sorry to Bruce. But I was spending more time in the pub than I was on the training ground. He might have been a success, but he didn't have a chance when the club captain wasn't there. And there were problems with other players. But he loved Dennis. I could see that.'

We'll never know, because just before the 1996-97 season the former Scotland captain and Bolton manager was summoned to a meeting at Highbury. Rioch, now retired and living in Cornwall, had realised early in his time at Arsenal that the board saw him as a stopgap appointment. He recalls: 'The chairman [Peter Hill-Wood] came back from Augusta, I believe it was, and I was called into the office with him and [managing director] Ken Friar and they just said "we are parting company". I have to say it wasn't a surprise. I was aware from a few conversations I'd had that Arsenal had been talking with Arsene Wenger. I knew that was in the background.'

Famously, Rioch fell out with Ian Wright, the club's leading goalscorer. After a pre-season match at St Albans, he'd called Wright a 'Champagne Charlie' in the dressing room and the relationship never recovered. Rioch: 'If I'm being absolutely honest, you could say: "Maybe you made a bit of a mistake there, maybe you didn't have to chew him out in front of the group." I wouldn't blame Ian at all. I would apportion more blame to myself, to say: "You didn't act in the right manner probably on that occasion."'

He was also struggling to cope with psychologically troubled players. 'There were a few who were having a lot of difficulties. When we went away on our first pre-season trip to Sweden, we had to take counsellors with us, for the players. They had to share rooms with the players. And I can remember one of the counsellors saying to me: "There are greater problems at this club than you realise." I won't say who, but I've had players come to me before training in tears because they're thinking of committing suicide. And I hadn't trained to be a counsellor! I think I did use the phrase: "I've spent more time at this club being like Marjorie Proops than I have being a manager." Several lads were absolutely incredible but some had problems. I'm not saying that these were bad lads, or bad people. Not at all. I'm just saying they had problems.'

Yet in many ways Rioch had done well. David Dein had brought Dennis Bergkamp to the club. David Platt, captain of England, had signed from Sampdoria and Arsenal began to open up, the team naturally playing more of a passing game than they had in the dog days of George Graham. In 1995 the club finished twelfth. Under Rioch the following year they finished fifth and qualified for the UEFA Cup.

'When you follow a man like George Graham, of course you want to keep some of the things as they were,' he says. 'So we kept the coaching staff but I also wanted to add my style and my players. Dennis and David Platt were the first but there were others I had identified like Rui Costa, Marc Overmars, Alan Shearer ... The coaching staff – Steve Burtenshaw, Stewart Houston, Geordie Armstrong and Pat Rice – all said: "Don't touch the back line, but we are short of goals in the team." Alan Smith had retired, Kevin Campbell and Stefan Schwarz had left the club and when I'd brought my Bolton team to Arsenal in the Cup [in 1994] – we beat them three-one – I'd seen more creativity was needed.'

Dennis was unaware of Rioch's plans to sell Wright and bring in Shearer and Rui Costa. 'I never ever heard about that! I only know how it did happen. Alan Shearer was a big player at the time, of course. But Ian Wright was really big, too. So I really don't know how it might have worked. Someone else was pulling the strings and I'm not sure the idea of buying these players was taken seriously. I think Bruce was thinking of attacking football in the British style, with a striker in front and maybe one behind. But somehow the way that I was playing I think it would have ended up with me more as a shadow striker.' Rioch's ability to buy players was limited because, following the George Graham bung scandal, the manager had little control over transfer business, which was handled by Dein and Friar.

Yet the Highbury crowd enjoyed the more attractive football Arsenal began to play. Is it too much to see in that year the beginnings of the revolution that ended with Wenger's Invincibles? Rioch himself is both modest and generous: 'Well, a little bit, but it was just a foot on the ladder. When I went to Arsenal I thought to myself: "I am with one of the great clubs of British football, so I've got to make them a great football team, which means not just winning a cup or trophy but making people remember." That was my philosophy and that's what I was looking for. But most certainly Arsene Wenger ... when you look at the team he eventually put together, everybody who has been involved in football over the last fifteen years will look at that team and say: wow! I think we would all agree that team was stunning. I mean just absolutely *stunning*. That to me is what you work for.'

Ian Wright, who disliked Rioch so much he had handed in a transfer request, was delighted to see him leave. But Dennis was surprised, angry and upset. 'I liked Bruce and got on well with him. People have different thoughts about people, which is normal. But when I came to England he was my coach and he helped me a lot and we just got on. In that season [1995-96] everything was changing for me. I was transforming my game, my mind, my private life. My wife got pregnant for the first time and we were staying in a hotel for six months. I'm in a new country. I'm getting back from a difficult situation where I felt *handcuffed* in Italy and couldn't express myself. So I've come to England and it's all fantastic. I thought: "I can open up again!" But I needed a year, maybe two years.'

Bruce supported him, encouraged him to play his game and taught him much about British football. 'Good things happened for me in that first year and he was part of it. He was my coach and he helped me to get used to England and the English game and English life ... If you were to ask me was he the best coach I ever had, well I think Bruce would say as well that's not really important. He was there at the time. In the end everyone moved on and I've only got good memories of him.

'For me, Bruce was a good guy, very positive, nice. So for me it came as a total surprise he was sacked after pre-season in the second year. But it was also strange for me. It's very difficult to explain. You come from a different country and you have a good year and you want to build on that. I was really ready to go [on] and suddenly the manager gets sacked without any warning! Without any reason that I could see. At that time it probably was the right decision [for the club], but only a few people will know why it happened like that. Especially after getting European football, it was really a shock and I was angry as well because I thought: "This is Italy all over again." The club makes promises and then they go the other way ... '

David Dein didn't reassure you?

'He did. I think he said: "Stay calm, just stay with us, good things will happen, changes will be made ... and somehow that was enough for me to stay. At the time I said it [leaving Arsenal] crossed my mind because I was really angry. But after two years at Inter I'd had only one year in England which I really loved, and leaving Arsenal would have meant going to a different club in England and that's not me. I needed some time to get settled and I didn't want to take that gamble. And of course very soon we heard that Arsene would come. It was a little bit of a secret in those few weeks but there were rumours and I knew about him at Monaco playing attacking football with four-three-three like Ajax. So I did stay calm.'

Bruce was obviously very hurt at the time. How do you see it now?

'I felt very sorry at the time. I didn't know what was happening. I visited him afterwards with my wife, not for "closure" or anything but just like "what happened?" and "how do you feel?" That sort of stuff. I think coming to Arsenal was a good step for Bruce. A good learning time for him, but leaving after one year . . . I think if he he'd had two or three years it would have been a good step up in his career and he could have gone to a bigger club afterwards.'

Rioch himself says he has no regrets: 'When I look back I enjoyed the opportunity of going to Arsenal. I enjoyed the opportunity to work with the players and to have someone of the calibre of Dennis on board was just fantastic. It was great.'

9

THE PLAN

'SOMETHING I OFTEN wonder about is: what were Arsenal thinking? Before I came it was Boring, Boring Arsenal. Then they buy me and David Platt. What's their idea? What did they have in mind for the future?'

Surely someone told you, Dennis?

'No. David Dein and Bruce Rioch said things like "We have big plans" and "We want to move forward" and all that sort of stuff. But everybody says that, so I thought "Yeah, yeah, whatever." I didn't take it seriously. But it wasn't like when Abramovich came to Chelsea and straightaway it was: "I want to win the Premier League and the Champions League, and these are the players I want ... *tack, tack, tack, tack* ... and here's the money and if it doesn't work that way we'll get the youth players and do it another way ..." I mean, there was a big picture from the start. When Sheikh Mansour went to Man City, I'm sure it was like: "Here's the ten-year plan." So what I'd like to know is: what was the bigger picture of Arsenal at that time? Was Rioch there just for one year? Was that already set up? Were Arsenal already thinking they wanted to get in foreign players and a foreign coach, change the playing style? What was the plan?'

Soon after Arsenal manager George Graham was sacked in February 1995 for accepting illegal payments from a Norwegian agent, Tony Adams received a phone call. 'I'm driving in Wandsworth and I get this weird call [*puts on an Old Etonian accent*]: "Oh Tony! It's the chairman speaking." The guy has spoken to me three times before. "Fuck off!" I say. "Who is this?" "No, Tony, this is Peter! *Peter Hill-Wood*, Tony!" He's calling from America. "I hear the shit's hit the fan back there. Don't worry! Good man on the way! The club is going in the right direction! Tally-ho! Goodbye for now! Speak to you later! Hold the fort!"'

He said, 'hold the fort'?

'"Hold the fort, Tony! Be back soon!" It was so bizarre I called back and arranged to go and see him.'

Adams, the club captain, was drinking secretly but heavily and amid the chaos of Graham's sacking, was getting phone calls from Alex Ferguson who hoped to sign him for Manchester United. Midfielder Paul Merson had revealed his addictions to cocaine and alcohol the previous November, and David Hillier had been convicted of stealing luggage at Heathrow Airport. Since winning the championship in 1991, Arsenal had declined. Meanwhile, their playing style had become a sort of English *catenaccio* relying on solid, massed defence and the goal-poaching talents of Ian Wright. 'We'd turned into a very good Cup team but we were nowhere near the League. It was a bloody mess!' recalls Adams. 'Dennis came into a bloody mess. He probably thought: "Jesus what have I done?" David Dein, who was in charge of the club at that point, probably kept telling him not to worry.' Actually, after Italy, Dennis found Arsenal nice and stable. 'Ha! Ha! Really? No, I can see that Dennis would have a different take on it. But the place I was in was pretty dark.'

Was there a plan? Adams sought assurances about the future of the club from Dein, Hill-Wood and Ken Friar. 'I remember going in and saying: "I've had enough! It's ridiculous us signing players for £325,000 like Glenn Helder. Where's our ambition?" I didn't know at the time about the money [director] Danny Fiszman had put into the club. They said: "Don't worry, we have ambition and everything's under control. We are going to get some good players at the club and we are going to go to the next level, and you're going to get a new contract. We're going to look after you. And we think we've identified a new coach ..." That meant Arsene Wenger, who David Dein had got through Glenn Hoddle. I think Bruce Rioch was just a stopgap.'

Dein takes up the story: 'Because I was representing England at UEFA and FIFA and I was moving in those circles, I saw a lot of what was going on around the world and I thought English football had to change, had to move in many respects. The players had to become more professional, more dedicated, more serious about their lifestyles. And the game itself had to change. It was fairly bland and basic. When we got Dennis we realised we had a footballing genius and he definitely changed football in England.'

But that wasn't your plan?

'I thought the club needed moving to the next level.'

What kind of next level?

'That was one reason we chose Arsene because we realised he was going to transform the club, which he did, straightaway with his training methods.'

Was there a blueprint? Did you have the idea that you could make a great new Arsenal and they'd end up playing Total Football?

'No. It evolved. Signing Dennis was a step in the right direction. In order to progress the club on the field of play, we needed better players, more technically gifted players. Dennis was one of those, but where it would lead to nobody quite knew at the time. I knew

Arsene, I knew his style of playing and I think the combination of Arsene and Dennis definitely changed the culture of Arsenal Football Club.'

BRUCE RIOCH WAS sacked just before the start of the 1996-97 season and Arsene Wenger arrived to take up the job a few weeks later. Ken Friar recalls an early conversation with the new manager. 'Arsene asked if it might be all right to have two foreigners in the team. I said: "The fans won't care as long as the team is winning." I think the public saw us signing Dennis as a positive move.'

But the board never stipulated or even envisaged what style of play might emerge?

'I don't think anyone woke up one morning and thought: "I want to change everything." It just evolved because of the players we had. It was an evolution rather than a revolution. We just had the players and they started doing it.'

Tony Adams sees the emergence of the great Arsenal of the late nineties and early noughties as the result of a series of happy accidents.

Adams: 'There was no blueprint. It wasn't planned. No one said: "We want to be Total." It was more a falling forwards. Bruce Rioch comes. He has his ideas but he's unlucky. The old training ground burns down, so they build the new one. My alcoholism is in there somewhere. Then I stop drinking and I get all this new-found knowledge and health, so instead of running to the pub I'm enjoying playing with Dennis, and enjoying training and playing free and being around. All these things fell into place at the same time. And Danny Fiszman's part in it has got to be acknowledged, because he got the finance into the club ... You know, this game is about money. And it's about players. And players go for money. I went from three hundred grand a year to a million. It was my first-ever decent contract. Under George Graham there wasn't the level of financing. We were on no money at all compared to later. Without Danny Fiszman's money there is no way we would have got Dennis, or David Platt, or Arsene. I wouldn't have stayed at the club. David Seaman wouldn't have stayed. Bouldy [Steve Bould] got his best contract. Nigel [Winterburn] got his best contract. Without Arsene we wouldn't have got Patrick [Vieira], or [Nicolas] Anelka, or any of the French lads from that untapped market. None of that would have happened if you didn't have the cash to support it. It's not one isolated thing, or one person.'

Finally we turn to Arsene Wenger, the French coach then working in Japan whom David Dein had wanted when the board appointed Rioch. Dein recalls: 'I'd met Arsene eight years before, when he was at Monaco. And we finally signed him in 1996. He didn't know he was auditioning all that time, but he was! I used to go to Monaco a lot and he would invite me to the games, and I would see how he interacted with the players, with the press, with the fans, with the board. And he was just different class.'

Was there a plan? What was the process that makes the great Arsenal?

Wenger: 'The process that makes the great Arsenal is that progressively I changed every player who played before into a more technical player. First in improving existing players. After, when they had to be replaced, by a player who could contribute more to offensive quality, to build up the game from the back, like Kolo Toure, Lauren, Ashley Cole, and bringing in Brazilian players like [Gilberto] Silva, Edu ... and progressively to change the whole environment ... to have in every single position a player who could really play both sides of the game. Attacking and defending.'

Which is very Total?

'Which is very Total. Yes. That was the plan. That's where in every position we could find the player who could absolutely absorb that.'

But you didn't tell people or make speeches saying, 'This is the new philosophy, this is what we do'?

'Of course we spoke about it many times. But I believe that your philosophy goes with the training session, and what you do in training. So I made slow changes. You know, when you go abroad you have first to test how far you can go. Because I was not in a position where I could come in as the Master who had done it all before. I was an unknown figure. I was like an English guy who goes to Bordeaux and explains to them how to make the wine! A French guy who comes to this country to explain to English people how to play football? They'd say: "Who are you? What do you want?"'

So you have to go cautiously?

'Yes, I go step by step.'

Was there resistance?

'Not really, I must say. No. In every country you have a culture. And in every football club you have a culture. And the more successful this culture has been, the stronger the resistance to change will be. Because if you are not immediately successful, people will question what you want to do. That's why I tell you, you have to slowly change. Today Arsenal is well-known to play a technically high-level game. But if you go twenty years back this was not the case. That shows you that the change, the trend, has worked. But it has been done slowly.'

So you had a plan, you just didn't advertise it?

'Of course. Of course I had a plan. But I did not shout from every rooftop that I had a plan!'

10

THE BODY MATTERS

Iᴛ's sᴀɪᴅ ᴛʜᴀᴛ before Arsene Wenger brought modern principles of physiology and nutrition to Arsenal, English footballers knew little about how best to look after their bodies. Tony Adams demurs: 'People say massage only came to us when David Platt came back from Italy, but David O'Leary was doing self-massage almost twenty years earlier. That's one of the reasons his career lasted as long as it did. I'm not saying Arsene didn't teach me a lot about my body, about preparation and recovery. He was brilliant at that. He's a physiologist and that's his strength. He's the best in the game. But I also remember a book by Dr Robert Haas. It was called *Eat to Win* and we had that in 1987, long before Arsene ever came to these shores. OK, we were drinking twenty pints of lager as well, but at least we were eating pasta!'

Gary Lewin, the hugely respected former Arsenal physiotherapist who is now the England physiotherapist, recalls plenty of unhealthy habits from the 'good old bad old days'. 'It's been well documented that George Graham liked to take the team away for a week somewhere and that would involve drinking. We had trouble all over the world, but that was the culture then. Talk to any of the old Liverpool lads and they'll tell you that when they won all their European Cups, drinking was part and parcel of it. It was part of team bonding. And before the match we used to have a bottle of brandy in the dressing room so players could take a swig before they went on the pitch – for courage! That wasn't drinking as such, just old school. And one of the first things you'd put on the bus for after the game was a crate of beer.'

Players' food was equally bizarre by today's standards. 'Even when Dennis arrived, players ate fish and chips after a game. And there'd be Mars bars and Jelly Babies in the dressing room. You're led by science and in those days the science said: quick sugars give you energy. It's changed dramatically now, of course, but in George Graham's time we'd pick up the fish and chips on the way home. Arsenal were actually one of the first teams to move away from that and have stewards serving cooked meals on the bus. But teams like Liverpool and Man United stuck with fish and chips. When they came to Highbury, they'd put their kit out then give me or the kit man a list of fish and chips for after the game. We'd then run the order down to the chip shop on the corner of Avenell Road and Gillespie Road, and they'd pick up their dinner on the way out! That was still going on when Dennis arrived. Of course, he never got involved in the drinking and he was always very careful what he ate. And then, with Arsene, everything changed completely. The training, the diet, the drinking, everything.'

Dennis recalls being astonished. 'Of course as soon as I joined the dressing room I realised there were a lot of things wrong. I remember in my first season the pre-match meal would be white beans in tomato sauce, bacon, scrambled eggs ... I could not under-stand it! And on the coach the other players would be eating crisps and chocolate. That was England in those days. I didn't get involved. I just thought: "You cannot do that" and brought my own food. For my first pre-season with Arsenal, we went to Sweden and trained twice a day. The first evening I went for a walk with my wife and saw eight or nine Arsenal players sitting outside a pub, drinking beer. I thought: "This is unbelievable! You've just had two hard sessions to prepare for the season, and now everything you did is going down with the alcohol! What's the point of being there?"

'The funny thing is you wouldn't notice it in training because they were so strong. Sometimes you could smell the alcohol in the morning but you could never tell from the performance because they always gave one hundred per cent. But I thought: "You can't treat your body like that." I'd come from the professional culture in Holland and Italy where it's really serious – apart from some players smoking. So it took some time to adapt. But I felt it was also a question of me respecting a different culture. I wouldn't be happy if players missed training because they were drinking, but if they trained in a professional way, giving one hundred per cent, who am I to say: "It's not good for you"? I won't criticise. They respected me for not doing that. Maybe they looked at me and realised the way I performed was connected to what I ate. Maybe they learned a bit from that. But the real change only came when Arsene forced the issue by putting different food on the table. All of a sudden, the minibars were empty in the hotels. And no room service! Not accepted any more. And it helped the players of course.

'To me, professional sport is just that, a profession. The better your body is prepared, the better you can do your work. In every other kind of work, if your tools aren't right you get fired. In football, if you're overweight, if you're not quick enough, if you don't recover well enough after a game ... well, to me that's not good enough. There's no research that says: "Don't worry, junk food is good for you! Take another burger, have six pints!" So I thought they were out of their minds drinking so much or having that kind of food. And the club allowed it! Then Arsene went to the opposite extreme. He went totally overboard. At the start with him, the pre-match meals were so boring. Vegetables with no sauce, white chicken boiled ... Oh, come on. I mean, I like a bit of flavour and, really, this was no fun. But slowly it got better, and it had to because there's the mental aspect as well. Normally, you only eat what you like. If that's bad for you then you have to find a balance, but you have to feel good about what you eat. So at the training ground, they started to use sugar in the desserts, for example. But not refined sugars. And the food started getting tastier and eventually it got much better. But those first few weeks were like '*bang!*' It was a real shock even for me.'

One aspect of the new regime Dennis did not favour was the use of mineral and vitamin supplements. Gary Lewin: 'Arsene felt that, due to the wear and tear of the season, players needed them, so you'd have Vitamin C drinks and Vitamin B tablets. Yann Rougier, a nutritionist from France, came over and did blood and hair tests to see which minerals and vitamins the players lacked. But Dennis really didn't like that. It wasn't his ethos. He felt he ate healthily so he didn't need supplements. But they didn't argue about it because Arsene was a bit like Dennis really: a discussion person. Rougier would sit down with every player and go through the blood tests and say: "You're low on that, so I'd like to give you such and such supplement." Dennis would say, "I don't like taking supplements," so Rougier would say, "Well, in that case we need to think of another way." So he'd ask Dennis to eat more liver, or spinach or whatever it was. That went for the whole team. About a third of the players didn't take all the supplements Rougier offered them. Another third took some. The others, with all respect to footballers, they'll just do what they're told.'

Dennis's approach to injuries and treatment was also unique –

and at odds with English tradition. For one thing, he was fascinated by the workings of muscles, ligaments and other parts of the body. As his physio at Ajax, Pim van Dord, noticed a few years earlier: 'Even as a junior player Dennis always wanted to know everything there was to know about injuries. That was striking, especially because he hardly ever seemed to get injured himself.' Lewin was also struck by his attitude: 'Dennis was much more aware of his body than any other player I'd met before. I mean in the *medical* sense. For example, he'd say: "My calf feels really tight," so I'd work on him. I'd say it might be a risk to train but Dennis would go: "No, I know how it feels. I can train today but if it feels a bit tight, I'll tell the manager."'

What's unusual about that?

'Well, Dennis's idea was: "Give the manager and medical staff the information and they'll make their own decision – and so will I." But in the old English football culture if you were injured you would never mention it. It was drilled into you: "Don't show any sign of weakness!" You didn't want to give the manager any reason to not play you. In those days it was still survival of the fittest. You'd never get on a stretcher, you played on like Bert Trautmann with his broken neck in the Cup final. Don't worry about the long-term consequences.' He remembers what happened to Bob Wilson in 1972. 'Bob absolutely slaughtered his knee in a Cup semi-final and while he's on the floor in agony the other players are swearing at him: "Fucking get up! There's nothing wrong, you tart!" Bob's knee is wrecked! It shortened his career! And they're shouting at him.'

Bob confirms: 'It was at Villa Park against Stoke and I knew immediately I was badly damaged. I'd snapped the cartilage and tendon. I tried to play on but I was absolutely disabled and a complete liability in goal. But there were no substitute goalkeepers in those days so everyone wanted me to carry on. Bertie Mee [the manager] came round and said, "You've played through injuries before, so come on, Willo, you can do it!" And I remember Peter Storey standing over me, effing and blinding, shouting at me that I was a "coward". The injury still causes me problems: I walk with a limp because of that one.'

Lewin continues: 'But that was the culture in the seventies. Even into the nineties that was still there. I've seen Tony Adams play with fractured bones, torn ligaments ... He'd say: "I've gotta play, gotta play!" He was so competitive. A bit like John Terry later.'

That wasn't Dennis's approach?

'Dennis would say: "Well, actually I'm having a *career* in football. I'm not going to jeopardise that for the sake of one game." And he'd be thinking of the team as well.'

At the end of the 1998 season Dennis had a muscle strain. Would he be able to play in the Cup final against Newcastle? If they won, Arsenal would clinch their first Double since 1971. Dennis was desperate to play ...

Lewin: 'We went through all the rehab and the running sequences and he felt really good. On the Friday he was training normally, with a view to playing on the Saturday. He trained and trained, and after about forty minutes he stopped and said to the manager: "I'm not right." As he walks in I say: "Has it tightened up again?" and he says: "No, but it doesn't feel right." And then he goes: "I'm not going to cheat those guys tomorrow. It's not about me." That was eye-opening for me because most players would have said: "Sod it, I'll start the game and if I come off, well, I played in the Cup final." But Dennis was so aware of his body and his limitations. And he knew the expectations of the team from the fans. You could call him dogmatic, or honest, but I saw it as him being *aware*. From a medical professional's point of view it's what you dream of when you're working with a player.

'He never had any very serious, long-term injuries, just the usual footballers' injuries – hamstrings, thigh, calf. Two or three-weekers, never more than that. With rehab, where other players would just ask: "How long is it going to be?" Dennis wanted specifics. "When am I going to progress into jogging? When am I going to progress into straight-line running?" Then he'd be very methodical about it. Other players put it all on you. They don't take responsibility. They just say: "OK, what are we doing today?" then moan that it's too much. Dennis would talk it through. Let's say I was planning a six-minute jog then some straight-line running. He might go: "I'm not sure I'm ready for that yet." So I'd say: "OK, let's do the jog first. If you don't feel it, we'll do another six-minute jog, keep it at that pace and see if you get a reaction. If you don't get a reaction, we'll step it up tomorrow." "OK, that's what we'll do then." He was always so aware of everything around him, analysing it all. You saw it tactically and in the way he managed the speed of the game. That's something they talk about in Holland and Italy, whereas in England it's all one pace for ninety minutes. Dennis could hold the ball, pass it simply to slow the game down, then speed it up when that was needed.

'Another part of what Dennis brought to the club was his education, and habits he regarded as being normal for a footballer. If training was at ten-thirty he would usually be there not later than ten, often at nine-forty-five or nine-thirty. And he'd check his equipment. If the shorts weren't right, or if the socks weren't right, he'd ask the kit man, Vic Akers, to change them. Not maliciously, just: "Vic, have you got a pair of these?" or "Can I have a pair of those?" And his footwear was meticulous! I've never known a player who knew exactly what he wanted from a pair of boots. He'd involve the company that made the boots for him. Remember, this was an era when players started changing their boots for fun, but Dennis was old school. He broke in a pair of boots during pre-season and wore them for the season because they were *his* boots and they were comfortable and if you change something in them it might change something in you. You could argue that was part superstition, but I think it was more what I call *good habits*, and the awareness that by changing things, subtle changes, it can affect you physically, mentally, technically.

'He was the same with strappings. He was the first player I'd met who wouldn't wear strappings during the week but would wear them for a match. I found that very interesting. From a medical perspective you don't want players to wear strappings unless they have to. Strappings are to stop you turning your ankle but usually, when an English player has had strappings once, that's it, he'll wear them for the rest of his career. But he's doing that for *non-medical* reasons. Partly it's superstition and partly he thinks: "If I have a strapping I won't sprain my ankle so I may as well have the strapping." What they don't understand is that when you strap a joint you restrict the range of movement, and by restricting the range of movement you affect the sensation – we call it *proprioception*, the sensation that comes through that joint. It will affect your balance, which could affect . . . everything. So what Dennis did was to train without strappings – because he wanted all the proprioception – and then, for games, when you are at three times' greater risk of getting injured, he'd wear a strapping, to protect his ankles from cuts and kicks and stop his ankles twisting. And I'd never seen a player do that before. That's an example of where I was learning from him.'

* * *

DENNIS IS INTRIGUED by Gary Lewin's take on his 'good habits'. I put to him a story involving Bill Shankly when he was manager at Liverpool.

Lewin's talk of manly old English football attitudes reminds me of Bill Shankly, who regarded injured players at Liverpool with something close to contempt. When one had a knee injury, Shankly got angry: 'Get that poof bandage off! And what do you mean your *knee? It's Liverpool's knee!'*

Dennis [*appalled*]: 'I don't know about the psychology of that, but I would never have accepted it. I own my own body and I'll be the judge of whether I can play or not. And the coach has to leave that decision to the player. I never had a problem in that way. I always wanted to play, always. And I don't say everything has to feel perfect. Ask any player: "Did you ever play without pain?" That situation doesn't exist! There's always something. And if you're limping, that's different. But if you feel something but it's not going to do you damage long-term, then OK, you have to play.

'Even in my time, when I came to England it was not accepted any more that a player had to play no matter what. I know those pictures of people like Terry Butcher with the bandage round the head, blood streaming down. But come on! To have a player limping on the pitch or who can't run? No chance! You need one hundred per cent players.'

Is that why you missed the 1998 Cup final?

'I'd had a hamstring injury towards the end of the season and missed the last few league games, including the Everton game, when we won the title. The week after was the FA Cup final, so I got my physio over from Holland, Rob Ouderland, to work with me. Gary Lewin was fine with that. He was really open-minded, and I appreciated it. All through the week I was getting better and better. I even missed my wife's brother's wedding because to play in the FA Cup final at Wembley was my dream since I was a boy. This was my first chance and who knows if I'd get another one? On the Thursday, it felt OK. Green light! I can do this! But Friday was team training and we thought: "OK we'll decide after that." I took a free-kick and I felt the muscle again. I stiffened up straightaway and that was it. And of course I was thinking as well that it wasn't the end of the season because the World Cup was coming up afterwards. The next morning that proved to be the right thought because it got worse. I felt pain just walking, so really it was impossible. I couldn't have played.

'Gary talks about my career. Well, yes. It was my ambition to play for as long as possible at the highest level, to enjoy the game and give everything, to put my name in the books, so to speak. You want to be the best there is. You want to make history. But you can only do it if you do it for a long time, and if you do it at the high-est level and if you stay healthy. On the other side, I understand about the old English idea of *manliness*, but I know players who played when they shouldn't have done.'

The playing career of Pim van Dord, the physio at Ajax who became a close friend, had been destroyed by corticosteroid injec-tions on an Achilles injury. Dennis took the lesson to heart. 'I learned that when it's a muscle problem and you put an injection into it, you don't feel the pain but it can tear. I always said: "I'm not going to do that. I want to feel my body. I want to know what's hap-pening." There are certain injuries an injection won't aggravate, so I've had injections. I've had them in my knee a few times, in my groin a few times at Inter. When I was at Arsenal I had a problem with my toe once and played four or five games with injections. They put the injection in quite deep so it was really painful and it took out the feeling in two toes. But that was OK. It's inside my shoe, no problem. I knew the difference between what could cause me damage long-term and what wouldn't. I was never going to take cortisone injections just to play a game, but it's different if you use them therapeutically, like "take this cortisone and then have three days no training..'

How did you become knowledgeable about medical matters?

'I was always interested in physiotherapy and, even without that, I was interested in how the body works. I wanted to learn about its structure. How do muscles work? That was the most intriguing question for me. I studied physiotherapy for two years at school and even when I got my first contract at Ajax I carried on studying and playing professionally as well. I always wanted to do something with sports so if my football career didn't come off, I could be a physio. Where did that come from? I really don't know.'

Gary Lewin became a physio because injury ended his playing career. I'm imagining it the other way round: you get injured instead of him, he's the player, you run on the field to help when he gets hurt ...

'[*Laughs*] I was always conscious of my body and what it needed and how to prepare myself, and that got more and more towards the end of my career. And I was always OK with food, with sleep. I took my rest. I'd love to be able to say I never got seriously injured because I looked after my body. Partly it is, but I was lucky, too. Of course, some of that comes from being aware of defenders around me, knowing when the tackle comes, knowing when to jump up, and knowing when to put your foot in. Sometimes I made a mistake and got injured. It's a combination of luck and awareness. Timing is important, and having quick feet. That was my main thing, really: "Stay away from the silly stuff." Paul Gascoigne hurt himself with a stupid tackle in a Cup final, didn't he? And Marco [van Basten] did something like that, diving into a tackle with a Groningen player when he was twenty-two. He was never quite right after that. That's where his ankle problem started. In the end, at twenty-eight or twenty-nine, it finished his career.'

Things changed for the better at Arsenal, didn't they?

'Oh completely. I give Gary a lot of credit. He was very open to new ideas. He thought things through and it all changed very quickly. Like having a masseur. In my first season David Platt had a masseur, and that was new. In my last year at Arsenal we had three masseurs who came in the day after a match ... So in ten years it changed from "Why do you want a masseur? To work on your muscles? Get lost!" to three masseurs! And of course all the clubs copied. Now everybody does that. It changed very quickly.'

So you got on well with the medical staff at Ajax and Arsenal. But how was it at Inter?

'Different! In late 1994 I had a groin problem. I'd had it for a few months and it was starting to get really annoying. I'd seen lots of doctors and tried everything. In the end I told the club I wanted to get a physio over from Holland. They wouldn't accept that. A physio flew down and came to the training ground and tried to be friendly and normal, but they just wouldn't let him be there. So he treated me at home instead. In the end, around Christmas time, I said: "OK I'm going home for a week and I'll get my treatment there." They said: "No, no! You must stay here!" I said: "No, I'm going home to my family. That's what I need and that's what I'm doing. And I'll get my treatment there." They said: "In that case we'll send a doctor over." "Fantastic!" I said, "no worries!" So back in Holland I'm finally getting the treatment I need and the Italian doctor comes over. It was just silly. While the physio is treating me, this young doctor from the second team is sitting there with a notebook, watching and hardly speaking. Why? For their files? I never found out.'

11

THE JOKER

IT IS LUNCHTIME at a pub in Kensal Rise and Ian Wright has begun to sing in Dutch. Quite loudly.

'*IT WAS in a discotheeeeekk! Zat ik VAN DE WEEEEEEKKKK!!! ... En ik VOELDE mij daar zooooooo AARRLLEEEEEEEEN!!!!*'

No one even looks up. Impersonating André Hazes, the sentimental, diminutive, melancholy, alcoholic, late Dutch crooner probably happens all the time in Kensal Rise.

How do you know that song, Ian?

'Cos of Dennis! Or rather, Glenn Helder *and* Dennis. Glenn taught it to me and when I sang it to Dennis he nearly died. ... *AND IT WAS warm en dreeeeee-EUUKKK! Ik zat eeen LEVEN CROOOOOK!!*'

You've caught its emotional overkill perfectly ...

'Yeah, I'm not bad like that. So then Dennis is on at me: "You've got to sing that on Dutch TV!" "No, I'm not going to do that." "You have to do it! They'll love it. They'll love *you*!" He's egging me on. So after that game at Leeds, that's what I did. I sang André Hazes on Dutch telly.'

Is there a video?

'There most probably is a video.'

IAN WRIGHT AND Dennis Bergkamp were not only a football act but also a comedy duo. As on the pitch, Dennis was the instigator, the ideas man lurking behind, setting up Wright for glory or, in this case, laughs.

Wright: 'People don't know that side of Dennis, but he was really a mischievous joker. I love that! I love that about him because it is a side I will be able to remember forever, but other people won't see it. All other people see when they look at Dennis Bergkamp is just pure genius. But I saw the man and I knew the man and feel very honoured. So you don't see that side of him, but he is really ... *funny*!'

Martin Keown was often on the receiving end of your pranks ...

'We used to get a lot of fun at Martin's expense. We all did!'

Why pick on Martin?

''Cos he's so fucking *intense*! Grrrrrrrr!! Know what I mean? He was *sooooo* intense! I remember when Dennis said to me to dress up in Martin's clothes. He tries so hard, but his clothes are so ... *rubbish*! Poor design and really very bland, rubbish clothes!'

Keown confirms: 'Dennis was all for having plenty of fun. He may have been seen as serious, because he was very exact in his performance. But off the pitch we would be laughing and joking all the way from game to game and then the same in the dressing room. Then it was like: "Let's focus now and win this one." It was a nice balance.'

I hear he didn't approve of your fashion sense.

'Ha ha! Yes, Dennis was, shall we say, the clothes manager. If you came in and what you were wearing wasn't to his liking then he would be hanging it up twenty foot in the air somewhere and you'd have to go and get step ladders and all sorts to go and reach it. I'd be furious: "Fucking Bergkamp, he's done it again!" But it was just part of the banter. Some players couldn't take it, but Dennis knew he could do it with me. One day I turned up for training and Dennis and Ian Wright had got together. Wrighty came to give me a big hug because he hadn't seen me for a while and I'm looking at him and thinking: "That jumper looks familiar," and I look at his feet and I'm thinking: "Those fucking shoes look familiar." Then I realise. He's wearing *all* my fucking clothes! Then he's running off towards the swimming pool . . .

'The little man Overmars was just as bad. People forget what a fearsome player he was. He struck fear into the whole Premiership because when Dennis gave him the ball he was unstoppable. Just so bloody quick. But don't let him in your room! If you had any chocolate or anything and Overmars has been in the room, it's gone. And let him anywhere near your washbag and you'll have deodorant in your toothbrush or something. It's a way of handling the pressure. A football club is almost like an extension of school, really. In school you've got your pranksters, you've got the people who want to make noise . . . and they're all talented. There was a lot of fun going on and Dennis was a big part of it.'

'Dennis had a more intellectual humour as well,' says Arsene Wenger, '. . . this dry sense of humour, and he could hit where he wanted, you know?'

Like when he said Ottavio Bianchi mentioned Maradona 'a few times . . . every hour'.

'Yes! That's a little bit Dennis! Very precise, like his technique.'

One day in 2003, provocative posters of Freddie Ljungberg, naked except for a pair of bulging Calvin Klein briefs, appeared on advertising hoardings all over London. In the dressing room Dennis led the congratulations. 'Freddie we're all really proud of you. But I hope you didn't forget about the lads. Could you get us all a pair of those Calvin Kleins?' 'Of course, Dennis, I can do that.' 'We'd really appreciate it. But we want the special ones like yours. The ones with a sock down the front.'

* * *

'WELL, IT REALLY was a strange poster,' says Dennis a decade later. 'Freddie has tattoos of panthers on his back. Somehow in the photo they were on his front. What's going on here? And, Freddie, we see you every day in the shower, and you're really not that big ...'

But why did you dress Ian Wright up in Martin Keown's clothes?

'I don't remember that.'

Martin and Ian both say you didn't approve of Martin's clothes so you persuaded Ian to make fun of Martin by putting on all his clothes. You don't remember?

'Not at all.'

You've probably committed murders you don't remember.

'I do remember putting Martin's clothes in high places. Whoever wore the worst clothes had their clothes put up high. Martin wanted to look nice, and he really made an effort. But sometimes he did things which were just not good enough in our opinion. Once he had a black leather jacket and we took some tape and I put T-Birds on the back, like John Travolta in *Grease*. It was fantastic. He's like: "What's going on here?!" But he took it well. Martin always took it well. And he's a really funny guy back, really sarcastic to everyone. He really doesn't care if it's to Thierry or Ian Wright or me or David Dein or whoever. He just doesn't care, which is great. He's got a fantastic sense of humour.'

People think of you as The Iceman but you're really not, are you?

'When I feel good in a group, when I feel confident, you see a different me. I always came across as cool. You know: "No emotion" and "He doesn't play with a smile on his face." It's different when I'm in a normal space with everyone. I've got my humour. I've got my things to say. I don't think I'm different from what people see, but I have a different side as well. It's not like I was joking around on the pitch or whatever. There I was concentrated and looking to do my thing and do it well. There is emotion there, but it's more inside. In a group I can be more extrovert.'

I have to ask you about this. I keep hearing stories about trousers. Ray Parlour says there was a craze for pulling people's shorts and trousers down – and you were implicated.

'Ha! We were playing pre-season in Austria in a training ground with a little stand. There were always Arsenal fans travelling with us, so there were about twenty or thirty people watching. I was doing Arsenal TV, I think, and while they're filming, Ray comes up from behind me and pulls my shorts down. Luckily I always have my underwear on. All the people were laughing in the stand. And Ray's laughing and I was like: "OK, I'll take that. No worries. Hold my hands up. Very funny." But I remember it. Three or four days later we're playing again, somewhere nearby. It's a friendly game with a lot of fans and the main stand is full. Ten minutes before the end we get up to go and walk past the stand and some fans stop us for autographs. Ray is doing autographs and I'm behind him and I think: "This is my moment." *Whooosh!* The shorts are gone, and there's nothing underneath. I was so happy.'

Yes, Ray tells that story, and laughs and freely admits he started it. But he also told me about Vic Akers.

'Oh that was great! I'm glad you mention it because I still talk about it now.'

You and Vic are really close. He's the kit guy and he goes with you by road to all the away games. The rest of the team fly, but you and Vic travel together by car or coach. And he keeps you entertained and cooks your meals and you watch movies together, and chat for hours. And he's your best friend at the club. And your families are close, and you're close. And you play golf and you socialise and he speaks about you so lovingly now, and you speak so lovingly about him.

'Of course, of course. He's such a special guy, a fantastic guy. I love Vic.'

He says of you that being your friend has been one of the great delights and privileges of his life.

'He doesn't need to say it. We don't need words between us.'

And yet you do that thing to him at the training ground!?

'Oh, it was fantastic! I'm still trying to do it with the physios here.'

Admittedly, Vic speaks warmly about it now. But, in your own words, what happened?

'Vic's got this big tummy and dodgy knees and he always wears shorts. At the training centre there's a big room next to the canteen with sliding doors. It's for media and meetings and stuff, and one lunchtime there's an event to sell grooming products to the players. There are sales girls in there and Vic is leaning on the door, chatting and flirting. He's leaning like this, arms crossed and one leg over the other, standing like this, very casual and looking very funny. And the players, we come in for lunch. So we're eating and watching Vic chatting up the girls. And I can't resist. I sneak up to him, and . . . *whoosh!* . . . the shorts are straight down! [*laughs*] And the reaction! Vic lurches forward to cover himself, and all the guys are still having lunch and they're all in tears because it took Vic ages to lean down to pull up his shorts. The girls are all laughing, too. People were laughing about it for weeks afterwards. You know, I've won some trophies. And I've scored some nice goals. But this may be the highlight of my career.'

IT HAS TO BE PERFECT

'Dennis thought about things other players couldn't even imagine,' says Patrick Vieira. 'And when you look at the way he dresses, and the way he played, you can understand that elegance and perfection are important for him. He dresses really simple but elegant. And when he played he was always on his toes, really kind of "nice Dennis". Alert. He is one of the very few players I would pay to watch. To make his kind of passes you have to like things to be perfect. I wouldn't be surprised if at home his clothes are really well organised. I would not be surprised at all.

'Dennis is always taking the piss out of me, saying: "I'm the one who made you" because, of all the goals I scored, ninety-five per cent were from his passes. That's what he is saying! I think it is true. I didn't score many goals but they were mostly from him. You know when you give the ball and you see the space and make the run? Sometimes you say: "Well, I'm not making the run because the ball is not going to come." But when it is Dennis, knowing Dennis, I know he will see the gap. I know I am not going to run for nothing. So I make the run forward, because I know the ball will get there and I will score because of the timing of the pass, and the quality of the pass. Like the goal against Leicester. I get the ball at my feet. I can't remember who I give it to. Is it Thierry? Thierry to Dennis? I don't remember. But I knew I was going to get the ball back. I give the ball to somebody who will give it to Dennis and he will find me because of the run and because he will understand. I knew it would happen. I knew Dennis would find the gap and would give me the ball. *It will come. I know it will.*'

Arsene Wenger observes: 'Dennis is a perfectionist. Until the last session of his training [at Arsenal] he was absolutely never neglecting a control, or a pass. And when it was not perfect, he was unhappy. But that is the characteristic of a top-level competitor: he is an unhappy person ... or *unsatisfied* more than unhappy because sometimes you approach perfection. Then you're happy, but unsatisfied. He wanted to do everything perfect and that is common for all the top, top-level players. They need perfection. And that was Dennis.'

'I love everything about Dennis,' says Thierry Henry. 'Every Single Thing! And you know what I love the most? The way he used to train. He is an example for me. If he missed a control – even if the ball was impossible to control – he'd be upset. Everything had to be perfect. Even in training. We're doing running and he has to be the one. We're in front of goal and every shot has to be perfect. We're doing passes and every pass has to be perfect. It's windy, so you see him working it out ... "OK, if I shoot it over there, the wind will take it in ..." EV-ER-eee-THING!!! If you took the ball off him, he'd chase you until you gave it back to him, or he'd foul you. In training! I've never seen anyone like that. Everything at one hundred per cent. He's a very funny guy. But when he was working there was no joking. "Cross the ball properly!" ... the control had to be perfect. Everything had to be perfect. Never "Oh let's have fun." Never! It was crazy. And I was looking at him and thinking: "I guess that's why he's Dennis Bergkamp." Anything and everything: he's on it. "This ball is too soft – change it." He changed me too. He changed my attitude and my way of training. Of course, as he got older Dennis was playing less. But the way he used to train! He could have been on the sidelines going: "I'm Dennis Bergkamp. I'm thirty-five now. Why should I try hard in training? I'm not even going to play this week." But he was always training so hard!'

Ian Wright recalls a goal Dennis scored against Spurs at Highbury [in the 1996-97 season]. On the right wing, Wright twists and turns, beats his man, then sends a high hopeful cross towards the far post. Dennis receives it with a single touch on the half-volley, knocking the ball back and inside, beating both full-back and goalkeeper in the process before finishing neatly into the opposite corner. More than fifteen years on Wright is still astonished by what he saw.

'It was one touch! *One touch!* We are talking about a ball that's just travelled *forty yards in the air* and he's killed it *dead*. Not only that, he's brought it across, and he's taken the defender and the goalkeeper out of play . . . His touch made my ball look great but, to be honest, all I did was lump it over to the back stick. I thought: "I'm just going to hit it in his general direction. I know Dennis ain't going to head that, but I know if I get the ball over *in his general direction* there's a chance he'll do something I haven't even thought of. When you watch it again notice how perfect that touch is. He's trapped, half-volleyed it back with the exactly right amount of pace and all he has to do is lift it into the goal. And look at his celebration afterwards. He's on his knees, arms pumping. That should have been the statue: where you see he's not 'The Iceman' but deep and powerful and you see the core of his passion. It's a beautiful thing. I will always say that even with Thierry and all these people, Dennis Bergkamp is the best signing Arsenal have made and will ever make. What he's done for that football club . . .

'When he passed the ball to me, oh Jesus!, it would always be . . . *in the path*. On the right side for me, the wrong side for the defender, without him even . . . I mean the ball would come to him and, *one touch*, he would put it in to me. I found I didn't need many touches once he played the ball. That's something I find only the greats can do because they don't have to think about it. Like Zidane. And I'll mention Gazza because I have to, and even Paul Scholes. It's so *precise*. I remember that all the time with Dennis. When his ball came through to me, the defender couldn't do anything, the midfielder couldn't do anything . . . It gave me time to do something and it was a gift. It was just . . . *bang!*

'Even in training he was very precise. I never saw him have one where "Oh my God, Dennis, that's way over the bar!" It was all very technical. I don't remember many times when you'd say: "Wow Dennis, that is sloppy work," whereas I am sure there were many times when you could say that to me, where a ball bounced off me and stuff like that. Now I don't know if it's something that happened naturally to Dennis where he didn't give the ball away. But I don't remember many times where his pass is wrong, his touch is wrong. When he first arrived at Arsenal some people were thinking: "Yeah he's good but he's not all that, 'cos you can knock him off the ball." But I can't remember too many times where Dennis's touch was off. What was always fascinating to me was he didn't seem to have to work very hard on the touch side of his game and the passing. It's obviously very natural to him. It's something I was quite envious of because I had to work very hard on that.

'In training he enhanced his skills, but how do you hone your skills to make sure you've already calculated all the angles, and you know where the defender is and where the midfielder is? How do you get to that? Dennis made a lot of my goals. I remember one up at Everton in his first couple of games. He gets it. I make my run. He whips it into the space, and I have one touch ... past the defender and the next one is literally ... in. I'm just running onto it. It's in my path. Same with a goal I scored against Aston Villa before I broke [Cliff Bastin's goal-scoring] record. You don't even need to touch it. It's just ready to go ... With other players you'd have to control it. But with Dennis, I never had to worry about the ball up and around my neck, or I've got to fight off the defender to get it down. He passed it at the right time for me, not the right time for him. There's nothing to do. He knew I didn't really want to get involved with holding the ball up and all that stuff. I don't think that was my strength. So he'd pass it quickly into the space and I'd be onto it. I worked hard on my game and playing with Dennis Bergkamp proved to me that I'd got to the pinnacle of where I was going to get to. He raised my game by thirty to forty per cent.'

Thierry Henry was the recipient of many of Dennis's perfect passes. 'Dennis respects the game and whatever the game is asking him to do he will do it. If he has to wait one more second to give me the perfect ball he waits one more second. If he had to put it on my left because that's the only way I cannot lose the ball, then he puts it on the left. If it has to be on your head, it will be on your head. If he had to play one touch straightaway, he played one touch straightaway. Everything he did was amazing.'

Some of his assists were spectacular, like against Celta Vigo in 2004: surrounded by defenders, Dennis pirouettes a full 360 degrees before setting up a goal with an exquisite reverse flick with the outside of his right foot. Is that Thierry's favourite?

'No, not that one. I prefer the one for Freddie Ljungberg against Juventus by a *distance*. The Celta Vigo one is great, but, by his motion, you can see the move. With the Juve one, Dennis is turning everywhere. Everywhere! Yet he still sees Freddie. He's waiting for Freddie to move, and he's toying with the defenders, but he still knows where Freddie is. And he still knows the right pass to make. If he puts the ball on the ground, a defender can stop it, so he lifts it waist-height. As a defender, that's the worst. You can't lift your leg to reach it, and you can't bend down to head it ... It's perfect. For me that's his best assist.'

Freddie seems a bit slow on the uptake. Dennis has to wait for about three seconds for Freddie to make his run.

'That's my point. Dennis *waits*. That's Dennis Bergkamp. Any other player would have played the ball first touch and then screamed about it: "Hey! You didn't move!" But Dennis sees the player isn't moving, so he waits and he's toying with all the defenders around him and he's like "Come on, Freddie ..." Aaaaaah, it's so beautiful ...!'

And these are Juventus defenders ...

'It's funny how people see it like that, but for me he could have done it against Yeovil and I would still say it's his best pass. It's not because it's against Juve, it's because of the *patience* he shows in order to give Freddie the perfect ball. A skill is a skill. And it's not the toying with the defenders that impressed me. It's that he had to wait three seconds, so he waited three seconds. If he had to wait one, he would have waited one. That's what makes the pass beautiful.'

* * *

DENNIS IS NO LESS KEEN to praise the team-mates whose movement, intelligence and skill made his assists possible.

What about your assist for that Freddie Ljungberg goal against Juventus? Your best?

Dennis: 'Yes, that one is my favourite. You create a certain relationship with players. On the pitch they know what I want to do with the ball, and I know exactly what they are going to do. That's the thing which in my opinion is the beauty of the game: that there can be just one look to each other, or just me controlling the ball and the body language means "Come on Freddie, go! GO!" And then he goes, because he understands. There's no shouting, it's just my body language. I'm keeping the ball, meaning: "Come on, come on! What are you doing?" And then he's going and I flick it. I had a lot of moments with Freddie like that, and with Marc Overmars. You just know each other. They know: "OK, Dennis is always looking for the pass so I have to go there, I have to do that." And when that works it makes defenders look silly.'

Because it can't be defended?

'It cannot be defended because he's gone with high pace and the defenders are standing still, all facing forward, and when the pass is given it is not offside, not by a mile, and he is controlling the ball five or six yards behind the defenders, so he has plenty of time to do something ... And that finish was nice, too. Freddie, eh? Amazing player! Very strong. Very quick. And the things he did! Certain players have a certain style, a certain movement. With him it looked a little sloppy – with respect I say that – but he did it on purpose. He knew exactly what he was doing! He scored a lot of goals like that. People underestimated him. But he never underestimated himself!

'It's true I always forced myself to make the best pass, to make it easy for the striker on the receiving end. Why? For myself, because I wanted to do the maximum. I always put myself in the position of making the best pass possible. And sometimes it goes horribly wrong but I learned from that, from those things, and go on again. Eventually it became automatic for me, normal to try for the best. Maybe every player does that, I'm not sure. In Holland I got accused of being an "all or nothing" player. People said: "He only wants to do the beautiful thing." Especially when I was younger, those "all or nothing" things went wrong. You have to put a little risk into your game. In my mind the idea is: "Make it a fantastic pass." But what is the best pass? For some people it's get it over the defender and the striker can receive the ball. To me that's not good enough. No, I have to beat the defender, and make the goalkeeper think he can get it, so he comes out, leaving space. And I have to get the ball in front of my striker or onto his head so he can put it into the corner ... It's a different way of thinking. But it also has to do with communication and knowing each other. When I started at Arsenal the other players don't know me. They have to learn that I'll give the pass so they can take a little bit more risk. They have to be thinking: "I know for sure that Dennis is going to put the pass there," so they can take another step away from the defender ...'

We spoke once about the way you could see into the future, rather like the clairvoyant girl in Minority Report. *Tom Cruise and Samantha Morton are trying to escape through a shopping mall. There's nowhere to hide and the cops are closing in. But she's seen the old man with the balloons so she says 'WAIT!' Tom Cruise doesn't understand why because they're out in the open. But when the cops arrive the balloons have moved so they block the view. Tom and Samantha escape. That's the kind of thing you did. You saw passes no one else could see, and delivered the ball through gaps that didn't seem to exist. How?*

'I always had a picture in my head of how it would be in three seconds or two seconds. I could calculate it, or sense it. I'd think: "He's moving this way, and he's moving that way, so if I give the pass with that pace neither of them can touch it because they are moving away from my line. With the right pace, and with the right player coming in ... *yeah!* Like with that pass for Patrick against Leicester at Highbury. I think it was our last unbeaten game. The one-one goal, or the two-one, I don't remember. [Vieira scored to make it two-one.] It was very crowded in the box but he just made his run and I could slip it just in between ... I was so proud! I can enjoy it really! And the pleasure is even greater because it was a goal that meant something as well.'

But how can you see two or three steps beyond what most people are seeing?

'A lot of it is about measuring. Cruyff talks about that with the youth at Ajax now. Measuring offensively, but defensively as well. It's all about distances. I know where the gap is, I know the speed of Patrick. So I know where the space will be in two or three seconds. But he has to keep running ... *orrrfffff!* ... or it looks like a silly pass!

'The other thing, of course, is the pass *before* the assist. I don't know if there is even a name for that, but there should be. Every now and then they would show one of those on *Match of the Day*. They'd say "Look at the goal, and look at the assist, but most important look where the attack starts from." That's interesting. Where does an attack start? What makes the difference in the end?'

Some of the old Arsenal players say a lot of your work was missed or was almost invisible to the cameras and the crowd. The smallest of touches, the spin you'd put on a ball ...

'Maybe. But when you're watching you have to be independent in your mind. I am not going for the goal or even the assist. But I want to make a difference with the earlier pass. The real football lovers see that – not that I play for them. But it gets appreciated, especially by myself. I think: "OK! That was a good pass. It made the difference even if no one saw it."'

Zidane, in the 2006 World Cup quarter-final, destroyed Brazil with something quite different. It's one of the games that defines him and looking at it again I realised that often when he juggled the ball or flicked it over a Brazilian head, he then just played a little sideways pass. It didn't contribute to the game in the way you're talking about. But he's killing Brazil all the same. He's showing them: 'This is your thing but I do it better than you.' He breaks them psychologically. You never did that.

'That's true and it comes from me being a team player. I have individual skills, but those skills are based on the idea there has to be an end product. Someone has to be on the end of my pass, of my move, or my one-two or whatever it is. That's what's in my mind. But I've never been a guy for one against one or a trick. Never.'

Nor one for dribbling from your own half like a Maradona?

'I don't believe in that. In my mind a great player is a player who will give something extra to the team. He can be a defender, a midfielder. Or he can be in my position. I am a player who gives something extra to the team by assists or setting other players free. I scored many goals, but by the end of my career I had more assists. And, not just assists but *perfect* assists.'

Thierry said he loves to give an assist when he knows he could score himself – and, when his team-mate scores, he sees the joy in his face and knows he made someone happy. He said: 'For me, scoring a goal is amazing, but nothing beats that … making someone happy.' I'm guessing you feel like that?

'I got so much pleasure from that! It's unbelievable what goes into it. First, of course, there's your ability. But you also need the understanding of the other players. Do they understand what I'm trying to do? At Arsenal we didn't have that in the first season but slowly, slowly they got to understand me. That means stepping up their own game. They think: "Oh wait a minute, this brings more to the game. He can do things." But I had to adjust myself as well, and that was a great process.

'The other thing you need is imagination. That's so important. Not just imagination from me but imagination from the players around me. You can compare it with the receiver and the quarterback in American football. Sometimes the camera from behind shows there is nothing there. Then the quarterback throws the ball and then slowly you see the picture expand. It's like a puzzle. Finally, where he's thrown the ball, you see the catcher move to receive it. That's a little bit like what I was doing. You need the pace on the ball, and both of you have to have the vision. In American football, of course, everything is about patterns and they practise it day-in day-out. But in football you can't practise. It's not like you have a timeout and the boss says: "OK Dennis, we're going to do this pattern and Patrick is coming this way . . ." It has to come up within the game. You don't know how their defence will be, either. But you see two or three defenders and you know what they're going to do in two or three seconds. You have to know that Patrick is moving, and then you make sure there's the right pace on the ball, and he's not offside. And the timing has to be right, and you have to get all angles and the maths correct . . . But I always liked that sort of precision. It's like solving the puzzle.'

As a small boy you were fascinated by geometry. Your mum told us you spent happy hours measuring angles and lengths and doing precise little drawings of triangles, semi-circles and rhomboids. Do you think any of your old school exercise books still exist?

'I don't think so. Why do you ask?'

Maybe we could see in the drawings the beginnings of your later understanding of the pitch?

'I don't think so and, anyway, it's just a small part of it. Geometry is what I like, of course. It's certainly a passion. Maybe it's my biggest passion. But there are so many other things: the pace of the ball, the touch. It's not only down to maths. In football it worked out well for me, but is it geometry? It's also the pleasure of knowing what other people can do and are going to do.'

So it's more telepathy than geometry?

'You read my mind.'

DRIVEN

WHAT MOTIVATES YOU, *Dennis?*
'I think about this a lot, especially now I'm a coach. You see players who have a hunger to succeed because they had a difficult childhood. You know, people often say: "You have to be down in the gutter to understand what it means in life." You're always thinking about which of the young players has the drive to have a great career. As a coach you're looking for that hunger. I know I had that drive. But where does it come from? That I don't know.'

You weren't in the gutter.

'No, no, not at all. I had a very secure, happy childhood. We could just about manage. Maybe you could say: "Then money is my drive." But it isn't.'

Is it just passion? Is it something within yourself? You're very shy and modest, but deep down inside you want to be the best in the world and that's your goal, your aim ...

'That's me. Sometimes you hear of people having drive because their parents divorced. My parents weren't divorced. Perhaps it was significant that we didn't have much money when I was a child. It doesn't explain my drive, but maybe it formed me in some way. Perhaps it made me feel that if you have a chance you go for it, and keep going for it. I really don't know. I know my feeling but I'm not sure where it comes from, if it's character, if it's childhood . . .'

What do you look for in the youngsters you coach now?

'Well, you see straightaway who has drive. But it can come from different things. Let's say this kid wants to be a millionaire when he's eighteen. That's drive. Is it bad? "By twenty-eight I want to have three sports cars and the only way to get them is to win trophies and play good football." If that's his conclusion, maybe it's OK. But if he thinks: "I'm making one million each year now and if I play for five years I've got five million and that's it, I can retire," that's different. Or "I'll stay in the reserves and just keep training as long as I can put gas in my Lamborghini." I'm not sure that's drive at all. It's not a passion from the soul. And that's what you're looking for: the real passion that comes from inside.'

What about the drive of the artist, where you don't have a choice: you have to do it, and do it your way, like the musician has a passion to make music and the painter has to paint. You need to express what is inside you . . .

'Yes.'

. . . and, in the end, perhaps the striving to improve becomes almost spiritual. Patrick Vieira says that with you it is both artistic and spiritual.

'Well, you set yourself goals, targets. And once you've got there you want to move on and go further. You keep raising the bar, and therefore it's never good enough. You want perfection. It's never good enough but it's within your reach. You climb one mountain and see the higher one. And I want to do it, I want to do that. That's probably what people have. But I like what you say that it's a passion – something within the soul, isn't it? It's deeper. Whereas ambition, for money or whatever, is more calculating. It can be satisfied. But passion is ... no ... you keep ... you want to grab it. You do the hard thing, always go for the difficult thing, and then you have to go for the next thing.'

Because it would be a betrayal of your deepest self not to do it in that way?

'Right.'

ARSENE WENGER HAS an interesting view about this. He says: 'It is a spiritual thing. I am convinced of that. I believe you have two kinds of players who play football. Those who want to serve football like you serve God, and they put football so high that everything that is not close to what football should be is a little bit non-acceptable. And then you have those who use football to serve their ego. And sometimes the ego can get in the way of the game, because their interest comes before the interest of the game. Sometimes the big ego is linked with what we call strong personalities, charisma. But most of the time, what people call charisma, is just big ego. I believe that Dennis was one of those who had such a high idea of the game and such a respect for the game that he wanted that to be above everything. I believe that the real great players are guided by how football should be played, and not by how football should serve them. If it becomes spiritual, it's endless, and you're always driven to going higher, and getting closer to what you think football should be.'

Then Wenger gives the example of a player who knows he ought to pass but takes a massive gamble and scores. 'If he really loves the game he'll go home and worry about it. He'll know he really should have passed to set up an easy chance for someone else. But he was selfish and got lucky. If he doesn't care about the game he'll go home and think: "That was great – I'll do the same next time."'

And he says that's the difference. 'That's why you have to teach the kids to respect the game, and treat the game a little bit like a religion, that is above you, where you want to serve the game.'

* * *

WOULD YOU TALK about this sort of stuff with Arsène?

Dennis: 'I remember when Arsene talked about players, sometimes he'd say: "Oh no, he doesn't love the game ..." This is quite a big statement from him. But I know exactly what he means. There are some players who, as soon as the whistle went at the end of training ... *boom!* ... They went inside, got changed, then straight in the car and away. But the real *liefhebbers* (the literal translation is 'love-havers', the guys who really have love for the game) stayed behind to practise. And not only players. David Dein and Massimo Moratti are people who really love the game too. At Arsenal it was always the same players, eight or nine, who stayed behind to work after training. And I guarantee if you do that you'll become a better player.'

I love the idea of a small group of exceptional guys all competing with each other and pushing each other. Artists and intellectuals in 15th century Florence did that and gave us the Renaissance. At Arsenal you end up as The Invincibles. So I'm picturing this group of players, all talented in different ways, sometimes perhaps rivals, and all stimulating and provoking each other. I'm guessing that to do well in this team, you have to be one of the players who stay on after training?

'Well, yes. That's part of it.'

And the ones who prefer to go home immediately leave?

'In the end, yes. I must say I don't have a real memory of who was who, and there were players who sometimes joined and sometimes didn't ... but there were always eight or nine players who joined.'

Freddie Ljungberg would stay?

'Well, yeah. And Thierry was always there. Robert Pires would stay. Others would stay and go to the gym, which is working as well.'

And you competed with each other?

'That as well. It's part of being a successful team. But I like what you said about pushing each other, challenging each other, in training as well.'

Bob Wilson said the old English approach was to teach young players to give the simple pass so that the receiver could deal with it easily. But you found that annoying. When you arrived at Arsenal you told everyone: 'Don't give me these soppy little passes, give me fast, hard balls because I can deal with anything that comes at me and playing faster is playing better. By the time Pires and Ljungberg are in the team, a few years later, it's moved on a long way, it's at a much higher level.

'Yes, always give me a strong pass because I want to challenge myself by controlling a difficult ball. You have to keep pushing and testing each other. Like you test your pace and strength against Sol Campbell. He's your team-mate, but in training you're against him. If you can beat Sol, who can't you beat in the Premier League? And if he can stop me or he can stop Thierry Henry, who can't he stop in the Premier League? That's the challenge: always trying to improve yourself. But it can only work when everyone is giving one hundred per cent. Like having goalies who try in training. At Inter they didn't try and it was so frustrating. But Jens Lehmann? David Seaman? Fantastic! Jens couldn't stand to have a single shot go past him. And if I tried to lob David Seaman ... *woaah!* If it worked, it was a fantastic goal and he was like: "Great, well done." But if it didn't work out, he got hold of the ball and smashed it two hundred yards away! He'd just kick it away and say "Get that!" and I'd have to go and get it. David is a nice soft guy – but not when he plays. That was his drive: "You're not going to fool me! Now get that ball!" I loved that attitude.'

There seems to be a critical mass. You have to get a certain number of people doing this, all with their different motivations and talents. Get the right number of the right kind of people together and somehow it works.

'It starts somewhere. Maybe, as the players say, it started with me because I was like that. I wanted to give everything and when training was finished I would go on and I would keep practising and going and going ... and suddenly there's goalkeepers staying on as well, saying: "Wait a minute, I'm going to have some of that." And then others would stay behind, too. But it's not like it wasn't done before I came. I am sure if you look at any successful team, and you look at their week in training, it would be like that. When you've got players staying behind and playing with a smile, they don't get tired. Do they smile because they play well in the matches? Or is it the other way round, that they play well in the matches because they stay behind?

'Look at Messi. There was a game last year where Barcelona were winning five-nil and the coach took him off and he was furious. "But the game is won!" "I don't care! I love playing. Don't rest me." When they score the fifth goal you see the whole team enjoying it. I can imagine that team in training just having fun. They love the game. They really enjoy it, they love passing the ball or putting it in the net or doing some tricks. And you can pick out the ones who would say ... "Oh, I'm going in now" ... and the ones who say: "No, I'm staying behind."'

Perhaps there's a child-like innocence to it as well?

'Yes'.

There's a lovely story in Rogan Taylor's book about Ferenc Puskas when he was a boy in Budapest. He wouldn't take the tram to school; he'd run alongside the tram, dribbling his football, doing tricks.

'Ah, that's fantastic. I like seeing clips of Maradona at Napoli, like when he scores direct from a corner and jumps up and down like an eight-year old. Bianchi probably told him to do that, eh? My favourite is the warm-up he did with the music in the stadium. I think it is Napoli against Bayern and the song "Live is Life" [by Opus] is playing ... *naa nan a na naaa*! He's there with his Pumas, laces untied, socks down, and he's got his tracksuit on. And while everyone else is doing the warm-up with sprinting and stuff he's juggling the ball *to the beat of the music ... naa nan a na naaa!* And he kicks it in the air, like this, you know. I'm not sure if he's singing as well. But it's rhythm and joy and it's fantastic! You have to look that up! It's really good.'

14

THE DARK SIDE

'SOME PEOPLE SAID Dennis was too nice,' says Patrick Vieira, hugely amused by the thought. 'I can't agree at all. Dennis is not a nice sweet guy! I would not want to play as a defender against him, because he's really clever. He looks like "the good son-in-law" on the field, but he's not just there to play football and the beautiful game. He has a nasty side which he can dig out when he needs it. He had a few red cards, you know. Not as many as me! But people know me and they don't know Dennis. He can be worse than me. He doesn't like losing games, not even in training. He doesn't like people making fun of him. And he doesn't like being kicked for nothing. He is a nice guy, a lovely guy. But if you need to go to war, Dennis you can take with you because he's got this competitive, tough side.'

As Ray Parlour puts it: 'Dennis had that little bit of . . . no one could bully him. You think, oh, he's got all the talent and all the skill, but he was hard as nails, too. He didn't muck about. If someone did him, he'd get him back somehow, but he'd do it in a really clever way.' Thierry Henry concurs: 'Dennis was clever in everything. He could be vicious in a good way on the field. And he was very brainy. Perfect. I mean, the way he played, there was never anything dumb about it. Nothing! Even when he wants to foul someone ... clever! Even when he got the red card he was always giving it [*makes innocent Dennis face*] "Who? *Me*? But I'm Dennis!" I loved it when he did that. If it was me, I'd get two red cards!'

Sol Campbell recalls that before they were team-mates, Dennis was perfectly capable of giving him a hard time. 'He was quite naughty sometimes. I mean, if he wanted to be naughty he could be *naughty*. Like putting the foot in ... big time! When he put his foot in, he put his foot *in*. And he was incredibly strong. Really good upper body strength. He could hold me off quite easily.'

But Tony Adams remembers the problems Dennis faced when he arrived in England. 'When Dennis first came he needed to be toughened up a bit. At that time, he wasn't as physical as he became later, but the English Premier League was very physical. At that time foreign players coming to England basically had a choice. You could say: "I just don't fancy this, it's too tough for me." I felt Vladi Petrovic was like that for Arsenal. Great talent but ... There were quite a few foreign players up north – I don't remember their names – who just folded and went home. They couldn't handle the physical side. But Dennis definitely could. He could get hold of it and go: "I can play bull as well here." He had a nasty streak in him in that respect. And I think he really benefited from us. In his first season he could be spiteful, reacting to things. He could get away with it because there weren't so many TV cameras on the go then. He wasn't very strong. But he got stronger, and when you play with better defenders and better players, I think it makes you better. I'm not talking about smashing him in training, but we made him play under pressure and do things early.

Remember, until the mid-nineties the tackle from behind was still legal. I enjoyed it and strikers had to deal with that. Back in the day I played against Kenny Dalglish. I'd tee him up and be waiting to go straight through him but, as the ball is coming, *he* backs into *me*. *Shoooooom*! I'm still going *aaaaaaargh* and he's gone! Alan Brazil used to do that for Ipswich. That's how it was then. The good support strikers knew the defender's going through 'em so they get it in first and then ... *bang!* ... they're off. Sure, Dennis had that. Later on when the rule changed and you couldn't do that, you had to get intelligent. As a typical number ten, you make one run for the defender, then you come short. And if you're a defender, you're reading it. Is he going to there or there? It becomes a thinking game. And, of course, Dennis could play both ways.'

* * *

IT'S QUITE A SURPRISE to realise how many cards you got at Arsenal. Four reds and 46 yellows. At one time, you almost developed a reputation for diving, though Ian Wright says this was undeserved because you were adapting to a new country. In Italy you'd go down, because you'd get a free-kick. Some English players didn't like that.

Dennis: 'In Italy you have two strikers against five defenders, so you have to find ways to protect yourself. You have to find ways of keeping the ball, doing your job properly and doing it well. So if you are up against five defenders and you get the ball and you get a little touch, you go down. Is it cheating? In England it is cheating. In Italy it's just part of the game. So you adjust to the Italian game. It's normal. And then you come to England and you realise, wait a minute, you can't do that here. It's not acceptable. I'm not sure ... I don't call it cheating. I have seen players who cheated. It's very difficult to say, but I sometimes used it. But I think most of the time I was honest.

Used it? Explain.

'A lot of times you get pushed or you feel a little touch and that stops you reaching the ball. If you run on you won't get a free-kick because no one noticed it. So you have to react a little bit more. And then you get the free-kick. (You exaggerate a little to bring it to the referee's attention.) But there has to be contact before I'd go down. I think cheating is something different. For me, cheating is if you go past the defender, there is no contact then you roll over, you go down. The *schwalbe*, as the Germans say. That's real cheating. I didn't do that. But if there is contact, it's a matter of how do you exaggerate? If you don't, you won't get a free-kick. If you do a little bit, you might get a free-kick or a penalty or whatever.'

But too much of that is also cheating, surely?

'Yes, but it's a really difficult area. For me, it's not acceptable if you don't get touched but go down because you still want a free-kick. I really don't approve of that. But where you are always battling with the defender and he's touching you and you stay on your feet, you're not going to get a free-kick. I think you have to act a little bit ... "Jeez, come on ref!" There are plenty of times where a foul is committed and you don't get a free-kick. What do you call that then? That's the other side of it. You get pushed and the referee doesn't see it. Is that cheating by the defender? That doesn't exist, does it? It's cheating. He's cheating. The referee didn't see it, but he pulls you back. That is the other part of cheating, I feel. Doing something behind someone's back and that happens all the time. I got really frustrated in my first season at Arsenal. I'm definitely not a cheat and I don't think people see me in that way.'

But you got away with things too. Like when you stamped on [Sinisa] Mihajlovic in the '98 World Cup. Because of your nice-guy image you got away with that, but you should have been sent off.

'Yes definitely. But on the other side there was a moment against Coventry when I went across a player and he goes behind me and trips me. I'm past him, one-on-one with the goalkeeper, I've got

Stillness in mid-air.
Highbury, December 2003.

'Which part do they think I didn't mean?' The goal at Newcastle, March 2002.

(Stuart Macfarlane, Arsenal)

Champions. Members of the Invincibles celebrate in the Highbury dressing room, May 2004. From left: reserve goalkeeper Rami Shaaban, Freddie Ljungberg, Jens Lehmann, Edu, Gilberto, Sol Campbell and kit man Vic Akers. (Stuart Macfarlane, Arsenal)

Celebrating with eldest daughter Estelle, Highbury, May 2004. (Stuart Macfarlane, Arsenal)

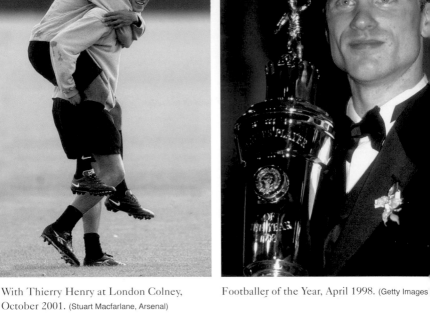

With Thierry Henry at London Colney,
October 2001. (Stuart Macfarlane, Arsenal)

Footballer of the Year, April 1998. (Getty Images)

Dennis celebrates his first Premier League title (and the first part of the 1998 Double)
with Marc Overmars and Ian Wright, Highbury, May 1998. (Getty Images)

Beating Tony
Adams to score
with a reverse lob
at Wembley, 1993.
(ANP)

With Clarence
Seedorf, Edgar Davids
and (in background)
coach Frank Rijkaard
during training at
Euro 2000. (ANP)

'Your life is leading
up to this moment.'
The goal against
Argentina, World
Cup 1998. (ANP)

Dutch fans with a cutout picture of Dennis, World Cup quarter-final, Marseille, 1998. (ANP)

Dennis applauds the crowd after his last appearance for Holland, the Euro 2000 semi-final defeat against Italy in Amsterdam. (Louis van de Vuurst, Ajax)

Dennis with Dad and Mum in their newly-built home, Wilnis, 1992.

Air ticket to Malmo, 1987. (The note explains that schoolboy Dennis will be accompanied on the plane by TV commentator Kees Jansma.)

In the garden of his home in Blaricum in 2013, with children Estelle, Yasmin, Saffron and Mitchel, and wife Henrita. (Jan-Dirk van der Burg)

With fellow members of FIFA's Pele-selected list of 100 best-ever players. Robert Pires, Patrick Vieira, Edgar Davids, Rustu Recber, Ronaldinho and Patrick Kluivert at a dinner at London's Natural History Museum, March 2004. (Getty Images)

Dennis's Arsenal, Holland, Ajax and Inter shirts at his home, 2013.
(Jan-Dirk van der Burg)

The perfect 10 – artwork by Bob van Persie (father of Robin) on the wall of Dennis's home, 2013.
(Jan-Dirk van der Burg)

Memorabilia at his mother's home, Wilnis, 2013. (Jan-Dirk van der Burg)

Dennis's first job as a coach: training the Ajax D-Youth team, De Toekomst, August 2010.
(Louis van de Vuurst, Ajax)

away from the offside, and this guy – Paul Williams, I think his name was – he brings me down! Maybe it's an accident or whatever, but he really tripped me. I want to keep going because I'm one-on-one with the goalkeeper. There's no advantage for me to go down. So what happens? The referee gives a free-kick and sends the defender off. But afterwards there was a lot of commotion about it because on TV, because of the camera angle, it looks as if he didn't touch me. But I was there! It was just a little trip, but when you are sprinting and both feet are in the air one little touch will bring you down, and that's what happened. But you couldn't see it on TV. And I was so upset with that because everyone called me a cheat! So my only comment afterwards was: "What do you mean? I'm one-on-one with the goalkeeper, I'm away from my defender, so why would I go down? Why??"

You're still cross about it.

'I am! I am! So we get a free-kick outside the box – it wasn't even a penalty! So why would I do that? "Yes, but it looks like ..." Yes, *I know how it looks.* I've seen the same footage. But I know what happened! That was a difficult moment because I was aware of what people were saying about foreigners coming over and cheating. And that's exactly what I didn't like! I love the English game! I love the honesty and the work ethic. I'm not going to go there to be a cheat.'

So you were getting criticised like Luis Suarez?

'Not to the same degree, no, not at all. But I had a few moments and this was one of them. But I tell you now, that's what happened. And I was really upset to be called a cheat. I don't want to be called a cheat. I don't do that! There must be contact. And if I exaggerate the contact a little then OK.'

So, basically, it's a sliding grey area, but for you it's a moral absolute that you are not allowed to go down unless there has been contact?

'Definitely that's my opinion. There has to be real contact. It's cheating where there is no contact at all and you're just trying to get someone sent off.'

When do you decide?

'It's not just one moment when I make the decision. Suppose there is contact. To go down or not to go down? Do I have an opportunity to score? Is the contact such that it deprives me of an opportunity to score? Have I lost a chance to make the pass or to score myself? Then I make the decision to make the most of it.'

Simon Kuper wrote that you often wasted energy reacting to provocations.

'My wife always said: "I hope in the first few minutes you get kicked because then you change." The biggest example was Southampton away at the beginning of my third season. There was a left-back who was English but he had an Italian name and he really was acting as if he was Italian – shirt pulling, leaving a bit in after a tackle or after I'd passed the ball. At one point, something happened again and I thought: "Jesus! I've had enough now!" I was really angry. I don't remember what it was. When it's a shirt pull or a tackle, or even just a defender intercepting the ball, I can get frustrated if that happens. But this time it was a physical thing and I really got upset, and then within the next thirty seconds I got the ball, and I think I held him off with one hand ... I was so angry I turned around, facing the goal, taking the ball with me and smashed it in the back of the net. And the celebration was fantastic because all the players came up to congratulate me ... and our fans were close by and I went up to the defender and celebrated right in front of him. All the Arsenal players were around him and he was in the middle of that, trying to push and get away.'

You turn into The Incredible Hulk?

'David Endt [former Ajax team manager] calls it "boiling milk". I understand what he means. But coming back to cheating, a lot of things happen between defenders and strikers that you don't see.

And I would call that cheating. My comment usually to the referee is: "Watch the first foul." They usually don't see the first foul. They only see my foul, the reaction. But maybe because they are watching the ball, they miss the first one from the defender. There are a lot of clever defenders.

'Generally, I think the English defenders are honest. They are straight. They put their foot in but nothing nasty. I mean there is a difference between leaving your foot in after the ball is gone and just going for the ball. Of course, some players are a little bit more nasty than others, but in reality and fairness most of them throughout my career in England were honest. You can talk about Sol Campbell or John Terry. They were just there to defend, to get the striker out of the game, which is their job. Martin, Tony, Bouldy ... all of them. Nothing nasty. Nothing. And I must admit those are the most difficult defenders to play against – the honest ones who put their foot in, who've got pace, who've got strength, who read the game. And it's not easy for them because they always play with a back four, with one line, which means they have to defend the space behind. In Italy they have the *libero*, but the English have two central defenders against two strikers, so they can't really cover each other. As an attacker I liked that because it meant you could play in between. They can't come off their line. So I used that. It was my strength, I think. But, defensively, it takes a lot out of you.

'Actually, I always loved playing against the best Italian defenders. I always had fantastic battles against them. You know, players who have a big mouth and make dirty tackles, who'll pinch you and step on your toes, and give you a kick off the ball when no one is watching. Maybe they'll even give you an elbow without a ball near you. That got me going as well. You would really try to have a good game against those players. Defenders in general who would have the attitude: "Look at me, I'm fantastic and it's all about me!" I can't have that. I can't stand that! I prefer players like Martin Keown who just do their job and maybe have big mouths in the dressing room but in a funny way. He's just a funny guy. He would really take pride in stopping someone else from scoring a goal. And he was a fantastic trash talker: "Come on, come on, let's have it . . . You think you can go past me? Yeah? Oh no you can't." And to his own striker: "You're fantastic."

'Guys like that would give it but take it as well. Martin would go in, but if he gets a kick it's not like he would be rolling on the floor. He would just take it and the next time do it back. That's so different to those players where if they do something to you and you do something to them they try to get you sent off: "Oi ref! The whole world is against me," and all that.'

Is that why you trod on Mihajlovic and elbowed Steve Lomas in the FA Cup quarter-final at West Ham in 1998?

'With Mihajlovic it's one of those moments where immediately afterwards you realise you've gone too far. It was a bit silly, but I could live with it. And getting away with it, I could live with. The one with Steve Lomas, I wasn't happy with that. He pulled my shirt from behind as we were breaking out from the corner, and I smashed him with my elbow. But he was bleeding and I felt bad about it. He didn't deserve that, not at all. It was meant like "Get away from me!" but when you do it in such a way that you hurt someone, straightaway you think: "That's not nice." It also hurt the team. They had to play for an hour with ten men. So the whole thing was not good. I wasn't hammered for it, because in England I think they want to know if you're sorry about it. And I said what I meant straightaway. There were a few incidents but the one with Lomas was the only really bad one. I was banned for three games. I thought: "That's not me," but these things happen in football. I think everyone gets into a situation at some time where you think: "I really, really want to win this tackle and if I'm gonna hurt him that comes with the sport." With certain players you get the feeling they always think: "Whatever it costs." But you want to get that out of your system. With me I was always a little bit embarrassed afterwards. "I shouldn't have done that, it was stupid." But if there are players who say: "No, he had it coming," then I think there is something wrong.'

15

LEADERS

WHO LEADS ON A football field? And how do they do it? Sometimes it's hard to tell because dominant figures come in a range of shapes, sizes, personalities and decibel levels. There's also confusion between different types of leader and teams usually have more than one. As well as formally appointed captains, there are 'technical leaders' and specialists. Old English centre-forwards, for example, were said to 'lead the line'. Goalkeepers dominate defence. Some of the natural leaders who have influenced Dennis Bergkamp's career, like Tony Adams in clenched-fist warrior mode or Johan Cruyff, who used to shout, point and tell team-mates where to run, are impossible to miss. Others, like Dennis himself, are harder to spot.

In fact some colleagues failed to see leadership qualities in him at all. At Inter, in the view of Riccardo Ferri, Dennis was 'too quiet'. To Ferri, the crucial point is that the leader must be vocal and gregarious. 'Dennis never became the technical leader at Inter. You can't just say: "He's the leader now." The team decides. I don't know how it was in the Arsenal dressing room, but at Inter if you don't socialise you won't be the leader. You can be Maradona but if you don't socialise you still won't be the leader. At Napoli, Maradona showed his feelings all the time. And he was very generous. When he was interviewed after a game, even if he'd scored three goals, he always praised someone else in the team. He'd say: "I couldn't have done it without De Napoli," though De Napoli was a very modest player. Maradona was generous to the whole team, outside as well. He invited everyone out, had dinner with everyone.'

Osvaldo Bagnoli makes a similar point: 'A team chooses who must be the team's leader. It is an automatic, unconscious thing. Subconscious even. It just happens. And that Inter team didn't choose Dennis. Maybe it was because of his character, his shyness, his loneliness, his "closedness". If he'd had more time maybe he could have become the leader. But he didn't.'

As Arsenal goalkeeping coach when Dennis arrived at the club in 1995, Bob Wilson saw the Dutchman differently. 'When you're a genius it's often very difficult not to be arrogant with it. Some people could misinterpret Dennis's aloofness at times. I saw it as shyness. He would never talk about how great he was as a player or anything like that. He was humble. But I'm seventy-one years of age now, and I've loved and followed football from the age of six or seven, and he is in my handful of top players of all time. I put him up there with Stanley Matthews, Puskas and Hidegkuti, Duncan Edwards, Pele, Garrincha to a degree, Cruyff, Maradona, Messi, Beckenbauer, Bobby Moore: players who without doubt made the game better. Dennis Bergkamp took the game to a new level. For all watchers of the game, I think he led them into almost an unknown area of how they viewed the game. It was his total mastery, *total* mastery, of the ball. He was like a juggler on stage, except people were kicking him. Was he a leader? Of course he was. He was the one the others would turn to and say: "Look Dennis, we're in trouble, we can't find a way through," and he would come up with something different. But without doubt the biggest thing that Dennis did for the players was to show them they didn't need to hide or be scared if they made a mistake. "Do it. You can do it! You're capable." He was never like Tony Adams or Frank McLintock. He was more like Bobby Moore. There was this presence and calmness about what he did that made people think: "My God, we'll try that." He was the leader of the pack. He was inspiring.'

Thierry Henry confirms this. 'People sometimes get confused between arrogance and confidence so they misunderstand Dutch players. Dutch players are very, very confident. People always go: "They're a bit arrogant." No! They are confident. One of the things I loved right away about Dennis was that he was super-confident and not arrogant at all. Sometimes I heard people say: "Why does he have to show off?" He's not showing off. That's how he plays. Like his goal against Newcastle. People cannot comprehend why Dennis did that. But for him there is no "why". The ball was coming this way, so: "OK, I'll control it the other way, get in behind Dabizas, make sure the spin is right to come back ... then finish." For someone else it's impossible. For him it's natural. I played with Zidane, with Messi, with Xavi, Iniesta, Ronaldinho, Eto'o ... Those guys were unbelievable. If you're talking about raw talent, Zizou was out of this world. He could do whatever he wanted. I mean the guy was *dancing* with the ball. Sometimes I was watching him and my mouth was just hanging open. Messi? He's doing stuff that I don't know if anyone will ever do again. Maradona? Incomparable! Cruyff? The same. Platini, the same. But I played with Dennis Bergkamp the longest and I saw him every day in training and the way he saw the game and the way he was ... and that's why I always say Dennis was the best that I played with. For me Dennis was and always will be The Master.

'When I arrived it was his team so it was always like that. When he left it was different, but as long as he was there it was his team. Don't get me wrong. Dennis has a big, big personality. But that's why I admire him even more. Any big players at that level have a big ego, but Dennis could control it. When he was in his prime he could have scored a lot more goals. But sometimes the game was asking him to pass the ball to the free man, and that's what he did. Dennis was for me and always will be The Man. It wasn't a case of "looking up" to him. It was just like having an older brother. But he was intelligent enough to know he didn't need to be the front man. He doesn't shout a lot but when he *looks* at you . . .! Dennis talks with the ball, which is the best way to talk.'

Tony Adams was more sceptical. 'Other people can be sentimental and tell you about his magic more articulately than me. But what you'll get from me is the reality, my experience. I had respect for Dennis but I wasn't overwhelmed. You've got to take into consideration where I was when Dennis came to the club. In 1995 I wanted to die. I didn't give a shit about Dennis Bergkamp. Then I got sober and the world was my oyster. I came to life and I had this fellow team-mate who was technically unbelievable. But there were a lot of players who came into that team, don't forget. So I'm just seeing it differently to everybody else. I went from being very sociable, one of the lads, but being masked most of the time, to going to AA recovery meetings. Suddenly I've got this new-found knowledge and health and I can enjoy playing with Dennis.

'But I'm still the captain. And that's like line management. You need to play a role at times. I couldn't be his mate. I didn't think it was my place. Maybe in another life, another place, another situation, we would have had a different relationship. But I had the voice of the manager. I was wanting to win and Dennis was a player who could get me to where I wanted to go. So I was going to make sure I was on him.'

On him? Driving him? Pushing him?

'Yeah. But he didn't need a lot because he was the ultimate professional. I didn't need to keep him on his toes. Only the once. That's all I needed to do, and that's all he needed to take. You know, I've played with hundreds, and against hundreds, of players in three decades. People like Maradona, Van Basten, Dalglish, Thierry ... unbelievable players. And I put Dennis in my top three. Top three. I'm not saying who the other two are, but Dennis ... For me, he was ten times the player Thierry was. But I'm also serious. I'm professional and I don't like waste and I just felt at one point that he was on cruise control, just going a little bit through the motions. Super, super player. But come on Dennis, it's about time you won the league, player of the year. That kind of stuff should be yours for the taking. This would have been 1997 or early 1998. We've come through the dark years. We've done the Bruce [Rioch] thing. We've got the team in place. We've got the finance. The next step is to win stuff. So we're getting on the coach after the Middlesbrough game and he's sitting there. On his own ...'

On his own?

'... We had a kind of set-up with the English boys at the back of the coach. It was more to do with us and nobody can kind of come in, like no one can just walk into an old East End family. We'd grown up together. Me and Bouldy used to drink together. Dicko [Lee Dixon] I've known for ten years at that point. With Nigel [Winterburn] we've known each other ten lifetimes, and Dave Seaman ... We'd lived and breathed, men together, you know? Like in the army. So we're sitting at the back and we're maybe to blame for not including other people in the squad ... But anyway, I go to Dennis and I say it. "Dennis, you've been here two-and-a-half years and you haven't won anything. It's time for you to win something. How much do you want it?" It looked like

I got a reaction from him, physically, in his face. As I was going, I was thinking: "He might just turn round and punch me."'

And did you sense a change after that?

'A few months later we've won the Double, Dennis is player of the year and he's just played the best football of his life.'

He's said your phrase stuck with him: 'How much do you want it?' It was kind of a revelation for him. It's a phrase he adopted and often uses now.

'Yeah, I remember him saying that. But it was all for me, really, because some players don't need motivating. He could quite easily have said: "Oh, for fuck's sake shut up, Tone." But he didn't. It was just part of my thing. "How much do you want it? Come on!" Passion, pride in the club, motivation. That's the way I kind of worked. It helped my concentration. Manu Petit was very quiet, but I was ... [*clenches fist, makes war face, bangs forehead*] WOOO-Aaaarr! I would be that kind of pumped up. The adrenaline going. Motivation! Martin [Keown] was like that as well, but he didn't calm down. He needed to calm down. Oh God, the number of penalties Martin gave away down the years with his impetuous tackles! And Dennis was so quiet I felt I needed to get him up now and again. But maybe he didn't need it. There was enormous self-motivation in there anyway. He couldn't have got to where he got to without having drive. I was learning about me and other people, and what makes other people tick ...'

To Patrick Vieira, Adams's successor as Arsenal captain, Dennis's secret lay precisely in his quietness. 'Dennis is not the one who will shout and he is not the one who will talk. But on the field we knew that he was our technical leader, the one who would bring the small magic that would help us win something. You knew he would be the one to make the assist, to create something.'

You were the captain, but Dennis was the leader?

Vieira: 'Dennis was our inspiration, he was the leader. We knew that Thierry would score, and we knew that Dennis would make something happen, and we knew that Sol Campbell would be the one who leads at the back and we knew that in midfield I would be the one who got the red card.'

How did the squad see him?

'He got the respect from people. That's why everybody likes Dennis. Of course he has got this kind of Dutch arrogance. I say it all the time. "We are the best, we have the best way," you know? [*laughs*] But everybody liked him because he respected everybody. And he was popular in the dressing room. Everybody was laughing and talking with him so we all knew that he was our technical leader on the field. But I think what was really good as well was that they brought in a manager who has got the same philosophy. You couldn't have in your team Dennis Bergkamp and a manager who would want to play kick and rush. If you didn't have Dennis and you had instead a player like Duncan Ferguson, that would not fit your team trying to play football. Because that is the way it is.'

* * *

DENNIS SAYS HE was impressed by Vieira as a leader.

'He is French, so he is moody sometimes and arrogant. I keep telling him that as well [*laughs*]. Off the pitch he is just a normal very polite guy and very charming. All the women say: "Patrick, he is so charming!" But he's got this personality. It's overwhelming when he comes into the room. Fantastic charisma. And he was a good leader as well. After Tony Adams, it was like "Who can take over?" Tony was the captain. Tony 'Captain' Adams. It was his middle name almost. Who is going to be next? But Patrick built that role fantastically in his own way, less clenched fist, more connecting to everyone, to the kit man, to the chef, the coach, the players ... That role doesn't suit everyone, but he could do it. He could play football and take that role on himself.'

This still leaves the question of how the role of technical leader works in practice and how, specifically, it worked with Dennis. Having failed to be accepted as a leader in Italy, he goes on in England to lead Arsenal not just moment-by-moment on the pitch but from boring football to Total Football. What exactly was the mechanism? Arsene Wenger has the most intriguing and perceptive explanation: 'It took Dennis a while to adapt. Because he was questioned a lot in the first year. But after that, he slowly became more and more important in the team. Was it linked with confidence? Was it linked with the fact that I arrived? Was it linked with the fact that there are more technical players around him? And some are improving technically because of his influence? It is ... certainly a little bit of all of that. It's very difficult to give a percentage to that. But the biggest thing was that everybody acknowledged his quality.

'Of course, I am a lover of the way the Dutch see football. They have a positive philosophy and they build the game from the back. The Dutch also have a philosophy that they put the 'brain players' through the middle, the technically gifted players, the thoughtful, clever ones. They put them through the middle of the pitch, in the heart of the team. And there is nobody better than Dennis as the symbol of this Dutch philosophy, because it is based on technical quality, imagination, the brain. When you're a manager, you can only develop that game if the player is respected in the team. That means the team accepts to play the game that suits the player. They do this if they feel they have an interest to do it. And the big strength of Dennis is that he was hugely respected by the other players of the team.

'I find similarities when I speak with my former players about Dennis, and when I speak with the former players of the French national team about Zidane. Without judging who was the better one, I find similarities between the respect and the admiration of their partners in the team. Once you have that, it's easy because when they say something, people listen. They understand that it is in their interest. Because a team has a kind of subconscious intelligence. And the game flows naturally through the strong points of the team. That means the game goes from Tony Adams to Patrick Vieira, from Patrick Vieira to Dennis Bergkamp, from Dennis Bergkamp to Thierry Henry. The team understands that it's in their interest to do that. It can sometimes become detrimental if one player is so strong that the team always goes through him, because the variety of your game can suffer. But it was not the case with us, because Dennis had such intelligence. What is quite remarkable, he was more ... He was a guy with a strong personality. Sometimes they say when a person enters the room that people look at him. To go in there, to give that impression, that person has to think: "I am the most important person." It is a subconscious way. I would say Dennis is the exact opposite. The *exact* opposite. But he still has a kind of aristocratic elegance in the way he walks, in the way he behaves. And he provokes attention through a kind of attitude and class, natural class, and elegance.'

Gary Lewin recalls how this worked in practice. 'When Dennis came into the club, he was fully aware of what was going on around him. Some things he liked, some things he probably didn't like. People around him could see what he was like. He would always talk before and during a game: "Try doing it like this ..." He would educate players in that way. But he wouldn't be in your face, he wouldn't be shouting at you, and he wouldn't do it in front of other people. He was more of a quiet-word person. Some people would say "introverted", but I don't think he was introverted. I think he knew exactly what he was doing.'

Dennis himself reflects: 'What is a leader? It's an interesting question. Cruyff used to stand with his foot on the ball gesticulating and point wildly to everyone, telling them where to go. He was a leader. But in my day I never had time to stand still with the ball. I would have been hacked down immediately! By the nineties, there weren't any leaders like him. In my day everyone coached each other. That's what I did. I was constantly coaching and I led players, too. I never hid, I always demanded the ball. I always tried to play a prominent role, to be the best. I was never satisfied, I always wanted to try even harder. As a trainer I'm like that, too. If one of our strikers misses a chance, I start thinking about it. What can I do to make sure he scores next time? I want to be such a good trainer that I can teach a striker to avoid missing *any* chances. I want to be good at what I do, and I want to be important, but I'm not after fame. That's why I have no ambition to be a manager.'

OK. There are all sorts of leaders – so what kind are you?

'You mentioned how Patrick Vieira was a totally different leader to Tony Adams, but they were both leaders. Patrick, of course, had a completely different style. Maybe you didn't really see on the pitch, but he led the team and all the people in the club. It's fantastic, and it's different. And, yes, you can be a technical leader as well, and I like to be that more, you know, leading by example. It's similar with coaches. You've got coaches who are loud and really out there shouting so people will say: "Look at him, he's a real coach!" Whereas Wenger is more a teacher, and he's teaching the right stuff. I never like people who are out there for show, the guys who shout all the time. At the lower level of the game, you see a lot of coaches and captains as well – 'leaders' – who are just out there for the armband and the show. To me a leader is someone who affects people, who makes changes, who makes other players or people better. It's the opposite of someone doing it for the cameras.'

Tony Adams is obviously camera-friendly, yet he also leads in the sense you mean, doesn't he?

'Oh yes, yes. You look at him and think he's the *prototype* leader, you know, with all the shouting and the clenched fists. But he's not doing that for the cameras. If you didn't know him, you might think he was, but he's like that in the dressing room, too. A real leader. Bergomi was similar, actually. Tony was rougher, I'd say, but within the team Bergomi was also very strong and he approached the game, the players and the coach in a way that was similar to Tony. He did it in an Italian way, of course, but almost military-like: "I'm the captain!" I kind of liked him, because he had this awareness and intensity. I thought he was a good guy. He had a presence. Tony's got presence as well. Actually, a lot of players have got presence.

'Patrick, of course, had a completely different style. You didn't really see on the pitch what he was doing, but, wow, within the team he really affected people and got them going. He lifts them and therefore he lifts the club and the team just by having little talks with people. Did Frank Rijkaard wear the armband? Hardly ever. But behind the scenes he was always talking to people, giving advice. There were no cameras around but he was one of the great leaders. For Ajax in 1995, Danny Blind was the captain but people still keep telling me how important Frank Rijkaard was. For myself, it's not really about being a leader or not being a leader. But players, ex-players and other people talk about me like they talk about Frank. He was well respected within the dressing room. He made a difference. OK, people looked up to me in a certain way and looked to copy me in certain ways. They were confident with me and knew I was an honest guy. I'm looking for that, but I guess that's a sort of leadership. Bob Wilson probably has that right. One of the other things as well: if you are a leader it comes by itself. I still believe that. So Bagnoli and Ferri are right. You can't just say "This guy is now the leader." If you give someone time, it just happens. It drifts to the surface. It becomes apparent. It reveals itself somehow.'

16

POWER PLAYER

'I USED TO LOVE, STILL love, and always will love to see a Dutch team play,' says Thierry Henry. 'In the history of the game we all know that it's not always the case that you win like that. But for me that's how you should play football: the Dutch way.'

Isn't it strange that Dennis's Holland side never won a tournament?

'Yes and I'm actually sad about that. In 1998 we [the French team] were scared of the Dutch. When Brazil won the semi-final on penalties we celebrated. I'll always remember that.'

Because Holland were better than Brazil?

'By a distance! That Brazil team wasn't bad. But the Dutch for me were definitely the best team of the tournament. Who knows what would have happened in the final? But at that moment we were very relieved. Trust me. More than relieved. I was young but I remember the older guys talking. They really didn't want to play against Holland because however you try to play against them, they're strong, they're fast, they're technically great, they have a lovely way of playing. Everybody wanted to avoid that Dutch team.

Always do, to be honest. And then they did the same thing in 2000. Again we didn't want to play them and, again we were on the other side of the draw, waiting. That Dutch team with Dennis didn't win anything – crazy! Too crazy for me.'

Why do you think it didn't?

'I don't have a single clue, but as a fan of the game it's upsetting. Having said that, if they had won something, then we wouldn't. So it's better like this [*laughs*]. But it's weird to see a great team like that not getting the reward you would like them to have.'

AFTER THE MR HYDE version of Dutch player power had wrecked their attempt to win Euro '96, Holland's national coach Guus Hiddink decided to get tough. Get tough, that is, in a very Dutch way: he drew up a code of ethics. He then asked all the players to sign a pledge to respect each other, members of staff, supporters and even journalists. Everyone signed except Edgar Davids, whose exile continued for a while. In place of strife, qualification for the next World Cup proceeded smoothly and Holland began to play some classically clever, fluid attacking football. Dennis, with seven goals in six matches as shadow striker, was at the heart of most of it. Meanwhile, a stroke of luck meant his decision never to fly again would not damage the best years of his international career. The only qualification games he had to miss were in Turkey (Holland lost without him) and San Marino. The two next major tournaments would be on his doorstep in France and Holland/Belgium. After that, he planned to retire. Meanwhile, Arsenal had accepted that Dennis would never travel by plane – though they had docked his salary accordingly. Dennis: 'They did the maths: "If he doesn't fly then he can't play a certain number of games and so such and such a sum will be deducted." But I didn't care. What mattered was that I no longer had to worry about it. I gradually got more and more into my stride. I felt like I was unstoppable there. I felt amazing.'

By the time the 1998 World Cup rolled around, the mood was so positive that Hiddink and Davids became friends again. Holland thus headed to France with one of their greatest-ever squads: united, confident, mature and selfless ... and with Dennis Bergkamp at the height of his footballing powers. The bulk of the team was made up of former or present Ajax men, including seven regulars who'd won the Champions League in 1995, and PSV men like Jaap Stam, Philip Cocu and Arthur Numan, who added steel and guile. Wim Jonk, Dennis's friend from Ajax and Inter, now at PSV, recalls: 'Everyone in the team enjoyed what Dennis showed in training. We were all good players, but he had such exceptional class that he was at another level. The other players found that beautiful. They really appreciated him. And he challenged you. Actually, we all challenged each other. That team was the best I ever played in.'

Dennis himself had only just recovered from the injury which caused him to miss the end of Arsenal's exhausting Double-winning season. So Hiddink left him on the bench for most of Holland's first match, a 0-0 draw with the defensive Belgians. The only thing most people remember about the game is Patrick Kluivert getting himself sent off for petulantly elbowing a defender in the chest. In the second match, however, the Dutch sparked gloriously to life and clobbered South Korea 5-1. The irresistible Dutch performance drew comparisons with those of the seventies team of Cruyff and Krol. Dennis, the 10 in a number 8 shirt, shredded the Korean defence with his elegant passing and movement, scored the third goal and even, at one point, dribbled past three defenders. In the final group match Holland surged to an early 2-0 lead against Mexico then relaxed (an old failing) and, with Dennis off the field, gave up an injury-time equaliser.

Instead of the chaos of 1996 the team had established a flexible, creative unity no autocratic coach could have imposed. Hiddink explains: 'The group was no longer as selfish as it was in 1996. The lads were unified and their enthusiasm was infectious. It was more like I had to rein them in than urge them on; sometimes I couldn't get them off the training pitch. The group was so full of energy, it was just a physical presence. There were no bosses in the group, but there was a kind of natural hierarchy. Frank and Ronald de Boer, Seedorf, Cocu, Jonk and Bergkamp automatically assumed leadership. They didn't spare each other and they dragged the rest along with them. They even wanted to play a five-a-side live game the day before a match. As manager, you would never agree to that if your team isn't functioning well. You'd be far too concerned that someone might get injured. But at the World Cup the group was so tight and the players were able to tolerate so much from each other, that I was happy for them to play those live games.'

The players were so angry with themselves for their slip against Mexico that they gave their own pep talks before meeting Yugoslavia in the next round. The tense and tricky tie was decided by a spectacular late Edgar Davids goal. But the game was almost a catastrophe for Dennis. In the first half he played well and scored. In the second he should have been sent off for that crazy foul on Sinisa Mihajlovic, an opponent he knew from Italy, bundling him over near the corner flag, then treading on the side of his chest. Dennis: 'I really don't know why I did that. I haven't the faintest idea. I didn't like him, but that was no reason to do something like that to him. I was startled by my own behaviour ... what I did was incredibly foolish, a moment of insanity.' Remarkably, Spanish ref José Maria Garcia Aranda turned a blind eye, thereby setting Dennis up for one of the defining matches of his career.

The story of the quarter-final against a powerful Argentina side in the heat of Marseille is well known. The match was as dramatic as Argentina's clash with England in Saint-Etienne four days earlier, but the football from both sides was even better. The match turned on two astonishing pieces of Bergkamp brilliance. Two? We'll come to Dennis's famous last-minute winning goal in a moment, but his touch for Holland's first goal was scarcely less magical. Ronald de Boer danced through the Argentine midfield then drilled the ball at midriff height towards Dennis on the edge of the penalty area. Falling backwards onto his knees, he somehow cushioned a header to lay the ball perfectly into the path of Patrick Kluivert, who lifted it neatly into the net.

Everyone seems to have forgotten it, but I reckon that's one of your best assists.

Dennis: 'That's what I say! People forget that. It was with my head, guiding the ball. Really I couldn't do a lot with it, except a cushioned header, and I'm very proud of that. No one ever talks about it, but I don't mind! And it was a good finish by Patrick as well.'

What about the last-minute winner?

'That's my top goal, I think. Also because of everything around it. It's a goal that gets us to the semi-final of the World Cup, a massive stadium, lots of people watching and cheering … My reaction afterwards was very emotional.'

You covered your face as if to say: 'I can't believe I've just done that!'

'I didn't know what else to do! It's funny. Every boy has a dream: "I want to score in the World Cup." Score the winning goal in the final, of course. But in this way … to score a goal like that, in my style? The way I score goals, on that stage, in a game that *really* means something, because that's important to me, too … I love good football, nice football, but it has to *mean* something. It has to bring me somewhere. And that's what happened with this goal. At that moment I thought about when I was seven or eight years old, playing football in the street outside my home. This is *the* moment! It's a good feeling.'

You're a long way off the ground when the ball comes. For a wide receiver

to catch that with his hands would be difficult. You do it with your foot!
What were you thinking? How much was planned? How much improvised?

'It's a question of creating that little space. So you get to that ball
first. You've had the eye contact . . . .Frank [de Boer] knows exactly
what he's going to do.'

You asked for the pass?

'Yeah, yeah. There's contact. You're watching him. He's looking
at you. You know his body language. He's going to give the ball. So
then: full sprint away. I've got my five, six yards away from the
defender. The ball is coming over my shoulder. I know where it's
going. But you know as well that you are running in a straight line,
and that's the line you want to take to go to the goal, the line where
you have a chance of scoring. If you go a little bit wider it's gone.
The ball is coming here, and you have two options. One: let it
bounce and control it on the floor. That will be easier, but by then
you are at the corner flag. So you have to jump up to meet the ball
and at the same time control the ball. Control it dead. And again,
like the Leicester one, you have to take it inside because the
defender is storming [the other] way. He's running with you and as
soon as the ball changes direction, and you change direction as well,
then he's gone, which gives you an open chance. Well, it's a little bit
on the side but it gives you a chance to shoot.'

It's an astonishing piece of control. How did you manage it?

'I've talked about balance on the ground. This was balance as
well, but you have to be in the air. You've got to be as still as possible, as if you are standing still . . . but in the air, and controlling the
ball. If you've got a lot of movement, and try to control with the
inside of the foot, then the ball could go towards the defender. So
you want to keep it on the top of your foot. That gives you the best
chance, and the best chance of controlling it. I'm not worrying about
the angle of my foot because that's something you do all the time.
I know I can control almost any ball that comes to me. But I want

to be *very* stable. I didn't realise how high in the air I was. But you know you want that ball in that position. Not there but *here*. So you have to jump up to meet the ball.'

How much looking back were you doing while the ball was on its way to you?

'You first look back when the ball comes, of course. But there wasn't much wind, so I'm looking forward, to keep sprinting, to meet the ball. You know the line, and at the last moment you think: "OK, now I have to jump." And when I'm in the air it's going to meet my foot. There's a little bit of calculation at that moment. But it's experience.'

And after you had landed it?

'You just think: that's step one. You want to get the whole moment, the whole sequence. It's three touches. Everything can still go wrong at that moment, so you are concentrating on doing it step by step. But you don't know the steps. You can only do the second step if the first step is right. If the ball shoots on a little bit further, then you have to adjust again.'

So you've killed the dropping ball, you touch it inside to get rid of Ayala [the defender] and make a better angle, and you don't take the shot with your left foot but with the outside of your right.

'Yes, because I feel more confident with that at that time. It's in the middle of my feet and I have the confidence, and it's not the right angle to take it as well with the left, because that's a different kick. So I choose to take it with my right – ideally, the *outside* of the right – and aim it for the far post, then let it turn in ...' It curves, even. 'That's what I wanted. Take it away from the goalkeeper and let it come in.'

Did it cross your mind that he might save it?

'No. You know, sometimes you have these moments where you think: "This cannot go wrong! No way!"'

And that's the moment you're in ...

'Yeah. What can you compare it to? Different sports, like running the hundred metres in what you know is going to be a good time, or a darts player who is ... in that moment. That's the feeling you've got ... After the first two touches ... that moment ... You give absolutely everything, like your life is leading up to this moment ...'

I thought it was the best game of the tournament.

'Yes, it was for us as well. That really was probably our peak moment – and then it all fell apart. It's a shame ...'

I didn't realise you were exhausted when you scored the goal. Hiddink left you on in case you did something amazing. And then, two days later, you had to play Brazil in the semi-final. And you outplayed them for long periods.

'I started the game well but as it went on I could feel the strength draining from my legs. I felt I had just enough power left if an opportunity came my way, but it didn't happen. I was shattered, but adrenaline kept me alert and, in the shootout, I scored my penalty. I got very upset with the penalties. Ronald [de Boer] just slowed down, slowed down ... it's not the way I would have taken it. Cocu missed as well, but he put it in the corner, I felt, and it was a good save. But I was distraught. I felt a whole range of emotions, but you didn't see it. I kept it all deep inside.'

You were furious, too, at Ali Mohammed Bujsaim [the referee from the United Arab Emirates], who failed to award a clear penalty when Pierre van Hooijdonk was pulled down by his shirt in injury time by Junior Baiano.

'Pierre got a yellow card for diving, but the ball should absolutely have been put on the spot. And I would have wanted to take that penalty. Even though I was dead tired.'

DENNIS HAD DECIDED to retire from the national team after Euro 2000 – but made a point of not telling anyone. 'I wanted to avoid creating a sense of farewell. "The last time Bergkamp will do this or that, his last pass, his final steps in an Orange shirt ..." I wanted to avoid that at all costs.'

The sense that time might be catching up with him was evident in the run-up to the tournament, which was being held on Dutch home soil as well as in Belgium. New coach Frank Rijkaard sometimes used newcomer Ruud van Nistelrooy and Patrick Kluivert as twin strikers, telling Dennis it was just an experiment. 'I was no fool,' Dennis remembers. 'I'd been in football long enough to sense there was something else going on and I could be relegated in the pecking order. Perhaps Rijkaard wanted to switch to a system with two strikers and he saw me as third choice. I was actually a bit off my game at Arsenal at the time and it concerned me.' As it turned out, the two centre-forwards were too similar for the partnership to work, and Van Nistelrooy then tore a knee ligament. Now there was no question about Dennis's role in the team: he would play in a slightly deeper version of the shadow striker, behind Kluivert.

The Dutch press, remembering him from his Ajax days, were puzzled that Dennis was no longer scoring goals. 'I'd become a different kind of player at Arsenal, more of a playmaking midfielder, an *assister*. At Arsenal they accepted my scoring less because they saw the number of my assists rising. In England I scored one hundred and twenty goals and provided one hundred and twenty assists, but in the Dutch team I didn't have that reputation yet.'

Dennis got on well with Rijkaard. 'As a manager he gave me a good feeling. We worked systematically and with concentration and Johan Neeskens also contributed tremendously to that as assistant. What surprised me were Rijkaard's talks. He'd always argued well. Now he told us we could achieve great things, the kind of things he himself had experienced. But we'd have to put everything else aside. He convinced us we would become European Champions if we were to focus one hundred per cent on that objective. Winning the European Championships really became a mission.'

In the first two group games, Holland, with Dennis conducting the team from his new deeper position, overcame stubborn Czech and Danish resistance. They then beat a reserve French team in a dead rubber before the quarter-final in which Dennis inspired a devastating 6-1 win over the Yugoslavs. Patriotic football frenzy now gripped the Netherlands. Towns and cities were awash with flags and bunting and the entire village of Hoenderloo, where the Dutch team was staying, painted itself orange. It made Dennis uneasy. 'It's great when the people are behind you, their enthusiasm really gives you a kick. But this was over the top, too much hysteria with all those orange masks and wigs. When you're abroad you hardly notice what's going on at home. When you turned on the TV during the World Cup in France, it was lovely and relaxing, it helped you forget football for a while. But in 2000 every time the TV was on, orange hysteria burst into the hotel room. Almost every programme was about us, about the Championship we'd apparently already practically won. You couldn't shut out the craziness.'

Beating the Italians in the semi-final in Amsterdam would surely be a formality. And so it should have been. But one of the strangest, most one-sided of matches produced a bizarre ending. Italy, playing with ten men after the sending-off of Zambrotta, had just one clear chance. Holland had more than twenty chances, failed to score from any of them and even missed two penalties in normal time. In the shootout they missed three times. By that stage, however, Dennis, who would surely have done better with his spot-kicks than Frank de Boer, Jaap Stam and Paul Bosvelt, was no longer on the field.

In the 77th minute, coach Rijkaard had replaced winger Boudewijn Zenden with Peter van Vossen, the 32-year-old who'd had a mediocre season with Feyenoord. When he came on Van Vossen urged the crowd to make more noise but otherwise contributed little. He and Rijkaard were close, but surely the manager would not have been swayed by sentiment during a major semi-final? Then in the 84th minute Clarence Seedorf came on for Dennis. Dennis was bewildered. Fine all-rounder though he is, Seedorf was not known for Bergkamp-style match-winning moments – and didn't produce one. Rijkaard's third change, in the 95th minute, was the strangest of all: Cocu off in place of 33-year-old midfielder Aron Winter. The substitution enabled Winter to break Ruud Krol's record for appearances, but did nothing to break down the Italian defence.

Even though the game was clearly headed for penalties, the two renowned pinch-hitting strikers and penalty specialists, Pierre van Hooijdonk and Roy Makaay, were left on the bench. Rijkaard later said his idea had been to inject energy into his sagging team. But Dennis remains unimpressed. 'I still think they were peculiar changes. I thought: "Come on, man, why don't you leave me on the pitch? Remember Van Basten in 1988 against the Germans, Bergkamp in 1998 against Argentina?" I felt I was capable of producing something like that again. I was still in the game, I wasn't tired and I was sure I could do it: give the deciding pass or score myself. But Rijkaard brought me off and I was very, very unhappy about that.'

As at the World Cup, the French were amazed to see their most feared opponents fall, and went on to beat Italy narrowly in the final. Patrick Vieira observes: 'I never understood why that Dutch team didn't win. They had everything that generation: Kluivert, Bergkamp, Overmars ... I remember watching them play against Argentina and they were unbelievable. Unbelievable! That was a good game of football! One of the differences between Holland and France at that time was that we had maybe less quality but we had more physical power. If you look at our back four, physically it was unbelievable: Thuram, Lizarazu, Desailly, Laurent Blanc ... We were winners. We were putting our heads where the Dutch would put their feet. And maybe the Dutch would not put their head where we were putting our feet. That was the difference.'

Dennis reflects sadly on the two tournaments that got away: 'I still don't know how we didn't beat Italy. Losing on penalties like that was humbling, but it was less shocking and less long-lasting than 1998. The World Cup is much bigger than a European Championship and you sense that. When it was over, we thanked the crowd and I knew: "OK, that's it then. Now I have to make an announcement and bid farewell."'

But '98 still haunts you?

'We shouldn't have lost to Brazil. That's definite. We were better than them. In ninety-six we know the problems of course. I'm not sure if we could have won that, but we could have got into the final, I think. But in ninety-eight it all clicked, it was all good. We should have won that. We should have beaten Brazil. And then we could have given France a real good game. They didn't want to play us, from what I understand. And the same with Euro 2000: we should have beaten Italy easily to get to the final. I think our game didn't really suit France. They liked being technically better than their opponents, but we were technically better than them. So in the end we knew we were really good players but we couldn't take that extra step. That is disappointing because ... After tournaments we always say: "But we are only a small country ..." We do have fantastic players. But sometimes I feel you need a bit less of the same, you know? We are all technical players, all thinking, playing football, all passing the ball, doing it in a good way. But sometimes you need a defender who just puts it in the stand, or just takes pleasure in his striker not scoring. And upfront, as well, we needed to be more clinical sometimes. You need to have differences in a mental way as well. But, yeah, it's so disappointing. We should have won one of those tournaments.'

THE PENALTY

'Isn't it every little boy's dream?' Dennis wonders. 'You're playing in the World Cup final. It's one-one and just before the final whistle you're awarded a penalty. And you get to take it. In your dream you put it away without effort. But in real life most kids cave in under the pressure because fear of failure suddenly kicks in. But that didn't affect me. Of course, taking a penalty can be scary but – and maybe this sounds weird – I liked that scariness. I enjoyed that tension.'

It's 14 April 1999 and something close to the little boy's dream is about to be enacted. It's 1-1 in a throbbing FA Cup semi-final replay at Villa Park between the two great English teams of the day: Arsenal, the reigning Double champions, and Manchester United, champions in four of the previous six seasons. United are a man down because Roy Keane was sent off. Just before the final whistle, Phil Neville clatters Ray Parlour to give Arsenal a penalty. *Every boy's dream* ... Dennis, Arsenal's most reliable penalty-taker, places the ball on the spot and runs up to take the kick that will surely send his team to their second successive FA Cup final and set up an unprecedented double Double.

'I'd scored our goal. It was deflected but it had gone in. And I'd played well. So I felt confident enough to take that penalty. I was up for it. Of course, it's against Peter Schmeichel. He's a great goalie and he's got plenty of reach to the corners. So you have to hit it firm. And that's what I do. I pick my corner – as always – after I walk back from the spot. That was my routine: put the ball down, walk back, then decide. I'm going to hit it there: bottom right corner. Don't show it too much to the goalkeeper, and hit it firm and then it should be OK. But here, Schmeichel's got – like a cat, you know? – a better reaction than I expect. Maybe he sees something, or maybe he guesses correctly. And as soon as you kick it, you look up and you can see him going. Then you know it's not good enough. You already know before he stops it. You look up. You don't see the details, but you see ... it's like a shadow ... a little flash ... And then it's ... you realise it's a miss. Yeah. It was a bad moment.'

Manchester United survived and, to everyone's surprise, including their own, went on to win thanks to Ryan Giggs's solo goal after a mistake by Patrick Vieira. Another error cost Arsenal the league title at Leeds four weeks later, when substitute Nelson Vivas left Jimmy Floyd Hasselbaink free to head the decisive goal. Manchester United went on to win the Cup, the Premier League and the Champions League: the Treble. Ray Parlour remembers it all too well: 'In them days it was only us and Manchester United. It was such a close call between us! I mean, Dennis, if he scores that penalty we win the Double again, because Man United would have gone. If we'd won the semi-final their heads would have gone down and they would have dropped points in the league. It was amazing how close we were to winning the Double again. One kick away! Then that game at Leeds ... oh God! It was nil-nil and we only needed a point. And we let in a goal in the last minute! I played with Hasselbaink later at Middlesbrough and said: "What were you doing, Jim? What'd you do that to us for?" And he had a big grin on his face. Even the Leeds fans wanted Arsenal to win, so Man U wouldn't win the league. But Jimmy was obviously a Dutchman and didn't realise!'

Was it a bad penalty from Dennis or a good save by Schmeichel? Parlour: 'Look, at the end of the day, if you blaze over the bar or miss the target completely, it's a bad penalty. But Dennis hit the target. It's all about the keeper going the right way, isn't it? But, oh dear! Dennis didn't speak for days. We all said: "Dennis, it happens: ups and downs, football's like that, you're going to get bad days, good days. And this was a bad day for all of us, not just for you. It just wasn't to be." Then look back to the '03–'04 season. At Old Trafford, Manchester United get a penalty against us in the last minute and hit the crossbar! You'd bet your house on Van Nistelrooy scoring. If he scores that, we lose in September. Instead, we go the whole season unbeaten. That's how football can change sometimes. So it's a little bit of fate at times, and Manchester United especially had a bit of [good] fate that year.'

Tony Adams remembers Dennis's distress. 'It's the last time he ever took a penalty, isn't it? I think he said he'd never take another one. We didn't blame him. Never ever. But it was a trauma to him. I could tell because he was even more quiet than usual. Vulnerable, weak human being that I am, I always kind of left him alone because he seemed like he could manage. He's like Becks, who's emotionally intelligent as well. After that Argentina thing [Beckham sent off as England lost to Argentina in the 1998 World Cup] I made him laugh. At least I think I did. I said: "It's all right for you. You'll get another chance, but it's my last World Cup and you've fucked it right up for me!" And it kind of broke him out of it. But he was in bits and it was completely normal. And the reaction of Dennis was completely Dennis.'

* * *

IT WASN'T YOUR last penalty was it?

Dennis: 'No, I still took the odd one, without problems, without hesitation and without missing. But that miss did bother me for quite a while, and the next season Thierry Henry became our penalty-taker. That didn't bother me. If someone else is better at something than I am, then they should do it, it's better for the team. Anyway, by then I was becoming more of an assister than a finisher so I didn't really need to score that extra goal any more.'

What was your immediate reaction?

'Well, I'm not a person to just drop, you know? It's more that I was angry and you just get on with it and want to make up for it. It's still one-one. We're still a man over. Then, afterwards, Giggs scored. Yeah, it's strange. Sometimes winning is a question of habit. Man United had the habit of winning. They expected it. This is football. It's not our day. It's not my day. It's their day. It's their season. You can't catch those things, you don't know why it happens. What is luck? What is form? You can work for it, but, really, what is form? You don't agree with it, you want to fight it ... Afterwards you realise that it's one of those things.

'I should have done better with the penalty, but everything came together for them that season. If you look at the Invincibles, I'm sure there were forty or fifty things that happened in that season where it could have gone the other way. It could have gone the other way against Man United in the fiftieth game as well. If we'd had a draw then our unbeaten run would have carried on for another twenty or thirty games. These things are really strange in football.'

It can't be analysed?

'I don't think so, because you're talking about a level where everything is so close. It's not like a difference of three goals. It's close. Sometimes you're better on the day. Sometimes you've got the better players who are more in form. And sometimes it's the other way. "Why didn't that ball go in? I've done everything right ..." That was my first reaction on the penalty as well. "I've done everything right, but Schmeichel is a great goalie." But then you're fooling yourself, because the penalty didn't go in, so it wasn't good enough. I was so disappointed with that. And then the Leeds game. It was just disappointing, especially after doing the Double in ninety-eight.'

People say that was the decisive moment when you could have broken United. Not only would they have missed the Treble, but a second Double for Arsenal might have established dominance.

'Well, I'm not sure you can hang all that on one kick! I'm not sure if it's that big an influence. From the inside, I would say it hurts your team, but it's not like: "Oh, we have to start all over again." You're very close and you realise that. For the next few years we're first or second. And at least ninety-nine showed that ninety-eight wasn't a one-off, a fluke. We were good enough to compete with them now, which wasn't the case before. In my first and second seasons we were nowhere near. So we were making steps, and that was all through the club. The idea was, "We're not that far off now."'

LOOKING BACK, IT seems odd that even during the best years of Arsenal, say from 1998 to 2004, United are a bit ahead. They win the league four times, Arsenal three. And they've won more since, of course. I asked some of the old players about it. Patrick Vieira says: 'I think first you have to give credit to United. They came back stronger every time we won the league. But what is really difficult is not just to do it once, but to win the league two or three times in a row. We didn't know how to keep doing it. We were missing something and we lost games that we shouldn't and small details ...

The difference was that as a club United had been doing it for years. If you think you are a winner, you can win. And it is not just the leading players. It's the whole club, all the way down to the ground-staff, from the bottom to the top. United knew how to win and we were behind them in that. We were striving to be successful, and that is not the same. We were building a domination and United had it already. So we were a few steps behind.'

Thierry Henry points out the economic mismatch: 'At that time everyone within the club knew we had to keep the team we had in order to have the new stadium. Basically, everything went towards the new stadium. We didn't do badly in the meantime, but Man United always added one or two or three players a year. And we were losing one or two or three every year. Marc Overmars and Manu Petit went together to Barcelona. Later, Robert [Pires] went to Villarreal. Patrick went to Juve. David Seaman went to Man City and retired. Lee Dixon retired. Nigel Winterburn went to West Ham and retired. Freddie went to West Ham, the MLS, came back ... I don't like to talk about stuff I don't know about, and I don't know what was going on with the board. But I'd say Arsene has done extremely well in the last few years. If you compare it with Manchester United then maybe you'd say: "Oh, maybe not." But given the limited resources, Arsene hasn't done badly.'

And, as Ray Parlour says, United were really a top team, too: 'Look at their midfield: Keane, Scholes, Beckham, Giggs in his prime. Then you add the strikers: Cole, Yorke, Sheringham comes into the side, and Van Nistelrooy. And Stam at the back ... Quality. It's a hell of a team. We had a very good team ourselves, but you can see why they did dominate a little bit as well. They were such a force and the games with them were massive, massive. As soon as that fixture list comes out, the first team we look at – "When have we got 'em? Where have we got 'em?" – is United. Season 1997-98 was amazing because we were twelve points behind, but we knew if we beat them at Old Trafford we could go on a good run. Little Overmars scored and we beat them one-nil and I think we won ten in a row. We won the league with three games to spare in the end. We knew we had a good side then. We knew we could compete for many years, because we were all quite a good age. And now we knew Man United would be looking over their shoulders. Because they used to walk it some seasons too easily. But now Alex Ferguson was like : "*Wooah* . . . this team's strong. This team is the one to beat." We pushed them close every single season.'

* * *

DENNIS: 'WINNING IN football is sometimes about habit. We were close enough to compete with them, but to change that habit? That's history. Not only in my time, but with the whole history of Man United.'

I wouldn't say that.

'Wouldn't you say that Man U is a bigger club than Arsenal?'

Depends how you look at it. In the 1930s, Arsenal were giants and United nowhere. In the 1950s United had the Busby Babes, who were wonderful and died. Then ten years later their resurrection team – Charlton, Best, Law – won the European Cup, which the Babes had been trying to win when they died. That's where the club's mystique comes from. But then they went into a long decline and didn't win the league for 25 years.

'But on average? I mean, weren't they second all the time?'

I don't think so. Let's look it up . . . OK . . . between 1968 and 1992 United were second . . . four times. And won some Cups. And got relegated one year. For a few years Leeds were the giants. Then for 20 years Liverpool were the giants. And when you arrived, the reigning champions were Blackburn Rovers. Admittedly, United were on a roll. They became champions in '93 then did the Double the next year. And in your first season they did the Double again. But the idea of them being this mega-club who won all the time was recent.

'It's strange because I had a different impression. When I first came here, it felt like it's a big achievement to compete, not only with them but other teams as well. In my first season we qualified for the UEFA Cup. Everyone was happy about that. And United had everything to be a successful team for many years. I didn't feel that at Arsenal. We didn't feel we could compete for the championship. It wasn't normal. In my first season it was like "UEFA Cup! Yay!!" And where did we finish? Fifth? But the steps we made afterwards … In my opinion, in those years, those five, six, seven years, we were really equal to Man U and even in a few of those we were better. In the Invincibles season, definitely, and maybe one or two seasons before and after that. Those were big steps, big steps.'

Can we take it back to penalties? It's not fair to remember Villa Park when for years your penalties were rock solid. You hardly ever missed for Arsenal, Inter, Ajax or Holland. Your technique was no frills and no risk, wasn't it? Hard and straight into a corner after a no-nonsense run-up which was neither too long nor too short.

'I didn't make a song and dance out of it. I always approached penalties seriously, even when we were four-nil up. I just wanted to score every time. It was another goal for my total. In particular I felt that at Ajax. Because I was top scorer and goals are your lifeblood.'

Did you ever consider a 'Panenka' or varying your run-up?

'During training, just for the fun of it, but not too seriously. The Panenka was a stroke of genius, an amazing solution at that moment. Panenka knew his best chance was a lob down the middle because Sepp Maier always went to a corner. But from then on the Panenka became a risky proposition. What if the keeper stays put? It's like the Cruyff-Olsen penalty. When Cruyff played the ball sideways [from the penalty spot] and [Jesper] Olsen ran into the box everyone stood and gaped. No one understood what was happening [Olsen drew the goalkeeper, then squared the ball back to Cruyff to put into the net]. But nowadays your opponent would respond immediately. For a while it was fashionable to saunter in to provoke some movement from the keeper. I did that a few times, but it didn't feel comfortable. Because there's hesitation in your run-up, you can start to doubt yourself. So I quickly went back to my tried and trusted method: a straight run-up and straight shot, actually one continuous, highly energised action.'

Why did the Dutch national team have such a terrible problem with shootouts?

'I played in five tournaments, and four of them we went out on penalties. It was so frustrating . . . and even more frustrating when you score your own penalty. You do what is expected, but penalties are never in your hands.'

Watching from afar, something seemed very wrong. Was it that you were all so good technically that you didn't see shootouts as a special discipline requiring a German-type approach? Was it a wrong attitude? Did the Dutch not take penalties seriously enough?

'How can you not take a penalty seriously?'

I don't know. Why did Seedorf keep taking penalties and missing?

'You think it's a matter of practising more?'

Did you practise enough?

'Enough is never enough. What is enough? You can never simulate the same pressure. You can practise and practise but it's still different when you get to a real shootout. So, first you have to be good enough to take penalties. Then you have to deal with the pressure. Of course it's a mental thing. It's not only Seedorf. Other players as well went up for the penalty thinking: "I'm going to take it, and I'm going to do it in a certain way." Maybe it's a Dutch thing. Maybe an arrogant thing.'

Do you mean making it too complicated like Ronald de Boer against Brazil? His dummy ended in disaster.

'That's what you say.'

You said yourself: 'It's not the way I would have taken it.'

'Well, you can try something. But you're playing with it. You're underestimating the pressure. It's not that you're not taking it seriously. He [De Boer] is. He thinks: "This is the best way," and maybe he's done it in training. But when there's pressure ... I wouldn't have done it that way because it's not the best option. But I think it's very difficult to say: "You should have done this" or "You should have done that." Of course you should have done better. You missed the penalty. But I don't see a difference in me aiming for the corner and it being saved or someone else kicking it over. You make a decision, and that decision is based on "This is my best play", but a near-miss is still a miss.'

There's been lots of work done by academics on penalties and shootouts. Game theorists have their theories. Number crunchers have data on the habits and patterns of goalkeepers and penalty-takers.

'OK, but in the nineties we kept on getting knocked out of tournaments on penalties. And we're now twenty, almost twenty-five years later ... There must have been plenty of studies, but no one comes up with a result! I've still never heard: "This is why you didn't win that penalty shootout."'

Well, we know some things, like the coin toss is important because the team shooting first has a 60-40 advantage.

'But can you influence a coin toss? I agree with the figure, but it's still a gamble. Whatever you do, it's still a gamble. You can practise enough, you can win the coin toss, you can hold each other's hands, you know, and be confident and whatever, but still it's down to taking that penalty. And that pressure is something you can't simulate in training.'

But surely we know what a good penalty is? Some of Holland's missed penalties were just awful. Jaap Stam against Italy: crazily high over the bar. Paul Bosvelt: weak and too near the goalie. Ronald de Boer against

Brazil ... Seedorf against France ... These weren't good penalties. So what happened technically or psychologically? Is it panic? Everybody says, 'Be clear what you're going to do' and 'Vary your patterns.' All these kind of things ...

'Then you assume the Dutch never thought about that?'

Well, what was the thinking? Why did Van Basten miss in '92?

'You think Marco didn't take Denmark seriously? Didn't have enough holiday? Or that he's arrogant because he's Dutch?'

I don't know. What do you think?

'He missed the penalty.'

He leaned backwards.

'Did he mean to do that, do you think? People most of the time, they want to have a reason why they missed. Oh, I leaned backwards, I must have taken about three million shots in my life, and this one I leaned backwards, but why? Because it's a penalty? Because it's Schmeichel? Because I'm nervous? That's very difficult to say. There's an element of chance as well. You don't know. I think Marco took lots of penalties in Milan that season. He always had the same rhythm, he always took it the same way ... it's difficult. There are a lot of studies. A lot of people have opinions about it. But you don't know unless you've been there. And I'll tell you, Marco did practise. He did ten penalties before the game. What would you say? "Yeah, but ten is not enough, he should have taken fifty." You know? What is enough? What's good? What's bad? I find it really difficult.'

But you can't say, as the English have for years, that it's 'a lottery'.

'And you can't criticise people by saying: "You took a bad penalty, you should have done better." Of course, I should have done better against Schmeichel as well. But are people going to criticise me that I didn't take it seriously? That I didn't take Schmeichel seriously? That I didn't practise before? Come on!'

No, but when Frank de Boer winks at Toldo then takes a terrible penalty, what's the psychology? It's a textbook example of how not to do it.

'Now you're judging? With all due respect, you've never been in that situation. And still you're judging someone who has been there?'

Yes.

'You're telling him he took the penalty wrong?'

He did take the penalty wrong. It was terrible.

'No, it was a miss.'

It was a terrible penalty.

'He missed the penalty, therefore it's not good. You can't have a good penalty that is saved. I've tried to explain that . . .'

But surely a penalty missed because of a great save isn't the same as a penalty skied almost out of the stadium?

'I don't see that.'

But the Dutch had to find a way to do better at shootouts somehow?

'Of course.'

The Dutch have tried a change of policy, but Dennis is not convinced by the approach. After the Italy fiasco, the KNVB instituted a new rule: to improve the nation's penalty skills, all junior matches would henceforth end with a penalty shootout. Dennis: 'But you can't *only* train the lower youth teams to take penalties! If the KNVB wants to make a change, that's good, but implement it across the board, with all ages and persevere. Look at Germany. They panicked after Euro 2000, too, because they finished bottom of their group. The DFB (German Football Association) was already talking about reforming their academies after the 1998 World Cup. Then after Euro 2000 they made really radical changes. They switched the emphasis from training power and athletic ability to technique, more like the Dutch way. Now you see the results. Germany now has the kind of footballers you wouldn't have seen fifteen years ago: Mario Götze, Marko Reus, Thomas Müller, Toni

Kroos ... wonderful players, and attractive football played by Dortmund, Bayern and the national team. They worked systematically to change things across the board, and it has produced incredible results. In Holland, the lowest youth team still practise taking penalties ... but nothing else has changed! You know, we won on penalties once [against Sweden in the quarter-final of Euro 2004] so no one was really bothered any more. But that's not how it works. Once you identify a problem you have to start working on solving it at the bottom of your organisation. But you mustn't stop there. You have to work all the way through, right up to the top. If you're convinced, as KNVB, that you have to teach Dutch footballers how to take penalties, then you have to really do it seriously. And that's what we're trying to do at Ajax now. I'm not just talking about penalties. I'm talking about everything. The Germans looked at the Dutch and learned. And now we're looking at them, and trying to do exactly the same thing: working in a systematic and concentrated way to implement changes and train our talents differently. And we will succeed.'

18

THE MEANING OF MEANING

IAN WRIGHT: 'THE touch! The turn! They should slow that goal down with some classical music and put it in a museum. Yeah! And make people see that it's a real bit of poetry in motion.'

Thierry Henry: 'You're talking about a great goal, but talking won't do it justice, so just *watch* it.'

The two most prolific strikers in Arsenal's history are talking about the goal voted by fans as the club's best-ever, the one scored in a league match at Newcastle in March 2002. To recall the essentials: receiving a low, driven pass with his back to goal, Dennis Bergkamp conjures a never-previously-imagined turn to beat defender Nikos Dabizas, flicking the ball right, spinning himself left and meeting the ball goal-side before calmly opening his body to side-foot past the advancing goalkeeper, Shay Given. Arsenal officials hoped to immortalise the moment in bronze when they commissioned a statue of Dennis for the Emirates Stadium. Sadly, this proved technically impossible. As film-maker Paul Tickell observes: 'It would need Boccioni back from the dead to sculpt that goal.'

'That goal at Newcastle is a genius moment, so people have to cast doubt on it,' says Ian Wright. 'But I've seen Dennis do stuff like that in training so when people ask: "Did he mean it?" I say: "Of course he fucking meant it!" He's an architect of space, so I reckon he's done the drawings, measured everything and built it all in a split-second. And if someone says: "But he couldn't have done that flick on purpose," I say it makes no difference 'cos the speed of thought was such that he was able to readjust and finish with *aplomb*.'

Thierry Henry rebukes doubters in a slightly different fashion. 'When people ask me about that goal I just go: "Dennis Bergkamp." And they say: 'Yeah, but did he mean it ...? Do you think ...?" So I say it again: "Dennis Bergkamp." That's my answer. I didn't play in that game. I was watching at home and my first thought was *"What!?"* But you have players like that in history. Like Cantona was Cantona and Zizou was Zizou and Maradona was Maradona. You don't have to comment on everything. Sometimes you just have to witness. Only Dennis can tell you what happened and I will believe him. Most of his goals he thought about before he received the ball. That's Dennis Bergkamp.'

* * *

BUT HOW DID Dennis do it? And why do people still wonder if he 'meant' his masterpiece?

Dennis: 'The whole question is strange. What do they mean by *what did I mean*? Which part do they think I didn't mean? Do I see it all in advance? Do I think: "I'll put it there, turn this way, then push?" Of course not. The situation creates the move. A few years ago I asked myself: "How can you describe a good footballer?" and my answer was: "The best players are the players who adjust to the situation they're given in the best way." The question is always: "how do you adjust?" I want the pass from Pires to my feet, but it comes behind me. It's not what I expect, so I think: "I need another idea here." It's like when Messi sets off on a run. The first defender moves that way, so he goes this way. Did he "mean" it before? Did he plan it? No, he's responding, inventing. "There's a defender here, so I go there. Oh, there's another one there, so I drop my shoulder ..." If people ask: "Did you mean the goal?" I say: "No, when I got on the coach to Newcastle I didn't mean to score a goal like that." The ball came in a certain way, so I turned and twisted and did this and that.'

When your left foot goes to the ball, surely the idea is to flick the ball one way and spin yourself the other? Your foot goes to touch the ball to the right but the rest of your body is already spinning left.

'Of course. The pass is coming like this, but I want to go that way so the creativity in my brain goes: "OK I'm going to try this ..." It's the all-or-nothing part of my game. I could have gone for the safe way, control the ball and knock it back. Or maybe turn. But I know the defender is stepping in and the pace of the ball can help me. With a small touch the pace will still be there, so I can spin the ball and keep it within reach.'

Tony Adams thought you must have tried this kind of turn before. Was it a move you'd imagined ahead of time and practised, then executed when you got the opportunity?

'No, no. It was nothing like that. If my first thought is: "I want to control the ball," then I would never make that turn. But my first thought was: "I want to go to the goal and I'm going to do whatever it takes to go to the goal, no matter how the ball comes to me." Ten yards before the ball arrived I made my decision: "I'm going to turn him."'

Did you calculate Dabizas's reaction?

'Not that. But you know where the defender will be and that his knees will be bent a little, and that he will be standing a little wide, so he can't turn. And he won't expect it. The thought was: "I'll just flick the ball and see what happens. Maybe the defender blocks it, or the flick is not wide enough, or he anticipates and gets two yards ahead. But maybe he'll be surprised and I'll be one or two yards in front of him." As it happened, I still wasn't in front of him, so I had to push him off. So you need some luck as well.'

So it's a foul?

'Never! You end up with the ball somewhere in the middle and you have to decide. Maybe you choose safety. Take it with your right and you open up the goal for yourself. Maybe the left is your weaker foot. It would have to be more of a good hit. You can't really place it. But with your right foot . . . at the last moment I can go low, or high [he is pointing to the four corners of the goal]. And then you just open it and take the far corner.'

So you're calculating at incredible speed?

'It is more instinctive because you know from training sessions and from other games. You know how the ball will bounce, and how the defender will turn. You know when you push him where the ball will end up, and where the goalkeeper is. It's not like you've done that for the first time, that shot and that push. You know from previous times.'

Thierry Henry observes: 'You know my favourite thing about that goal? The way Dennis puts his body in front of Dabizas. Dennis makes the turn and then blocks the defender, and that's what gives him *all the time in the world* to finish. Usually when you do something amazing you get carried away. How many times did you see a guy do a great control and then rush the finish? Dennis did something amazing but then he stayed composed. That's the difference between great players and normal players. A normal striker would be so happy to have made the turn he would try to blast it in. No! Calm down. Calm down! You did the most difficult thing. Now relax. Watch Dennis. The way he put his body between Dabizas and the ball was just amazing.'

*

SURELY, DENNIS, THAT must be your favourite goal.

'No.'

Why ever not?

'There's a lot of luck involved. If the defender takes one step back then it's finished. So it's not pure. People talked so much about that goal I decided to watch it on TV. It was interesting because it looks quite different to what was in my mind. On TV you see the defender. I knew he was there, but I never saw him. I felt him a little bit, his presence, and I knew he was on this side. So those are facts. The ball was here. I want to go there ... *boom!*

'Generally, though, I don't like tricks. I can enjoy it when other people do them, or when they work out for me. But it's really not something on my mind. I don't look for the chance to do a trick. It's just not my game. My game is about first touch, control, passing. With one pass or one control, can I get myself or someone else in front of the goalkeeper? Can I create space to give a pass ... That's my passion, my speciality. For me, a trick is just ... well, that's all it is. For me, everything has to have a thought and meaning behind it. What does a trick contribute? It has to be functional. Art for art's sake isn't interesting.'

But that goal relies on a trick.

'Yes, and it looked quite special, but only because there was a goal. That justified the trick which then becomes part of something bigger. The trick makes the goal and the goal makes the trick.'

Ian Wright says he knew you meant every millisecond of the Newcastle goal because he saw you score a similar one – perhaps even better – in training.

'Really? I don't remember.'

He says Martin Keown, who was the best in the business at that time, was marking you tightly and you had your back to goal. The pass comes from the side and you somehow flick the ball not around Martin but inside

him. Ian says it was one of the most amazing things he ever saw because
Martin was always full-on, even in training.

'Yeah, he was.'

Apparently everyone just stopped and applauded – even Martin.

'I'm not sure. Let me think . . . Oh yeah, I think I know the one
he means. It was in training, but at Highbury. Sometimes you have
these Junior Gunners training sessions and I believe I did it in a
game there.'

So lots of people saw it?

'Eighty-eight people probably! Maybe it was seventy-seven
and a half. Anyway, Martin was in the back four, left central
defender. I'm pretty sure of that. He's marking me, and I'm running from the left towards the middle and he's close behind and
slightly to the right. It's difficult to describe, but I think the ball
comes from the touchline. That means it's going across my body
from my left. Martin expects me to control the ball and keep going
across him. There's no danger from his point of view. But, instead
of controlling the ball with my right instep, at the last moment I
pass my foot over the ball and flick it back with the outside of the
foot.'

What?! You're running and suddenly stop and twist inside out??

'Well, no. It's coming across me and I go over it and . . . *chack*! . . .
now I'm going back the other way. You have to be in balance, and
you have to make sure you don't hurt yourself. It's like this: foot
over the ball and flick back, but all in one step. Normally you'd
control the ball without changing direction. Here you turn the foot
to the right like a stepover with the ball moving, and foot over the
ball – don't touch it! – and now your foot is on the other side of the
ball and you can touch it back inside. It's the contact with the ball
that makes the difference.'

Then you stop?

'No. I go over the ball and make a turn. It's a sharp turn, not a stop. I know I'm going to turn. The defender doesn't know. So I do my turn and he's out of position and I have my two yards and I get my shot away and it goes in. I tried it a few times, actually. It's a simple movement. Creative again, knowing what to do and where to go. It's a shame there is no footage. Martin would appreciate seeing it.'

19

THE CHEF

On 28 September 2002, three and a half years after losing the title at Elland Road, a very different Arsenal team walked off the same pitch to huge applause – from the Leeds fans. Yorkshire supporters understand the game as well as anyone and the powerfully inventive technical football that swept their team to a 4-1 defeat had been astonishing. As the home fans queued for Gunners' autographs, Leeds coach Terry Venables declared that the new Arsenal were better than any of the Manchester United teams of the previous decade and comparable to the great Ajax of the early seventies.

It would be two years before anyone called Arsenal the 'Invincibles', but they were rewriting the record books almost every week. The game at Leeds meant the reigning Double champions had scored in 47 consecutive matches and racked up 22 away league games without defeat, beating records by Chesterfield and Nottingham Forest. Most observers assumed – wrongly, as it turned out – that Arsenal would walk away with the league and the BBC's website posed a question that was already a cliché: 'Are Arsenal England's best-ever side?' Arsene Wenger didn't usually draw attention to the near-fulfilment of his Plan, but after the match he noted that his team was changing positions all over the field, posing danger from everywhere and playing 'great football, Total Football'.

In retrospect, one of the most intriguing things about the match at Leeds was the Bergkampian assist for the fourth goal. A 30-yard pearl-handled dagger of a pass pierced the heart of the home defence to put in Kanu. But Dennis was not on the field. He was 33 now and, along with Robert Pires and Freddie Ljungberg, was rested after the no-less majestic 4-0 Champions League destruction of PSV in Eindhoven three days earlier. Rather, the pass against Leeds was provided by 19-year-old Jermaine Pennant, destined to play just 12 times for Arsenal. Another promising young talent, Pascal Cygan, was a rock in defence and Arsenal's domination was such that by the end, two substitutes, Francis Jeffers (who would end up, at age 32, playing for Accrington Stanley) and Oleg Luzhny (the reserve right-back playing in left midfield) were gleefully swapping passes deep inside the Leeds penalty area. None of these four stayed long at the club or would ever be considered members of the Arsenal pantheon. Yet here they were playing divine football. How?

According to the principles of homeopathy, water will take on the characteristics of whatever substance it is shaken with and will retain those characteristics even when the original substance is no longer present. Thierry Henry has a simpler explanation: the whole squad was influenced by Dennis Bergkamp. 'He was an example to us all. If you are intelligent and you don't know how to feed off Dennis then you are an idiot! He doesn't have to talk. Just watch. He doesn't have to come to you. Just *watch him*!'

In similar vein, Ray Parlour remembers how he and Edu thoroughly outplayed the Inter midfield when Arsenal won 5-1 at the

San Siro in 2003. 'They had some very well-respected players but we pulled all the strings. They couldn't get near us. After the game the Italians were saying: "We didn't expect you to control the whole game!" But at that time, technically, I was just getting better and better.'

Because of Wenger or because of Dennis?

'Both. Dennis was always a big factor. He would always see everything around him, and he was such a clever, clever player. He affected all the players at the club. And Wenger was always making you think. With him it was always top-quality, high-intensity training. And he always likes a bit of movement. He loved it when people were changing positions in the game. You fill the gaps, don't you? If the attack breaks down, you don't just think: "Oh, he's got to get back in there." You fill in. It just happened organically. It's part of a good team. If you play a section on the field, you've got to have a good understanding with the people around you. I wouldn't have a lot to do with whoever played left-back or left-winger, but I'd know to go into the box, to the back post if they get to the line. You have pockets in the team and you all know where you're going. And a good team ethic always needs different sorts of players: technically good players who can open things up, like Dennis or Pires, workers like myself and Patrick Vieira, who can control and try to win the ball back in good areas, and good defenders.'

Did you realise you were creating something new in England?

'I don't think we thought about that. We just got on with it. We just played and enjoyed it. Everybody wanted the ball, which was very important. There was no one who would hide in that team. You'd have some bad games here and there, but generally it was very good most games.'

Thierry Henry, top goal-scorer and increasingly the team's dominant personality, was an admirer of the Dutch style and knew exactly in whose steps Arsenal now followed. When he arrived from

Juventus in 1999, Thierry had hoped to wear the number 12 shirt in honour of his hero Marco van Basten, who'd worn it at Euro '88. Since that number was taken, he accepted the number 14 instead and he went on to add lustre to a number first made famous in football by Johan Cruyff. Homage to Cruyff was never his intention, but sometimes Thierry even resembled the Dutchman in his speed, skill and tendency to drift to the left and cut in from the wing. He was also aware of the old *totaalvoetballer*'s influence on the new Arsenal. 'Cruyff took the Dutch game to Barcelona when he became the boss. And Arsene made it his way. At Arsenal we used to play four-four-two and you might say: "That's not Dutch." Sometimes it was three-four-three or whatever. But the formation doesn't matter. Whatever way Arsene sent his team out onto the field the mentality was Total Football. If it's four-three-three or six-four-zero with no strikers, I don't care about that. It's still Total Football. Attack at any time. Everybody attacks. Everybody defends. That's the Dutch idea. But along the way, you make it *your* style of Total Football.'

And what a gourmet style it became.

Thierry: 'Dennis and me, and Robert [Pires], Sylvain Wiltord and Kanu were on the same page. We were giving goals to each other all the time. People say the other guys were feeding me. I fed them, too. A hell of a lot. So we were feeding each other, but Dennis was the *chef*. He was feeding us all. That was the beauty of that team. I don't know how many goals we scored in that two or three years with passes *inside* the opponents' box ... *boom! boom! boom!* It was a lot! No one wanted to keep the ball too long. If just one guy had kept it too long ... *wheeeeeeeuuw* [*mimes crashing plane*]. Disaster! Every single pass: one-two-go! Not only in front of goal but everywhere. "He's alone – give it to him! He's alone – give it to him!" *Fast*! Everything opens up when there is understanding and you have a clever team and a certain way that the boss is asking you to play. We were opening teams up just like that. And remember, Highbury was not a big pitch. To do that at Highbury was not easy at all. People said: "It's easy, they're not defending," and I'd say [*deadpan sarcastic face*]: "Yeah, I know – but we are moving."'

As Arsene Wenger explains: 'The football I like is of a high technical level, based on movement and on team play with a build-up from the back. Why do I like that? Because I just think the game is created to give everybody a chance to express what it is in him, and not to be just a servant for everybody else.' To Wenger, that's the moral difference with defensive football. 'What brings you to the game is the pleasure to play. And just because you are professional doesn't mean you should get away from that pleasure of playing. It's all just based on the positive philosophy of the human being and the right to express who you are.'

Wenger prefers a musical metaphor. 'For me, football is an orchestra. The more they are inspired by the same music, the more they have a chance to play a good song. The players are all professionals. They know how to play Mozart. They know how to play Verdi. Intelligence, sensitivity and guidance from outside are also important because I am like a conductor.'

The team's golden age ran roughly from 2001 to late 2004. Bob Wilson still marvels at the wonder of having Dennis Bergkamp and Thierry Henry in the same side. 'I still think we will not see anything like that unbeaten season again in my lifetime and I don't think that team has ever received the recognition they deserve. It was nearly the perfect club side, the perfect jigsaw. Both Dennis and Thierry were extraordinary footballers and at the same time you had wonderful defensive players in the team as well. It wasn't just one player who would make a big difference but several. You had Vieira, you had Bergkamp, you had Henry, you had Pires ... In any normal era, Pires would have been the superstar. It was absolutely amazing.' The team won the League and Cup double in

2002, the FA Cup in 2003, the League again without losing a match in 2004, and extended their unbeaten run to a record 49 matches in October 2004. Only the Champions League eluded them.

The rhythm of the team's famously deadly counter-attacking was rehearsed at London Colney. With mannequins standing in for defenders, the team practised moving the ball from one end of the field to the other within seven or eight seconds. As with the Henry–Bergkamp breakout from a Spurs corner which led to Patrick Vieira's goal in the championship-deciding game at White Hart Lane in 2004, the results were often spectacular. Mostly, though, Arsenal just attacked and improvised. Thierry: 'If you arrived late at Highbury – ten or thirty minutes late – then you had a problem because we were already three-nil up. Before you step on the field you have that feeling you are going to be two-nil up in ten minutes. You start to talk before the game about *how* you're going to score, and *when* you're going to score. Even if you were playing Man United, still you had the feeling you're going to score. To have the feeling that you will win by two, or three ... it's *weird*. You don't fully appreciate it at the time, but I do remember we said to each other: "I hope people realise what we are doing." We knew we were doing something special. It was the same feeling at Barcelona later. You'd look at the ref like: "Please don't blow the whistle! Can't we have another minute? Can't we just have another *twenty* minutes?" It's the beauty of mastering something. You see in the eyes of the opponent they are accepting it. And you're not just grinding out results. You're playing the right way and making opponents give up. You don't force it. You don't bully anyone. Your team is just playing well and doing what you're supposed to do. You see the other team thinking: "OK, you won, whatever, please stop now ... " We didn't win the trophies Man United did, but we won some. And the biggest trophy for me was when people were stopping me in the street when I was in Italy or France or Spain and saying: "I don't like Arsenal, but you guys could play!" I'm a competitor and usually the only thing that matters is to win. But that was the exception to the rule.'

Arsene Wenger's preference for his players – especially attackers – to be under 30 is well-known: 'At some stage I doubt the players,' he explains. 'I had always the same respect and admiration for Dennis, and he never let it drop, his focus. Of course, when you get older, thirty-four, thirty-five, thirty-six, up front it's more difficult. The capacity to win a decisive fight diminishes. But he adapted remarkably well to his evolution. He didn't drop too much physically in his quantity of work. And because he had exceptional vision, he still served the team by the quality of his passing.'

As Dennis headed towards his mid-thirties, rumours of his impending retirement became a feature of every summer. Yet he defied expectations and played on, signing yearly contracts. By the time his testimonial game became the inaugural match at the brand new Emirates Stadium in 2006, Dennis was 37 years old. But he had almost left before the 2003-04 season – which is to say that the Invincibles almost never happened. Arsenal's offer in the summer of 2003 was less than half his existing contract. Dennis felt insulted and, for the only time in his career, authorised his agent Rob Jansen to place a story in the press about the situation. Embarrassed, David Dein rectified matters within a day and Dennis reported for pre-season training.

The team almost failed to become the Invincibles for another reason, too. Thierry: 'I remember we clinched the title at the Lane and the boss said we could go the whole season unbeaten and we really weren't very interested. I think we had four or five games to go. The boss had been in the game a long time and he understood. He's going: "Come on guys! To go the whole season unbeaten! No one has done that in history." We were like: "Whatever. Come on, man, we've just won the league." Going unbeaten sounded OK, but it was more like: "If it happens, it happens." When we won the

Double in 2002, we didn't lose any of our away games. That's also not bad. People forget about that. And then the following season Arsene came up with the idea and said: "This team can stay unbeaten." Why would you say that and try to provoke everybody? But that's Arsene. He wasn't trying to provoke anyone. He was just saying what he thought.

'After we'd won the title in 2004, it's not that we wanted to take it easy. I use the analogy of the boxer. The boxer will never go another fight for fun. In the next games you have nothing to lose because you're already champions. So you're thinking: "If that guy makes his run, I don't have to cover because even if we concede a goal, even if we lose the game it doesn't matter because we're champions. Even the fans won't care." Our next game was Birmingham at home and it was shocking! It was one of the worst games we ever played at Highbury. No one was running. Nothing. Not even an opportunity. And then we went to Portsmouth and we were one-nil down at half time and we all had a go at each other and decided: "OK, let's play for this now." And we ended up going unbeaten for the season and everyone still talks about that side. But it's crazy how you don't think about it at the time. I also had the opportunity to play with that great Barcelona team, and with the great French team, and we didn't think about it either. You don't think you're making history. OK, when you win the World Cup and lift the trophy it's obvious. But at Arsenal we never talked about it. We never said: "Oh man, can you believe we're still unbeaten?" And the following season I'll always remember when we passed Nottingham Forest's record of forty-two games unbeaten. But we nearly blew it against Middlesbrough: three-one down with twenty-seven minutes to go at Highbury and we won five-three.'

How important was Dennis for the Invincibles?

'Very important. The way he was on the field, the way he conducted himself, the way he approached the game, the way he was brainy ... His vision, the way he used to see the play three or four seconds before anyone .... I think even in the dressing room he could see the play! We were so lucky to have that man in the team. I'm not talking about age but about guts. What I liked about him all through that [later] period was his attitude. Whenever he had to step off the bench and make the difference, he made the difference. He could have gone: "I'm not playing. I'll try to score when I come on but I won't do more ... " But do you know how many times we played him as a holding midfielder? Or on the right? The guy was defending! Tackling! Trying to score! Dennis Bergkamp at thirty-five! That's why Dennis was The Man at Arsenal. He has ten minutes at the end of the game to make a difference and you see him coming on with the right attitude. That's why I say: "Yes! He was so important for that and everything else. When I saw Dennis Bergkamp on the field, tackling someone ...'

By the early noughties you're the main goal-scorer, a lot of the movement goes through you ... yet you are led by Dennis?

'And even more so when you see his eyes. He wants to kill someone – in a good way! That's Dennis. That's why I love him. He would come on the field with ten minutes to go and you see him playing so *hard*. You see his commitment, and his desire and the love of the game that he has. When he came on the field even for one second he would try to do something that would win the game. Really, he was our example. He didn't need to talk. He was a huge factor in that team. Accepting the fact that you will play less and understanding it, and embracing it, and doing more than that! *Doing more than a kid would do*?! That was magnificent for me. It was just an honour and a privilege to play with him.'

* * *

MANY PEOPLE LOVED the Invincibles but when Bruce Rioch says it's his football ideal, it seems especially touching.

Bruce got quite emotional about the Invincibles. He said: 'That was beauty! It was ballet! Art! They could play the opposition any way they wanted. As a player, do you enjoy playing in that team? As a manager, do you enjoy watching that team play? As a supporter of any team, do you enjoy watching that team play? Of course! Of course!' What do you reckon?

Dennis: 'Well, it's true. And it's nice from Bruce. He's a good guy and has no regrets and doesn't hold anything against anyone. And he's right. I saw a quote from myself from that time where I said something like we were rewriting football. I think that's true, too. What Arsene said about me trying to reach perfection was true for the whole team at that time. We were really close to perfection. Of course, you had some silly games where you can't kick a ball, but most of the time we were just unbelievable, really close to the way I think football should be played.

'Thierry mentioned that feeling of going onto the pitch knowing you are going to win. Yes, that's what it was like. You don't know by how many goals, and you don't know when you're going to score, but you know you are going to win. You have to take that from me and from Thierry, but it's an unbelievable feeling. Like running in the hundred metres and you're Usain Bolt. That's something unbelievable for a sportsman. It's what you try to aim for. Perfection. And that's what we had in those years. You knew you were the best team in the league and everyone was smiling and everyone was happy and everyone had a contribution to make ... It was fantastic. You knew exactly where to put the ball. You knew exactly what kind of run the other players would make for you, because you knew what they were thinking. It's really interesting within a team. At the time you just experience it. But when you look back ... it was an amazing period. Amazing performances. It's funny to me how Thierry remembers all the details. I look back and it seems it was a very short time between me arriving at Arsenal and the team starting to have success. In fact, it was about two and

a half or three years, but in my mind it was like half a season. Then
we had success. Then it slows down a bit. Then you come to that
period where it really flows, and you stay at a certain level and set
yourself different standards.'

Can you compare the Invincibles to other teams you played in or saw?

'Everyone talks about the Dutch team in 1998 and 2000, which
played really good football. If you look at other teams, then of
course you come to that AC Milan team but in my opinion the team
that stands out is the Barcelona of Guardiola. When they beat Man
United [in the 2009 Champions League final] ... I mean that was
just from a different planet, with all the movement, the one and
two touches, and one player, Messi, who just made a difference
every single time he was allowed to make a difference ... That was
football that all other teams had to live up to. They set the standard
and other teams start brainstorming and thinking what can they do
about it.'

All teams with Dutch roots – or is that just my obsession?

'I don't think so. Lots of people really love Dutch football. You
look at Sacchi's Milan and Guardiola's Barcelona. Is it a coincidence? Then you ask the captain of France who his favourite
player is and Patrick Vieira says Frank Rijkaard. Thierry Henry
says Van Basten. Arsene Wenger: "I love Dutch football." All those
teams that made a difference played in a different way and got the
admiration of a lot of people, but they all had roots in Dutch
football. At the same time, it's interesting to see where the Dutch
influence ends. At Arsenal, where does the Dutch bit end and the
French bit start? At Milan, where does the Dutch bit end and the
Italian begin? And Spain ... For me, there are lots of great teams,
but they don't all rewrite football. Of course, Manchester United
was a big team, but what did they do different to what other teams
had done before? The Liverpool I remember was the late eighties
team of John Barnes. Other Liverpool teams won more trophies,

but that John Barnes team played the most fantastic football. They could pass the ball all day long. Other Arsenal teams played some good football and won trophies. But who are the teams that play football that stays in your mind? Then you come to teams like AC Milan and you think: "Wait a minute, they really changed the game."'

There's an argument among Arsenal fans as to which of the two of you was the better. Thierry is very generous and says you were the Master, it was always your team and so on. How did you see it?

'The easy way, of course, would be to say Thierry was the bigger player. We've got so much respect for each other that we would say that about each other. But look at the things Thierry achieved at Arsenal. In a short time, he became the main goal-scorer and won trophies. His pace and goal-scoring were *unbelievable*. And he always had such drive. People talk about my drive, but look at his. In training he made others look silly. I always felt Thierry had a point to prove in every game, in every training session, which was quite similar to me, though I did it in a different way . . .'

Like you, he came to Arsenal after being insufficiently appreciated in Italy. When he heard Juventus planned to move him to Udinese on loan as part of a deal for another player Thierry told Luciano Moggi [the Juventus general manager later sentenced to jail for corruption]: 'I am not a piece of meat' and as he's leaving the room he turns round and says: 'And by the way, I'm not playing for the team again, and when I leave I want to go to Arsenal.' That night he flew to Paris, by coincidence met Arsene on the plane and told him he wanted to come to Arsenal.

'Meeting Arsene on a plane doesn't sound like me! But, yeah, it was a little similar at the beginning of Thierry's time at Arsenal. You didn't really see his potential. Then he scored his first goal against Southampton. And when he changed position and got comfortable in the team and was happy . . . *wow*! He really made a difference.'

I remember you saying Patrick Vieira was remarkably like his hero

Frank Rijkaard as a player and a person. How would Thierry compare to Marco van Basten?

'Totally different. Thierry had more pace and more skills, more fire, he was more explosive. Marco was more the out-and-out striker who could finish teams, finish games, finish defenders ... he could finish their careers! He was operating in a certain area of the pitch, whereas Thierry needed more space and could come from all angles. And that's just talking about football. Their characters are totally different as well. Thierry is really down to earth outside football. Thierry is saying I'm the biggest player at Arsenal, I'm saying the opposite ... You know at one stage people were comparing me to Van Basten? It's really not fair to compare because each player is unique, but if you look at the best players over the last thirty years they would both be there near the very top, definitely. The goal-scoring, the finishing ... at big clubs, at big moments.'

Thierry described his freezing technique.

'What?'

This is what he said: 'Most strikers control the ball then finish. The great strikers know how to pause. You control the ball – then you pause – then you finish. Sometimes you saw me finish fast because I had to do it that way. But when I can I take my time, I advance ... I look at the keeper ... and then I try to finish. I'm not looking at the ball. I know where it is. Actually, there are two ways of doing it. You can finish like Romario. He always waits for the keeper to jump, then finishes while he is jumping. With Romario, you always saw the goalkeeper caught in mid-air. That's one way. Or you can do what I would do and what Dennis would do. Control it. And when the goalkeeper makes the motion of coming out to you ... that's when you pause. And when you pause you look at the goalkeeper. And he freezes. *You've got to freeze him*. It doesn't have to be too long. But you have to freeze the goalkeeper. Let's say he wants to rush at you. If you're looking down at the ball, he'll rush at you and you won't even see him. That's why you have to look at him. So ... control ... put your head up ... and freeze him by looking at him.

'You know that game, what do you call it? Grandmother's footsteps? Where you creep up behind the guy but you have to stop when he looks at you? It's like that with goalkeepers. It's the same when I dribble past someone. And Robert Pires was the master of doing it. Control the ball, look at the guy ... and push it! But you know how hard that is? If you let the defender have the momentum to run with you, he will run with you! So you stop. Like Chris Waddle! And go. *Stop* ... and *go*! You know how hard it is to start again when you stop ... but you've got to *freeze* the goalkeeper or the defender. Freeze him! Dennis understands this. He has it, too. Dennis knows you've got to toy with them a bit. He used to love to toy with goalkeepers. For me it's very important. When you don't look at the goalkeeper, they can sometimes read where you're going to put it. But if you break his momentum ... sometimes the finish doesn't even have to be that great. Freeze him! It doesn't matter who the goalkeeper is. It works with everybody. With Dennis, you can see everything he does is what he meant to do. If he needs to touch it three times, he touches it three times. I love it when a striker scores a goal and you can see right from the start that's what he meant. A lot of Dennis's goals are like that.'

Thierry said you froze opponents, too.

Dennis: 'That's fantastic because I had the same feeling and I try to explain it to the players I teach, but ... I'm going to use that now! We say "stabilise yourself in front of goal, be calm, hesitate for a split second ... ," but the way Thierry puts it – *freeze the goalkeeper* – yeah! I like that.

Didn't you ever talk about that sort of thing?

'You don't. Every day you are on the training pitch and when you've finished your career you talk about other players and how they were, and what they're doing now. Every now and then a player might mention something in an interview but most of the time you are just doing your thing. You're not going to sit down and tell each other: "This is what I think of you!"'

Is that just part of a footballer's code?

'It's more that football goes so quickly. Everyone is focusing on the next game, or the next training session, so there's just no time. You're not going to sit down and *commend* each other for an hour or so. It's not done!'

I guess you do the opposite? Jokes all the time . . .?

'You do that. But a little nod or a little smile is enough to realise what you think of each other. If I gave a great pass from midfield to Freddie or whoever, Thierry would look at me in a split second and I would know that he acknowledged how good the pass was. You don't really need words: maybe just a nod, or a little smile or just eye contact.'

Bob Wilson said that in another era Robert Pires would have been the superstar.

'Robert was a big player, a great player and his role suited him fantastically. But I felt the fact that there were other technical, intelligent players around him helped him to reach his full potential. He could really destroy teams with his runs, his passing, his intelligent football and goal-scoring. Yeah, he was a fantastic player.'

How was it that squad players could play so well – like in that game at Leeds?

'I always feel that any club in the Premier League can make a good first eleven. But it's all about the numbers 12 to 16, and 12 to 21 in the Champions League. It's all about how they get pushed in training. If your first eleven is training at the highest level, the squad players will get to a higher level. If someone needs to be replaced, will the team still play at the same high level? It's always a puzzle for the manager. But I felt in those years guys like Luzhny or Jeffers weren't first-eleven players, but they could play in the team because every day in training they were forced to play at that high level. That is so important. To achieve that is the main focus for the manager all the time. Arsene said it right. The team is always about five or six main players. Then it depends on your weakest link. If he's good enough to keep up with the five or six players in your team, well, then you're happy. But when you're annoyed or scared that one player will cause the level to drop, then you've got a problem. The more players you have who can make a difference, the better chance you have that the other players will get to a higher level.

'But it's also about what Arsene said about respecting the game. You don't need one or two big players and all the attention goes on them, because maybe ten or fifteen games a season they will decide the game, but they won't win you the league. The league will be won by a team that has players who can make the difference but who also respect the lesser players and therefore the lesser players respect them. That is so important.'

In retrospect it seems even stranger than it did at the time that you never won the Champions League. People blame playing home games at Wembley in the first two years.

'Some of our defenders hated Wembley, because it was a bigger pitch so they had to defend more space. But as a striker you've got more space so I always really enjoyed it, and I liked the atmosphere with seventy thousand people for every game. But as a team I felt we weren't really ready. If we'd have played there a few years later we would have destroyed teams. I mean, can you imagine what Thierry, with his pace, or Freddie, or Robert would have done at Wembley?'

Thierry blamed the fixture pile-up for what happened in 2004. You had to play Liverpool in the league, Man United in the FA Cup semi and the two Champions League legs against Chelsea ... all in eight days. Your legs

were bound to go at some point and it happened in the second half of the
second leg against Chelsea. He says the FA should have moved the Man U
game.

'That season we thought: "OK, now we are ready to win the
Champions League." I felt we had a great team then and if we
could have got through that quarter-final we would have gone all
the way. But we had it so many times: you come to a certain period
when you have one or two weeks with a quarter-final of this, a semi-
final of that and a key game in the league. And you have to use your
biggest players. If those players are tired from earlier in the season,
or from international duty, you know you'll struggle. It's no
excuse ... at that level it happens.'

There's a bit of a debate about how significant your absence in some
Champions League matches might have been. Sol, Patrick and Thierry all
stressed that they respected your non-flying, but thought Arsenal could have
won the competition if you'd played in every game.

'Well, you never know, but I don't believe in a one-man team.'

You were a big part of that team.

'Yes, but in the beginning, when I was at my peak, I went by car
to some games, like Fiorentina and Barcelona. You just never know.
Still. I'm not convinced if I would have made a difference away
from home in difficult games. I mean, that would be putting
Thierry Henry down, for example. In his peak time. He did rather
well at Real Madrid and Inter – the five-one. I played in the home
game when we lost.'

So you play and Arsenal lose 0-3. You miss the game and Arsenal win
5-1?

'Yeah! So you just never know. I really can't tell.'

But you look sad.

'Well, that's the sad thing about football. If you miss games. I've
said it many times. You can miss games through injury and you can
miss games through suspension. It's a sad thing. On the other hand,

I was coming towards an age when it was very difficult to play three games a week at the highest pace. The club was OK with that. I was OK with it. I could play the weekend, take the week off then play the following weekend.'

That was the pattern from about 2002 onwards?

'I would think so.'

You played most of the second Double season?

'I think so. Only when I was thirty-two or thirty-three ... then it starts going down a bit. I start ... not exactly picking my games but ...'

You're not the first name on the team sheet any more?

'It was the first time that it happened. Usually Kanu would play in my position, but I don't really have it clear in my memory. Kanu or Wiltord, those sorts of players ... But it also went parallel with my going from being a striker and goal-scorer to being an "assistant". That was already happening with Ian Wright, of course, and with Nicolas Anelka: sometimes I would just remain back a bit and they would be the goal-scorer. I always played like that. I don't think I was ever top scorer in England and towards the end of my career my position changed a bit more and it suited me. My pace wasn't really important in that role, though sometimes I showed it and people were surprised. I scored from the halfway line at Leicester. I think it was a sprint with Matty Upson and I flipped it over the goalkeeper. "Look at his pace!" But I wasn't usually in that position. It looked like my pace had dropped, but it was because I was playing in a different way rather than because I was getting older. Well, it was both.'

By the 2005 Cup final your pace seemed to have gone ... that game where Thierry was injured so you were on your own up front. It was a strange game with Arsenal defending most of the match and winning on penalties ...

'It was a very weird game. But I still had my pace for sure. But in short bursts rather than all through the game. Thierry was so quick he made me look slow. But my pace of controlling the ball, passing and so on ... that was always faster than my running.'

I asked Arsene about how you adapted in your last years and he said you never let your focus drop but you found it more difficult.

'I think the club was searching to find the next step. They thought: "We've had this great team, but Dennis is coming to a certain age and Thierry is becoming the main man and it's not the philosophy of Arsene to have a main man, because when everything goes through one player you're vulnerable ... " So they had a problem. And at that time a lot of the old English players had left and I wasn't young enough to guide the new players ... So they thought I'd have a big influence of course in the dressing room. But they were worried: how would I react to playing less? I think those were the questions.'

Didn't they discuss it all with you? You'd think the obvious thing would be for Wenger to sit down with you and say, 'How do you see it going ...?'

'That's funny in football. I mean, nobody does that! And of course I'm too proud to just say: "Well, let me just play twenty games, I'll be happy with that." I can't do that! So that was the clash. I wanted to play every game, of course. And if I didn't play I was angry with [Wenger] until I played and then it was OK. Sometimes we really fell out with each other. He used statistics on me and one time I said to him: "Where in your statistics does it say that I changed the game with a killer pass?" And he'd say: "You run less in the last thirty minutes and you're more at risk of getting injured, and your pace is dropping." That was his thing: "You're dropping pace." Which I was. No problem. But then again I'm the one who can make a difference for you so ... And sometimes we fell out about that and he would say: "You only think of yourself." So I was the bad one!' [*laughs*]

Would voices be raised?

'Not many times but it did happen. But with respect: no swearing or name-calling. It would happen on the field when he told me I wasn't playing. Even later, when I was thirty-five or thirty-six, he would say: "Do you still want to come to the game? Do you want to be on the bench?" And he'd leave the decision to me. And most of the time, of course, I'd say: "I want to be on the bench." I don't know what he was thinking. Was it like: "I'd rather not have you there" or "I've got so much respect for you?" Of course I knew when I was thirty-five or thirty-six that I couldn't play every game. But within yourself you think you can.'

And you didn't want to come on for just twenty minutes?

'Well, in the end I wouldn't mind. If I was on the bench anyway I wanted to come on. But to be fair I think most of the time, if his decision wasn't obvious, he would tell me what he would do. So the respect was there. The arguments we had were only about those sorts of football-related things. Me playing or not playing. It was very childish [*laughs*], but it came from the heart ... from both of us.'

So by that time Jose Antonio Reyes would be ahead of you?

'Yeah.'

Which now seems a bit weird.

'Yeah.'

And who else would play instead of you?

'When we had Kanu, Wiltord, Henry and me, it was four strikers for two positions and it was all about rotating systems coming into football. "You can't play every game," and all that sort of bullshit. And later it was Adebayor and Reyes ... Yeah, that was a strange time but for me, it was like: "OK, I understand. I respect your decision, boss. But, come on, it's *me*. I can do something for you, I can make a difference." Sometimes, if the game was too chaotic he would put me on for the last twenty minutes to control the pace of the game, keep the ball, get a passing rhythm going again. It was kind of:

"Give the ball to Dennis and we can relax a little bit and get into position," because a lot of players would lose the ball too quickly. I didn't mind because I was playing and I was still important but in a different role. I think this would be my last two or three years at Arsenal. By that time Arsene would say: "I don't see you as a first-team player any more. Of course you're important for the team – what do you want to do?" Then I mentioned I would like to go one more year, finish at Highbury, which has of course been my home for eleven years, and do it like that. Largely, I accepted my role. No worries.'

No raging against the dying of the light?

'No, it was acceptable, although it was disappointing at the end of course with the Champions League.'

The Champions League final against Barcelona in Paris in 2006. It could have been the most fantastic swansong. Then Jens Lehmann gets sent off, Arsenal are down to ten men, Sol scores, you almost hang on to the lead, but in the end they score those two late goals, and you never got a chance to come on ...

'Arsene was disappointed as well. I think he had a different scenario in his head.'

Like you're 3-0 up, with ten minutes to go, and you come on for a last bit of glory ...

'Something like that. Or even two-nil down. You know, just to give me those minutes in the final. We had that sort of relationship in the end. It was somehow ... You're building up and building up and getting all the trophies and getting personal success and in the end you get to the Champions League final at last. "Jeez! If only I'd been five years younger!" But that was probably the most we could have hoped for. The team wasn't what it had been two years earlier. We weren't the favourites. We could have won, though, I wish there was something more in it, but .... we were happy with that. And I was happy with that moment.'

20

THE GOLFER

RAY PARLOUR REMEMBERS taking Dennis for his first game of golf in England. 'We used to play every Wednesday and Dennis said: "Mind if I come?" and we said, "No, Dennis! Of course you can! No problem at all." We weren't very good ourselves at the time, so we're a bit worried. We're thinking, he must be good, he's good at everything. Anyway, we're all sitting by the tee, about five to two and Dennis pulls up in his car, and gets out looking *immaculate*. He had all the proper gear and we're all like, "Oh my God, he's going to be so good." He comes up to the tee, and we say: "Dennis, you play first, you're our guest today." So we're looking down the fairway. It's about a mile. Dennis gets his big club out and as he swings, we're all like this [shielding eyes against the sun, peering into the far distance] … "Where's it gone?" … "I dunno" … "Did you see it?" All of a sudden Dennis says: "You see that bush there …" So we're all looking for his ball. Next thing he's on the green, putting for thirteen – and he writes it down! "*Thirteen* …" Next hole, nine. Next hole, twelve. It's getting dark! Oh my God, he was really bad! He shot a hundred and eighty-odd. We were like: "How are you at darts, Dennis?" He shook all our hands, and said, "I really enjoyed that, lads." We didn't! He was losing balls all over the place!

'The following week he comes out, and he's getting better. This is the sort of man he is. He kept every single card, and he was improving every week, by five, six, seven, eight shots. I think his wife played a little bit as well, and he started having lessons. He didn't tell us he was having lessons. And all of a sudden he got the hang of it. He just started picking it up. He began getting his score down to just over a hundred, then under a hundred. You could see the swing was getting better. It's just a game, very similar to football, and he worked hard. He had the eye-hand coordination. He loved golf and knew he could crack it. We used to go every week after training, and you could see him improving. I hate to think what his handicap is now. With Dennis I think anything he'd do in sport, it would be similar. If he enjoyed the sport, he'd make sure to become good at it. That's the sort of character he was in football. He made sure he'd be a top-class player.'

Vic Akers recalls the only time he ever saw Dennis flustered. 'We used to go and play golf together regularly and on one occasion we went to Woburn. Ian Poulter was there. He's an Arsenal fanatic so there was Dennis, Ray, myself, and my son, Paul. We were the last full group going out, and Poulter says: "I'll come out with you. I'll play one hole with you." Poulter had all these pros with him on the tee, just behind us. And Dennis goes: "I've never been so nervous. This is worse than playing in front of seventy or eighty thousand people." It's because he wants to be good at everything. He doesn't want to be a duffer, you know? And this fantastic professional golfer is watching him. Fortunately, we all got decent shots off the tee, and we were mighty relieved, but I've never seen Dennis in that sort of state before. He was unbelievable. He'd turn up immaculate every time we went out to golf. He'd turn up with the golf balls immaculate. Everything he did would be professional. Like for training. From the minute he walked in the building, to when he started putting his kit on, to the minute he changed and went home, everything was perfectly in order. *Everything.* He knew exactly the way he wanted to approach the day. Attention to detail in everything. Not as a sort of obsessive compulsive, but because he wants to be the best. And it *never* changed. He wanted to achieve the best, and the way he was rubbed off on everyone else.'

* * *

DENNIS RECALLS: 'There was a golf club next to my house at Hadley Wood, but when I first started living there I couldn't get in. I said: "OK, cool, but I really like golf and I would like to be a member." Then I asked Arsenal and I think they wrote a letter, but I didn't get in until my last few years in England.'

Ken Friar says they probably didn't like the idea of a footballer at the golf club. They thought footballers were loud and drunk and would urinate on the greens or something. He said he had to pull some strings to get you in.

'I didn't know about it. I mean, I could understand they had their reservations but it was a nightmare. You had to be nominated by *nine* members of the club. Then you had to go for an interview. It was really something else. I just want to play golf! And there's this fantastic club right next door! Finally, I started playing with some dads from school who were members and after that it went quite easily to being a member.'

Are Ray and Vic's stories accurate?

'Ha ha! I don't remember exactly like Ray tells it, but his version is better. It's true I always wanted to look good and in the beginning I couldn't hit the ball. I mean I could hit the ball but not like they could. But I was motivated. I really enjoyed the game, and I started working on it. Of course, I'd played a little in Holland, and my wife likes golf as well, so we played a few times in Italy. They have some good courses. But I didn't play enough to really improve. Then I got to England. I remember going to Scotland pre-season one year. Most of the team flew and I went on the bus with Paul Merson and the bus was full of golf bags from all the players. What's going on here? They all liked golf! Whenever they had a free morning, they'd play one or two rounds. It was just a matter of taking the first step, but it was difficult because I heard them talking: this one had a handicap of two, that one a handicap of four, and I'm still playing off thirty-six!

'Slowly I improved. I played a lot of times with Ray Parlour and Ray knew Ian Poulter. We went sometimes to Woburn as well and I just loved those courses where every hole is a new challenge, especially those bigger courses when you're off the green. You go through a pathway to the next hole and it's totally different, and they change the position of the pin every week. I just love that! I don't know if it's being in nature, or the challenge, or the fact that you can never have a perfect game. You're playing against yourself. You're playing a little bit against the elements, but it's got a whole mystique . . .'

It seems to be a very spiritual game. The novelist Anne Kinsman Fisher wrote a book called The Masters of the Spirit *where old golf champions teach life lessons. It's a game where you're competing against yourself and striving for perfection all the time.*

'Right! I'm at a really low level but you find sometimes that you've got five or six holes where you really are in some sort of zone, where everything works and you can find the concentration to hit every ball right. Then you think: "I can play golf!" Then suddenly – *boom!* – it's gone, it's totally gone! I can have that in the middle of a round where I just completely miss-hit the ball. After so many rounds of golf you should be able to at least hit a ball, but then you just top it. Funnily enough, you see the professionals do it, too. Even Tiger Woods. The other day I saw him completely shank a shot. I really love the game. It's a challenge ... In the two years after my career when I was still in England, I played many rounds by myself t Hadley Wood. No caddy, just carrying the bag myself. All weathers. I'd play in the rain. I just loved being out there.'

There's a ball, but it's very different to a football. And there's no passing, and no team-mates ...

'Yes. You're just trying to get the ball where you want to get it. And to do that is really interesting. So I'd watch a lot of golf on television, on Sky, and sometimes they would analyse a player's swing very closely. They're very good at that ... and they've got the images. They're very technical about it, so I'd watch and listen to them, then combine that with my own feelings ... and that's how I'd try to improve. And it works, of course. When you do something a lot of times, you definitely improve.'

So here's a game where nobody is paying you, no one is watching, and nobody knows anything about it. It's purely your passion – and it sounds like you're doing it rather in the same way you do football. Is that right?

'Yes, that's why I love to be out there by myself, just self-teaching, on the range. We have some ranges here in Holland and for the first time I took some lessons as well. And Ray was always funny. One day he said: "I know a course near Bedford. It's a new course and we'll play a round for charity." I said: "OK, I don't mind, but what kind of charity is it?" and he's like: "Oh don't worry, it's for my friend." So we arrive and there are about two hundred to two hundred and fifty people waiting for us! I said: "Wait a minute. I'm not that good yet." And Vic's there and Ray's already laughing. I think: "All these people are watching, so I'll take an iron and play safe." I was so nervous but it was quite a good shot. "I'm really glad that's over ..." Then that whole group of spectators starts following us down the course! Ray was just laughing all the way, going "Sorry, Dennis!" Fortunately, after a while the spectator group got smaller and smaller, because we really weren't interesting to watch if you love golf! By the end they'd all gone. But yes, I got really nervous'.

It's odd that you played football in front of tens of thousands of people in stadiums, and hundreds of millions more were watching on TV, and that was fine. But a few hundred people watch you doing something else and you go to pieces.

'It's so strange. When you go into someone else's arena you want to do well. That's just how I am. I want them to go home and tell everyone: "That Bergkamp, he can play golf." So I get nervous. It's not like I'm afraid to fail. I just want to do so well. I want to leave a good impression on people and therefore you raise the bar maybe far too high for yourself. You put yourself under pressure so people will say: "You know, I played with Tiger Woods, but Dennis Bergkamp could hit that shot even better ..." It's silly, but it's not an ego thing. I just want to do well. I want to be good.'

And you won't just put on a shabby tracksuit ...

'No! It has to be the full gear, to be perfect. Everything has to be right. The right pants, the right shoes ...'

I'm guessing that the actual movement and control of the ball fascinates you in the same way as the football fascinates you?

'The annoying thing for me is that I can hit a golf ball now, and I can make it do different things. But it's not *real* control. I *almost* know how to do it, but I don't *really* know. Like I can sort of get the ball to move from right to left, but it's not quite there yet. And I've got backspin a few times, but I don't know how I did it. It's so frustrating! With a football I know every shot, everything. So I keep coming back to the golf course, I keep trying ...'

How is it with tennis?

'Similar. My agent organises a tournament every year where it's golf, tennis, poker or whatever, and one time it was tennis and we played in the doubles final, Marc Overmars and me, against two other players. And there were ex-pros sitting on the sidelines watching us, like Jacco Eltingh and Paul Haarhuis, a fantastic doubles team who won a lot of Grand Slams. Again you've got the feeling: "OK, I want to really impress them!" But of course tennis is easier than golf.'

Why?

'With tennis, you can put some things from football in there. You're working with your body and with your shape. You can use your pace, you can use your little skills. Whereas golf is so internal. One swing. Just ... *boom!* And that has to be perfect because a millimetre wrong on the ball is fifty yards wrong on the course. It's interesting.'

Are there ideal shots in your mind? Do you dream of a hole in one?

'No, nothing like that. And I don't think about putting either. It's more about depth. You see the shot, then you hit it and it just takes off exactly as you want, and it goes there. It's not like, "Oh, I need an eagle or a birdie." Not at all. It's more like: "I enjoy that approach. I want it to be the perfect approach."'

It sounds like the way you thought about the perfect pass and the assist in football.

'Could be ...'

Because somewhere deep in your soul you're always searching for the same thing?

'It looks like it, doesn't it?'

THE FUTURE OF THE FUTURE

AFTER RETIRING FROM Arsenal in the summer of 2006 Dennis played golf, relaxed and spent time with the family. It was delightful. For a while. By late 2007 the man with a drive for perfection was getting bored. A few months later he and Henrita decided to take the family home to Holland where he enrolled on the Dutch FA's fast-track trainers' course for former top players. Part of the course was spent at Ajax when Marco van Basten was the coach.

Ajax had fallen a long way since winning the Champions League in 1995 and had ceased to be a European power. When Dennis returned to the club of his first great successes to become a coach to the Under-12s he was, in effect, joining a bucolic backwater. To the casual visitor, Ajax seemed cheerful and tranquil enough. But the stage was being set for one of the most bitter battles in all of Dutch football history. The conflict would pitch Dennis into unfamiliar emotional territory and prove to be another turning point in his football life.

The key figure – as so often – was Johan Cruyff who had, for years, been criticising Ajax, usually through his weekly column in Holland's biggest-selling newspaper, *De Telegraaf.* Cruyff's principal complaint, even in the mid-nineties, was that something had gone badly wrong with the club's youth system. At a time when Louis van Gaal's team of tyros was the best in Europe, this looked like sour grapes. Yes, he conceded, results looked good for now, but he had seen the younger teams and it was clear to him that a few years hence the flow of exceptional players would cease. As he never tired of saying later, Patrick Kluivert was Ajax's last great home-grown striker. Few people paid attention in the late nineties, but a decade later Cruyff's critique found a more receptive audience.

An outsider might be tempted to take a more relaxed view and see Ajax's decline as inevitable. The global football economy had changed so massively and so quickly that complaining about the failure to produce new Van Bastens and Bergkamps was like worrying why the city of Rembrandt now had so many graffiti artists. Due to forces beyond anyone's control, Ajax's football Golden Age had passed. In any case, there was still second-hand glory to be had. Seven of the 14 Dutchmen who played against Spain in Johannesburg in the 2010 World Cup final had started their careers at Ajax. Most clubs would take pride in having produced half a World Cup final team.

But Ajax was not most clubs. Even the directors were worried by the long decline and had commissioned a study, known as the Coronel Report, focusing on structural problems, which was to be presented at a members' meeting in February 2008. Few people ever read this report, because Johan Cruyff gate-crashed the meeting and pulled off a stunning coup. In style it recalled one of his most legendary exploits. In 1980, at a time when he had no formal link to the club, Cruyff was a spectator in the crowd watching as

Ajax trailed 3-1 at home in a Cup match against Twente. So angered was he by Ajax's performance that he walked out of the stadium, came back in through the players' entrance, made his way onto the touchline and sat himself down in the dugout. Having thoroughly upstaged coach Leo Beenhakker, Cruyff suggested a few changes – and Ajax promptly rallied to win 5-3. The TV cameras caught every moment of his intervention, and the match became a symbol of his near-superhuman footballing powers.

Now, in February 2008, Cruyff produced another game-changer: he turned up unannounced at the members' meeting. The crowds that greeted Ayatollah Khomeini when he arrived in Tehran from Paris in 1979 had nothing on the enthusiasm of the Ajax members that night. They acclaimed Cruyff ecstatically, and when they urged him to save the club, he graciously agreed. The power of the old board simply melted in his presence; it was the smoothest of velvet revolutions. Soon the chairman had resigned and Cruyff's candidate, Marco van Basten, was installed as coach. Just 17 days later, however, the revolution ended as suddenly as it had begun. Van Basten had declined to follow his mentor's advice to sack most of the youth academy staff. So Cruyff simply turned around and flew home to Barcelona, saying: 'Then I've got no more business at Ajax.' Wrongly, this turn of events was interpreted as a humiliation for Cruyff. In fact, he and Van Basten remained on good terms and the deeper significance was missed: Cruyff had revealed his extraordinary influence as club icon and fan favourite. As the new chairman Uri Coronel would later say bitterly: 'Cruyff is not just anyone. He's a demi-god here, or maybe a whole god.' By the time the old hero was ready to renew his assault in late 2010, conditions had changed once more. Van Basten's reign had failed: he left after less than a season, admitting: 'I can't live up to Ajax standards.' Cruyff was now free to direct his withering fire on yet another board-appointed coach of whom he disapproved, Martin Jol.

Meanwhile Dennis Bergkamp, from his vantage point as youth coach, had reluctantly come to a conclusion of his own: something had gone badly wrong with the club's youth system. He was dismayed by the prevailing attitude: 'Things were really going downhill, but no one seemed to notice or perhaps they didn't want to see,' says Dennis. 'Everyone seemed to be saying: "Hey, we're Ajax, we're the best, look at 1995 when we won the Champions League." I thought: "What's all that about? Nineteen ninety-five is thirteen years ago."'

The club's youth teams were still good enough to win trophies, he noted, but the academy (immodestly called *De Toekomst* – The Future) had turned into a soccer version of Stepford. 'It was as if all the kids had been made in the same factory. It felt strange. They were all good, tidy, rather technical players, but they weren't special or flexible or creative. They did what was asked of them. They knew their positions, played their roles, but even in the first team they had so little creativity. When they had to improvise they'd look helplessly to the touchline as if to say: "Now what do we do?" All the teams played four-three-three the way you're supposed to at Ajax. But it was completely uninspired, totally lethargic. The right-winger kept nicely to the right wing and did all the little things a right-winger is supposed to do, like getting to the goal line and putting a cross in. The left-back played exactly like a left-back and the defensive midfielder played like an Ajax defensive midfielder. It was all by the book, but the heart was missing. I didn't see one of the typical old Ajax lads with that cheeky attitude: "Let me have the ball, I'll do something good with it."'

For Cruyff, meanwhile, Ajax's humiliating defeat at Real Madrid in September 2010 was the final straw. The score was only 2-0, but Ajax had managed just one shot on goal and Madrid could easily have scored ten. In the glory years, Ajax had measured their greatness by their crushing victories in the Bernabeu. In 1973, Gerrie

Muhren had juggled the ball there en route to Ajax winning their third European Cup in a row. In 1992, Dennis Bergkamp scored one of his great goals in the stadium. And when Van Gaal's team produced a sensational performance there in 1995, Real's poetic coach Jorge Valdano waxed lyrical: 'Ajax are not just the team of the nineties, they are approaching football utopia.'

The pathetic Ajax performance of September 2010 revealed how bad things had become. Cruyff had already spent months ridiculing Jol's counter-attacking style and his signing of expensive but mediocre foreign players and had said that the sight of overweight Egyptian striker Mido in an Ajax shirt made him feel physically ill. Now he stopped being polite. Jol's shambolic outfit was the worst Ajax team he had ever seen. Ajax was no longer Ajax. The manager and the board would have to go. Cruyff had an alternative plan.

Around that time, Dennis received a call from his old mentor. 'Johan thought it was time we caught up, and he invited Henrita and me to dinner. He wanted to know how I saw my future at Ajax. I told him I hadn't given it a lot of thought, that I would see how things developed. For the time being, I was just a rookie youth trainer. But Johan took a different perspective; he was thinking further ahead and began talking about a managerial role at the club, some kind of director's position as well as some practical work on the pitch. I listened to him talking about me, about Ajax, and I thought: "Hey, something's going on. Johan is up to something." It got me excited.' Cruyff was talking to other former players as well, preparing a cadre of ex-Ajax stars for an unprecedented revolution. His belief, nurtured over decades of battles with directors, presidents, chairmen and other 'suits', was that former top players knew far more about football than the grey men who ran the game. Great former players should therefore be in charge. Great former players like Dennis.

Cruyff's plan was now much more developed than it had been

during the off-the-cuff intervention of 2008. Urged on by his media allies, Ajax fans began chanting his name in the stadium. Jol's position was becoming untenable. One afternoon in December 2010, Dennis bumped into chairman Uri Coronel in the car park. Coronel said bleakly: 'Your manager has just been fired.' Dennis shrugged his shoulders. 'I just said: "OK," but I was thinking: "Now let's see what happens." Jol's departure set the wheels in motion. I had no idea that the next months would become a nightmare.'

Frank de Boer was appointed manager, with the approval of Cruyff, who was now working with the club in an 'advisory capacity'. But, as far as Cruyff was concerned this was just the first of many steps. He wanted to change the very DNA of the club. In April 2011 the Ajax board resigned, saying they found it impossible to work with Cruyff. A new, temporary board headed by a lawyer and psychologist called Steven ten Have took over. But Cruyff's campaign continued. He wanted his plan implemented in every particular.

The plan had taken physical shape in the form of a report written by members of a circle close to Cruyff and reflecting his ideas. The authors were Wim Jonk, Ruben Jongkind, an athletics trainer who specialised in improving performances and who had worked with Jonk on an experimental training programme, and Todd Beane, Cruyff's son-in-law, an American coach who had spent eight years developing the international dimension of Cruyff's football institute, which helps educate youngsters who want to build a career in sport – and prepares them for life afterwards. The report envisioned a root-and-branch transformation of the club through its youth. The old, Van Gaal-style focus on tactics, systems and teamwork would be swept away and replaced by a new intensive approach to developing extraordinary individuals. *De Toekomst* would become less like a football factory and more like a workshop for encouraging and educating genius: not so much a vocational

apprenticeship, more like an Oxbridge college or a French *Grande
Ecole*. The greatest of former Ajax players would become tutors,
imparting their knowledge, wisdom and experience to exceptional
young talents who would in turn become not only spectacularly
good footballers but wise beyond their years. The roles of technical director and head of training would be abolished and replaced
by a sort of revolutionary committee known as 'the technical heart'.
This would consist of manager Frank de Boer, Wim Jonk ... and
Dennis Bergkamp. A canny financial dimension was built into the
plan, too. The unplanned career paths of men like Cruyff, Van
Basten and Bergkamp would now be used as a prototype business
model. By educating their own junior players to first-team standards, Ajax would both save money and ensure a steady stream of
players for the first team. These players would be much better than
the mediocre foreigners the club had been buying. And later, the
young players and Ajax would share the financial rewards when the
stars were sold on to Europe's elite clubs after a few years in the
Ajax first team.

During the transitional year of 2011, the men Cruyff dubbed
'suits' balked at his radical ideas, offering instead small reforms and
concessions. The suits argued that anything else would cause tur-
moil and cost the jobs of cherished employees. Cruyff pushed on,
insisting on implementation of his *entire* revolutionary programme.
Civil war now raged, with bitter accusations, insults and rumours
flying around the club and in the media. Even the quarrelsome
Dutch had never seen anything quite like it.

Dennis recalls the strain: 'It was an awful period. I would come
home in the evening and say to my wife: "Riet, you don't want to
know what's going on over there. There is so much tension it's
frightening." Wim [Jonk] and I were the enemy at Ajax. We wanted
change and many people within Ajax didn't. They were comfortable in their positions and the only thing they wanted was to

remain comfortable. That's why they resisted us, tooth and nail. At *De Toekomst* the atmosphere was positively hostile. Conversations would stop when Wim and I approached. That's when you know they're talking about you. All sorts of things were going on behind our backs, but we soldiered on as best we could.'

For a while an uneasy balance held between the *ancien regime* and the revolutionaries. Then matters came unexpectedly to a head. Interim chief executive Martin Sturkenboom – hired without the knowledge of the Cruyffians – started handing out disciplinary warnings to his opponents. Wim Jonk received two and was in danger of being fired. Then Danny Blind (now in the anti-Cruyff camp, though the two had been close twenty years before) was appointed technical director. Then came an unmistakeable attempt at a counter-coup. Ajax's supreme body was now a five-person board of supervisors, including Cruyff. The other four members, including Ten Have and Edgar Davids, having blocked Cruyff's candidate for the crucial post of chief executive, now, in Cruyff's absence, offered the job to his arch-enemy Louis van Gaal. When he heard the news, the astonished Cruyff shouted: 'Are they out of their minds!?'

Dennis: 'The resistance was so intense and so provocative that we had to act forcefully. Johan felt obliged to hire a lawyer and ultimately we had no choice but to go to court. Cruyff hated the idea of litigating against his own club. But there was no alternative. At that point, all the former footballers closed ranks around Johan and we said: "We're in this together." At first the judge simply annulled Van Gaal's appointment. Unwisely, the club appealed and unintentionally invited the decisive blow. In February 2012, the Amsterdam Appeals Court ruled that four of the five members of the board had acted premeditatedly and unlawfully by going behind Cruyff's back to recruit Van Gaal. The board fell. Resistance was broken. The civil war was at an end.

During the conflict, Cruyff was depicted by much of the Dutch media as the bad guy – irresponsible, vengeful, gangsterish – and his collection of former players were accused of being stupid and incapable of running the club. Dennis emphatically refutes all this and describes – off the record and in eye-popping detail – some of the dirty tricks deployed against himself and other Cruyff supporters. He prefers not to speak publicly on the subject, but believes Cruyff's side of the argument, and that he and his supporters were the ones most sinned against. At the time of writing it is too early to tell how the Ajax revolution will turn out. But the club, revived and re-energised and again using mostly home-grown players – coached now in the new methods – have won three Dutch championships in a row, a feat that matches the great teams of the sixties and nineties. As at Inter and Arsenal, Dennis's modest, patient but steely pursuit of footballing excellence – the defining characteristic of his entire career – has made him an agent of radical change.

* * *

THE OLD GUARD at Ajax saw your side as the aggressors.

Dennis: 'The way I describe it was that Ajax had become the ninety-five Club'. They'd say: "We won the Champions League in ninety-five, and in ninety-six we were in the final." OK. Well done, but this is 2013 now, and you have to evolve, you have to move on. And they'd say: "But look, we're making one or two little changes, so we are evolving." And I'd say: "No, you're not evolving. You're really not. You're still doing the same, but instead of one hour a week training with kids, it's one and a half hours. That's not change. You need a *complete* change every year to keep evolving." That's what they didn't understand.'

You see what you're doing now as an advance on the old Ajax system, and on Barcelona's La Masia, which is based on the old Ajax system?

'The outcome hopefully will be better. Because since Wesley

Sneijder and Rafael van der Vaart we didn't have one truly exceptional player coming through to the first team. Not one player who'd spend three or four years in the Ajax first team, then go to the first team of Madrid or Milan or Man United. It's still good, but the standard has gone down a bit. They go to lesser teams now, and sometimes they don't even get a first-team position in those teams. It's not what it was. So we have to do something else because we want to be different, we want to be unique. The idea now is that we are trying to create complete, exceptional players.

'We'd run into a wall. Wim Jonk had started doing individual training already, working with Ruben Jongkind, and it was accepted – but only in a very limited way, with only three or four players. Wim would work intensively with these guys on, say, finishing or controlling the ball or passing. He was very excited about this. He was saying: "This is the way forward!" He wanted to take it further. But the club would say: "We don't do it like that because it's a team sport and that's not our way of thinking. Maybe someday in the future ..." These were guys who'd been in the Ajax Youth Development since just before 1995. They simply wouldn't change. It helped when Johan made a few comments, and the fans were unhappy, too, because they saw a lot of bad things on the pitch. Ajax wasn't recognisable as Ajax any more, the way we played. It had to change.'

People complain that Johan continues to live in Barcelona and leaves the club to guys like you and Frank de Boer and Jonk. They say Johan doesn't take responsibility.

'But he does take responsibility. He has always been interested in Ajax, and always spoken about it. I don't see that as not taking responsibility. He puts his opinion out there again and again. That is taking responsibility by itself. People attack him for it. But he really says things the way he sees them. How many people in the world are brave enough to say: "This is wrong, you have to do it differently and I know how to do it differently"? Holland is a small country, so how can we succeed? And how did we succeed in the past? We succeeded by bringing exceptional talent, exceptional football to the world. As you said, it becomes almost a religious thing, being the best the Dutch can be. It's our philosophy.

'I believe in what we're doing here. And I believe that we in Holland should stop worshipping The System. For years we've talked and taught too much only about tactics. When I went to Italy for two years and to England, for thirteen years – eleven years' playing – I experienced other ways of thinking and playing football and I was like: "This is interesting." So now I want to bring that here too, to Ajax.'

So you're a bit of a heretic?

'Ha ha! Well, the old thinking was too narrow. What I liked about the things I saw was that they were new, they added something. And what we are doing now with Ajax is new again. It's *totally* new. And we believe – and it started with Cruyff again – that in the future teams, clubs, countries will copy this. We will be in the forefront again.

'When Todd Beane first came to us he talked about the high jumper Dick Fosbury. Until Fosbury, every high jumper had always jumped forward. Then Fosbury jumped backwards. They said he was crazy. He was doing something totally new. "Is he out of his mind?" Now no one jumps forwards. That's a little bit like our philosophy. Everyone says: "What are you doing? It can't be done." Our idea is: don't think about teams any more, just think about individuals. It's a team sport, but you're going to make individuals better. It's all about developing the individual.

'The only team that needs to win trophies is the first team. The youth teams don't need to win, they just need to make their players better. So what does the *individual* need at a certain age? Should you talk tactics to a player before the age of fourteen? At that age it goes in one ear and out the other. It really doesn't mean anything. So we start with that now *after* fourteen. Before fourteen, it's just playful skills and everything. And we have new ways of measuring and developing those skills, and developing good habits, like controlling the ball, and passing and positions, and we're also thinking a lot about the mental side. So in the end you have not just a complete football player but a person who is good for others, who means something in the world. He's not just a stupid football player, but someone with a good story to tell, who is outgoing; someone who is genuinely interested in helping or changing the world, for example, not just interested in girls and cars. A more intelligent person so everyone says: "Yes, that's an Ajax player!" That's the philosophy.'

JOHAN CRUYFF IS also optimistic about the future – and about Dennis. In a cramped and paper-stuffed room at the offices of the Johan Cruyff Foundation at Amsterdam's renovated Olympic Stadium, he draws up two chairs opposite each other. The foundation helps youngsters and the disabled to play sports. Cruyff takes the initiative, as he did as a player and as a manager, hurtling off on tangents in answer to some questions, answering others that haven't been asked. His words slalom, dribble, turn and shoot. It's fascinating and boils down to the following: 1) Dennis Bergkamp is *incredibly* decent, both as a person and as a man of football; 2) Cruyff is *incredibly* proud that his club is now being run by a group of former top footballers. It even makes him emotional; and 3) Ajax is on the right road, but that road will be a very long one.

What is your working relationship with Dennis now? Do you tell him what to do? Is he, as the victims of the revolution say, your 'executioner'?

Cruyff: 'No, Bergkamp, Jonk and the others in the technical heart call me. To confer. I've warned them never to blindly implement anything I say. They should listen to me and then make their own decisions.'

And what if those decisions are not what you want?

'That doesn't happen. We're too much on the same page for that. Their decisions will never be very different from the way I think about things, because we think exactly the same way about the main principles.'

But they do have to listen to you?

'Yes, of course, just like they have to listen to other people at the club who want their opinion heard. In football, you're dealing with a dictatorship within a democracy. Initially, everyone gets to give their opinion, but subsequently the decision is taken by whoever's in charge. He's the dictator. And that's not me. I don't have any responsibilities, I don't have an official job. At Ajax the technical heart and the executive board are in charge of their own turf. They are the dictators, and they only have to listen to me, those dictators.'

Where will the revolution take Ajax?

'All the way to the top.'

Which is what?

'The last eight of the Champions League on a regular basis.'

Is that possible, given football's completely unequal financial playing field? Don't you need financial fair play first?

'No, not necessarily, because if you have the eleven best-trained footballers in Europe in your team you will automatically reach the European top.'

And will Ajax train their footballers better than anywhere else?

'Yes, of course, there's no better place in the world to be a young player than at Ajax. Who can you learn more from than from great footballers like Dennis Bergkamp, Frank and Ronald de Boer, Jaap Stam, Wim Jonk, Richard Witschge, and the list goes on? I'm proud of guys like that. They were written off as ignoramuses. We were supposedly the nitwits who were incapable of anything, but we won out in the end. In the global history of football what has happened at Ajax is unique. As a group of footballers, we stood up against an executive board and a board of directors. And we won. I'm proud of what happened, incredibly proud, so proud that it makes me very emotional. And all those guys are doing this because they want to, not because they desperately need jobs or anything like that. They're not doing it for themselves, but for football, and they all think the same way about it. There's now enormous football know-how at all levels of the club, including the highest levels, and that is going to generate progress.'

And what about Dennis?

'Dennis sees everything. He maintains connections and drives people. You could call him a Jack of all trades, but I prefer to call him the playmaker within the technical heart.'

Cruyff won't say it directly, but it's clear that Dennis is the main man at Ajax now. At least *his* main man. 'Dennis keeps things in balance, because he's in balance himself. You can't pressurise Dennis Bergkamp. No matter how loudly people around him shout, he always remains calm and thinks. And Dennis is able to think more broadly, so he sees connections. He's always on top of everything, and when he has to he can pressurise other people. Then he gives loud and clear instructions: "First this, then that." Dennis Bergkamp is a truly amiable man, until he gets angry. Then you see genuine anger, but also intelligence. Then his comments are incredibly incisive, even hurtful, but always well considered. So when someone like that becomes prominent within an organisation, maybe even the most prominent individual, it makes sense. It happens automatically.'

* * *

NOW THAT HE'S such an important part of the future of The Future, how does Dennis see his own? Lots of people at Arsenal

would love him back at the club. Some of the top brass there see
him as a future manager.

Dennis: 'I want to be good at what I do, I want to be important,
too, but I'm not after fame. It's not about that for me. That's why
I have no ambition to be a manager.'

*Is that because it would be impossible anyway because you won't fly and
a manager has to fly?*

'Regardless of that, I prefer working with small groups. Let me
train strikers specifically. That's when I'm at my best. Of course,
I have opinions about the team as a whole, about how it should
function, but I have much less of a tactical overview than trainers
like Frank de Boer and Hennie Spijkerman [the Ajax assistant
coach]. Frank was a defender and Hennie a goalkeeper; that background not only gave them tactical insight, but also an overview.
I only have the insight. I'm still working on the overview. I played
at the front, or almost at the front. I always stood in a diagonal position so I could never see the entire pitch. They know how to
intervene tactically the moment the match requires it. Not me. I
need to see it all on the board first: where is everyone positioned
and what needs to change? How? I'm learning and improving, but
my ambition is not in the area of tactics. The greatest challenge for
me is improving footballers, especially strikers.'

That means working in other people's shadows.

'So much the better. I'm not attracted to the limelight, and I
certainly don't want to become the front man. That's not how I see
myself. As a player I also never saw myself as the face of Arsenal or
anything like that. Sure, as a player I wanted to be important for the
team, but preferably a bit inconspicuously. I needed a striker near
me who took things over from me, literally and figuratively: it was
Pettersson at Ajax, Wright and Henry at Arsenal. I needed someone to pass to or I needed someone else's pass to score. I had
insight. That was my great strength. Collecting and passing the ball

were my specialities and I could finish. I wasn't a Messi or Maradona who did it all by themselves. I never had the ambition to be a one-man show. Never. I didn't want too much attention or too much credit. Some people in football want all the attention and all the credit. There are even managers who are like that, too. But I was a team player, and that's my ambition as a trainer now. I want to add a lot of quality to the whole.

'On the field my greatest quality was seeing where the space was, knowing where you can create space. That's something I'm constantly focused on now as a trainer, too: where is the space in the opposing team? Is it behind the defence, between the central defenders and the backs, or in front of the defenders in between the lines? I make up drills for this. Running into space: how, where, when? I base this on my own experience and what I see around me. My speciality is optimising the sprints of strikers and deep-lying players. I know it's behind-the-scenes work, but it's fulfilling enough for me. I also prefer my organisational work at the club to be behind the scenes. I'm involved in some pretty significant decisions and I'm now officially part of the club management, but I don't make a song and dance about it.'

You're not interested in being a chief executive?

'No!'

Why not? You're intelligent and well-spoken – and you look good in a suit.

'Just let me be in charge in my own way, in the background. The stereotypical CEO is an extrovert, and I'm not. As a footballer I wasn't either. I've often been accused of not being a leader, but a leader is also someone whose way of functioning is an example to others. I was a role model on the pitch and now I want to set an example within the organisation.

'Being a show-off mouthpiece in a designer suit just isn't me. I want to be a leader who gets everyone on board by delivering good work. I'm good at observing, seeing our potential and our short-comings. I watch everything, and it bothers me when I see performances which don't meet the standards we expect. If anyone – *anyone* – isn't pulling their weight, then the details aren't in order, and that is unacceptable.'

What do you do then?

'We intervene. At the end of the season we do the same with the trainers, the medical staff, the people responsible for the pitches and the equipment as we do with the players. We review everyone and decide who is good enough to continue. Sure, we're very tough, but we want to be a top club and to accomplish that you have to be ruthless in maintaining the top standards.'

ACKNOWLEDGEMENTS

Heartfelt thanks to all the people who so generously gave their time and help and without whom this book would have been diminished:

Tony Adams, Vic Akers, Osvaldo Bagnoli, Leo Beenhakker, Estelle Bergkamp, Henrita Bergkamp, Marcel Bergkamp, Mitchel Bergkamp, Ronald Bergkamp, Saffron Bergkamp, Wim Bergkamp, Yasmin Bergkamp, Tonny Bergkamp-Van der Meer, Giuseppe Bergomi, Frank de Boer, Miel Brinkhuis, Jan-Dirk van der Burg, Sol Campbell, Amy Carr, Johan Cruyff, David Dein, Maddalena Del Re, Pim van Dord, David Endt, Don Farrow, Nellie Farrow, Riccardo Ferri, Ken Friar, Mark Fruin, Sophie Henderson, Thierry Henry, Mike Jones, Wim Jonk, Jane Judd, Martin Keown, Steve Kimberley, Momo Kovacevic, Simon Kuper, Gary Lewin, David Luxton, Stuart Macfarlane, Ian Marshall, Olga Mascolo, Marc Overmars, Ray Parlour, Tommaso Pellizzari, Robin van Persie, Stuart Peters, Bruce Rioch, Henk Spaan, Chris Stone, Dan Tolhurst, Patrick Vieira, Louis van de Vuurst, Tom Watt, Arsene Wenger, Tom Whiting, Bob Wilson, Ian Wright.